# STOCKS FOR THE LONG RUN

## The Definitive Guide to Financial Market Returns and Long-Term Investment Strategies

**JEREMY J. SIEGEL**

*Professor of Finance—
the Wharton School of the
University of Pennsylvania*

**McGraw-Hill**

New York  San Francisco  Washington, D.C.  Auckland  Bogotá
Caracas  Lisbon  London  Madrid  Mexico City  Milan
Montreal  New Delhi  San Juan  Singapore
Sydney  Tokyo  Toronto

**Library of Congress Cataloging-in-Publication Data**

Author:         Siegel, Jeremy J.
Title:          Stocks for the long run / Jeremy J. Siegel.
Edition:        2nd ed.
Published:      New York : McGraw-Hill, 1998.
Description:    p.  cm.
LC Call No.:    HG4661  .S53  1998
ISBN:           007058043X
Notes:          Includes index.
Subjects:       Stocks.
                Stocks—History.
                Rate of return.
Control No.:    98005103

*McGraw-Hill*

*A Division of The McGraw·Hill Companies*

1 2 3 4 5 6 7 8 9 0    DOC/DOC    9 0 3 2 1 0 9 8

ISBN  0-07-058043-X (HC)

The sponsoring editor for this book was Jeffrey Krames, the editing supervisor was Kellie Hagen, and the production supervisor was Suzanne W. B. Rapcavage. It was set in Palatino by Jan Fisher through the services of Barry E. Brown (Broker—Editing, Design and Production).

Printed and bound by R. R. Donnelley & Sons Company.

This publication is designed to provide accurate and authoritative information in regard to the subject matter covered. It is sold with the understanding that neither the author nor the publisher is engaged in rendering legal, accounting, or other professional service. If legal advice or other expert assistance is required, the services of a competent professional person should be sought.
—*From a Declaration of Principles jointly adopted by a Committee of the American Bar Association and a Committee of Publishers.*

McGraw-Hill books are available at special quantity discounts to use as premiums and sales promotions, or for use in corporate training programs. For more information, please write to the Director of Special Sales, McGraw-Hill, 11 West 19th Street, New York, NY 10011. Or contact your local bookstore.

This book is printed on acid-free paper.

# CONTENTS

**Chapter 3**

## Perspectives on Stocks as Investments   43

**PART 2**

# STOCK RETURNS

**Chapter 4**

## Stocks, Stock Averages, and the Dow Strategy   55

**Chapter 8**

## Taxes and Stock Returns   115

**Chapter 9**

## Global Investing   124

**PART 3**

## ECONOMIC ENVIRONMENT OF INVESTING

**Chapter 10**

## Money, Gold, and Central Banks   143

# A C K N O W L E D G M E N T S

Many of the same organizations who provided me with data for the first edition of *Stocks for the Long Run* willingly updated their data for this second edition. I include Lipper Analytical Services and the Vanguard Group for their mutual funds data, Morgan Stanley for their Capital Market indexes, Smithers & Co. for their market value data and Bloomberg Financial for their graphic representations.

On a professional level, I have benefited, as I did with the first edition, from correspondence and discussion with Professor Paul Samuelson of MIT, my former thesis advisor, about the equity risk premium and the degree and implications of mean reversion in stock prices. Tim Loughran of the University of Iowa provided me with invaluable data on value and growth stocks and Jay Ritter of the University of Florida provided feedback on many issues. As always, Robert Shiller of Yale University helped me better formulate my arguments through our lengthy discussions of the proper level of the market and the fundamental determinants of stock prices. I also wish to thank Brett Grehan, a Wharton MBA student who did an excellent job of isolating the data on the baby boomers and John Chung, a Wharton undergraduate who exhaustively researched the Dow 10 strategy.

But my deepest gratitude goes to Lalit Aggarwal, an undergraduate at Wharton who, at the age of 19, took over the entire project of updating, reformulating, and processing all the data that made this book possible. Extending the invaluable work of Shaun Smith in the first edition, Lalit devised new programs to determine and test the significance of many of the arguments, including the optimal funding of tax-deferred accounts, the market's response to Fed policy changes, and analytical measures of market sentiment. This edition would not be possible without Lalit's dedicated efforts.

A special thanks goes to the literally thousands of financial consultants and account executives of Merrill Lynch, Morgan Stanley, Dean Witter, Paine Webber, Smith Barney, Prudential Securities, and many other firms who have provided invaluable feedback on both the first edition and my new research. Their encouragement has motivated me to strengthen my arguments and pursue topics that are of concern both to their clients and the financial services industry in general.

I am especially honored that Peter Bernstein, whose written work is dedicated to bridging the gap between theoretical and practical finance, consented to write a foreword to this edition. No book comes to fruition without an editor, and Kevin Commins and Jeffrey Krames from McGraw-Hill Professional Publishing (formerly Irwin Professional) have provided constant assistance to ensure that the second volume has an even greater impact than the first.

Finally, a special debt is owed to one's family when writing a book. I can happily say that the production of the second edition was not as all-consuming as that of the first. Nevertheless, without their support through the many days I spent on the road lecturing to thousands of financial professionals and ordinary investors, this book could not have been written. Hopefully the lessons of this book will enable both the readers and my family to enjoy more leisure time in the future.

# FOREWORD

Some people find the process of assembling data to be a deadly bore. Others view it as a challenge. Jeremy Siegel has turned it into an art form. You can only admire the scope, lucidity, and sheer delight with which Professor Siegel serves up the evidence to support his case for investing in stocks for the long run.

But this book is far more than its title suggests. You will learn a lot of economic theory along the way, garnished with a fascinating history of both the capital markets and the U.S. economy. By using history to maximum effect, Professor Siegel gives the numbers a life and meaning they would never enjoy in a less compelling setting.

Consequently, I must warn you that his extraordinary skills transform what might have been a dull treatise indeed into a story that is highly seductive. Putting Professor Siegel's program into operation and staying with it for the long run is not the same thing as reading about it in a book. Practicing what he preaches is not as easy as it sounds.

Even on an intellectual level, investing is always difficult and the answer is never unqualified. On an emotional level the challenge is a mighty one, despite the mountains of historical experience. And despite the elegance of the statistical tools and the laws of probability we can apply to that experience, novel and unexpected events are constantly taking investors by surprise. Surprise is what explains the persistent volatility of markets; if we always knew what lay ahead, we would already have priced that certain future into market valuations. The ability to manage the unexpected consequences of our choices and decisions is the real secret of investment success.

Professor Siegel is generous throughout this book in supplying abundant warnings along these lines; in particular, he spares no words as he depicts how temptations to be a short-term investor can overwhelm the need to be a long-term investor. Most of his admonitions, however, relate to the temptation to time or adopt other methods of beating the strategy of buy-and-hold for a diversified equity portfolio. On the basis of my experience, greater danger lurks in the temptation to chicken out when the going is rough, and your precious wealth seems to be going down the tube.

I will relate just one story that stands out in my memory because it was the first time I had witnessed what blind terror can do to a well-structured investment program. In the autumn of 1961, a lawyer I knew referred his wealthy father-in-law to our investment counsel firm. Since we felt the stock market was speculative at the time, we took a conservative approach and proposed putting only a third of his cash into stocks and distributing the remainder over a portfolio of municipal bonds. He was delighted with our whole approach. He shook hands with each of us in turn and assured us of his confidence in our discretion and sagacity.

About two months later, in December 1961, the Dow Jones Industrial Average hit an all-time high. But then the market fell sharply. At its nadir, stocks were down more than 25 percent from the level at which we had invested our new client's money. The entire bull move from the end of 1958 had been wiped out.

I was in France during the selling climax, but when I returned my client was standing in the doorway waiting for me. He was hysterical, convinced that he was condemned to poverty. Although his portfolio had shrunk by less than ten percent and we counseled that this was a time to *buy* equities, we had no choice but to yield to his emotional re-monstrances and sell out all of his stocks. A year later, the market was up more than 40 percent.

I have seen this story replayed in every bear market since then. The experience taught me one simple but over-arching moral; successful in-vestment management means understanding ahead of time how you will react to outcomes that are not only unexpected but *unfamiliar*. Although you might intellectually accept the reality of market volatility, emotionally acceptance is far more difficult to achieve. As Professor Siegel concedes in Chapter 5, fear has a far greater grasp on human ac-tion than the impressive weight of historical evidence.

Although books should normally be read from the beginning, I suggest that you peek ahead for a moment and read the beginning of Chapter 5, *Dividends, Earnings, and Investor Sentiment*, and its opening section, *An Evil Omen Returns*. Here Professor Siegel describes what happened when the roaring bull market of 1958 drove the dividend yield on stocks emphatically below the yield on long-term bonds. Nobody even questions that relationship today, but as Professor Siegel points out, stocks had always yielded more than bonds throughout cap-ital market history, except for brief and transitory moments like the 1929 peak. Normality had turned topsy-turvy. This was not only a total sur-prise to most investors; it was totally incomprehensible.

I remember the occasion well. My older partners, grizzled veterans of the 1920s and the Great Crash, assured me that this was a momentous anomaly. How could stocks, the riskier asset, be valued more highly than bonds, the safe asset? It made no sense. "Just you wait," they told me. "Matters will soon set themselves to right. Those fools chasing the market through the roof will soon be sorry." I am still waiting.

In the years since then, other relationships sanctified by history have been blown apart. The cost of living in the U.S. was volatile but trendless from 1800 to the end of the Second World War, but it has fallen only twice, and by tiny amounts, over the past 50 years. As a result, we have seen long-term bond yields climb to levels more than double the highest yields reached in the first century and a half of our history.

As Professor Siegel explains in Chapter 10, the change in the behavior of prices is the result of the shift from a gold-based monetary standard to monetary system managed by central banks. This system means that the dollar is now a fluctuating currency and gold itself is rapidly losing its role as money and store of value. Dividend yields on stocks are currently little more than half what we once considered historically low yields. Differentiating between a blip and a wholly new set of arrangements is always difficult, but investors must understand that all familiar relationships and parameters are vulnerable to fragmentation.

The most powerful part of Professor Siegel's argument is how effectively he demonstrates the consistency of results from equity ownership when measured over periods of 20 years or longer. Even the stock returns of Germany and Japan, devastated by World War II, bounced back to challenge the total return of stocks in the U.S and U.K since the 1920s. Indeed, he would be on frail ground if that consistency were not so visible in the historical data and if it did not keep reappearing in so many different guises. Furthermore, he claims that this consistency is the likely outcome of a profit-driven system in which the corporate sector is the engine of economic growth, and adaptability to immense political, social, and economic change is perhaps its most impressive feature. Part 3 of the book, *The Economic Environment of Investing*, which describes the link between economic activity, the business cycle, inflation, and politics is the most important part of his story.

Nevertheless, I repeat my warning that paradigm shifts are normal in our system. The past, no matter how instructive, is always the past. Hence, even the wisdom of this insightful book must be open to constant re-examination and analysis as we move forward toward the future. Professor Siegel so rightly warns readers of this when he writes that "the returns derived from the past are not hard constants, like the speed of light or gravitation force, waiting to be discovered in the natural world. Historical values must be tempered with an appreciation of how investors, attempting to take advantage of the returns from the past, may alter those very returns in the future." Although the advice set forth in this book will very likely yield positive results for investors, you must remember that the odds are even higher that uncertainty will forever be your inseparable companion.

**Peter Bernstein**

# PREFACE

I wrote the first edition of *Stocks for the Long Run* with two goals in mind: to record and evaluate the major factors influencing the risks and returns on stocks and fixed-income assets, and to offer strategies based on this analysis that would maximize long-term portfolio growth. My research demonstrated that over long periods of time the returns on equities not only surpassed those on other financial assets, but that stock returns were more predictable than bond returns when measured in terms of the purchasing power. I concluded that stocks were clearly the asset of choice for virtually all investors seeking long-term growth.

The Dow Industrial Average was at 3700 when the first edition of this book was published in May 1994. With interest rates rising rapidly (1994 was by many measures the worst year in history for the bond market), and stocks already up 60 percent from their October 1990 bear-market low, few forecasters predicted further gains in equities. No one expected that, just seven months later, stocks would embark on one of their greatest bull-market runs in history.

As of this writing, the Dow Jones Industrial Average is above 7000 and most stock markets worldwide are far above their levels of four years earlier. Equity mutual funds have experienced a boom that surprised even their most ardent supporters, nearly tripling in value since the first edition of this book came out. *Indexing*, or investing passively in a widely diversified portfolio of common stocks, has reached record popularity. And a new group of "Nifty Fifty" growth stocks have been born, echoing the surprising results of my reevaluation of that original group that so captured Wall Street 25 years earlier. The popularity and acceptance of the concepts and strategies presented in *Stocks for the Long Run* has far exceeded my expectations.

Over the past four years I have given scores of lectures on the stock market in both the U.S. and abroad. I have listened closely to the questions that audiences have asked and contemplated the many letters and phone calls from readers. The second edition of *Stocks for the Long Run* not only updates all the material presented in the 1994 edition, but adds a great many new topics that have resulted from my interaction with investors. These include "Age Wave" investing and the fate of the baby boomers' huge accumulation of assets, the Dow 10 and similar yield-based strategies, the measurement and impact of investor sentiment on stock returns, the link between the Federal Reserve's interest-rate policies and subsequent movements in stock prices, and a broader look at the characteristics of value and growth stocks.

Throughout the writing of this edition, I have been very conscious of the extraordinary surge in the bull market and the possibility that the upward move of stock prices has been "too much of a good thing." I frequently thought of the late great economist, Irving Fisher of Yale University, who researched stock valuation in the early part of this century and strongly advocated equity investing. A popular speaker on the lecture circuit, Fisher stated in a public address in New York on October 14, 1929 that stock prices, although they appeared high, were fully justified on the basis of current and prospective earnings. He foresaw no bust and confidently proclaimed that "Stocks are on a permanently high plateau." Just two weeks later stocks crashed and the market entered its worst bear market in history.

Given my strong public advocacy of stock investing, I wanted to be sure that I was not following Irving Fisher's footsteps. I examined many of the historical yardsticks used to value the general level of equities. Most of these indicated that stock prices in 1997 were historically high relative to such fundamental variables as earnings, dividends, and book value, just as they were in 1929.

But this does not mean that these historical yardsticks represent the "right" value of stock prices. The thesis of this book strongly implies that stocks have been chronically undervalued throughout history. This has occurred because most investors have been deterred by the high short-term risk in the stock market and have ignored their long-term record of steady gains. This short-term focus has caused investors to pay too low a price for shares, and therefore enabled long-term investors to reap superior returns.

One interpretation of the current bull market indicates that investors are finally bidding equities up to the level that they should be on the basis of their historical risks and returns. My contacts with shareholders reveal a remarkable acceptance of the core thesis of my book: that stocks are the best and, in the long run, the safest way to accumulate wealth. In that case, the current high level of stock prices relative to fundamentals means that future returns on equities might well be lower than the historical average.

Yet the current premium on equity prices could also be the result of unprecedented domestic and international conditions facing our country. The overall price level has shown more stability in the past five years than at any other time in U.S. history. Furthermore, international conditions have never been more conducive to economic growth, as the U.S. is uniquely positioned to take advantage of the wave of consumer spending coming from developing economies. Lower economic risk and faster earning growth could most certainly justify current stock prices.

My judgment is that both factors—the unprecedented economic conditions and the surge of equity investing based on their long-term returns—are the cause of the current rise in stock prices. For that reason, there is no reason to be bearish on equities. Even if all the favorable economic factors propelling equities fade, history has shown that their long-term returns will still surpass those of fixed-income assets.

A more serious short-run problem involves investor expectations. The after-inflation stock returns during this bull market, which began in 1982, have been almost twice as high as the long-term average. This might have implanted unrealistically high expectations of future stock returns in the minds of investors. In that case, the current premium valuation that the market currently enjoys could quickly disappear and turn into a discount as expectations of future earnings growth fail to be met and optimism turns to pessimism. As I state in the conclusion of Chapter 5, "Fear has a far greater grasp on human action than does the impressive weight of historical evidence."

Yet even a market decline does not mean that investors should avoid equities. Although falling stock prices would bring some short-term pain, this will ultimately benefit the long-term investor who can buy and accumulate equities at these discounted prices. The fact that stock returns in the long-run have surpassed other financial assets through market peaks and troughs attests to the resiliency of stocks in all economic and financial climates.

# PART ONE

# THE VERDICT OF HISTORY

# 1

## CHAPTER

# STOCK AND BOND RETURNS SINCE 1802

*"I know of no way of judging the future but by the past."*

—**Patrick Henry, 1775**[1]

### "EVERYBODY OUGHT TO BE RICH"

In the summer of 1929, a journalist named Samuel Crowther interviewed John J. Raskob, a senior financial executive at General Motors, about how the typical individual could build wealth by investing in stocks. In August of that year, Crowther published Raskob's ideas in a *Ladies' Home Journal* article with the audacious title "Everybody Ought to Be Rich."

In the interview, Raskob claimed that America was on the verge of a tremendous industrial expansion. He maintained that by putting just $15 per month into good common stocks, investors could expect their wealth to grow steadily to $80,000 over the next 20 years. Such a return—24 percent per year—was unprecedented, but the prospect of effortlessly amassing a great fortune seemed plausible in the atmosphere of the 1920s bull market. Stocks excited investors, and millions put their savings into the market seeking quick profit.

On September 3, 1929, a few days after Raskob's ideas appeared, the Dow-Jones Industrial average hit a historic high of 381.17. Seven

---

1 Speech in Virginia Convention, March 23, 1775.

weeks later, stocks crashed. The next 34 months saw the most devastating decline in share values in U.S. history.

On July 8, 1932, when the carnage was finally over, the Dow Industrials stood at 41.22. The market value of the world's greatest corporations had declined an incredible 89 percent. Millions of investors were wiped out, and America was mired in the deepest economic depression in its history. Thousands who had bought stocks with borrowed money went bankrupt.

Raskob's advice was held up to ridicule for years to come. It was said to represent the insanity of those who believed that the market could go up forever and the foolishness of those who ignored the tremendous risks inherent in stocks. U.S. Senator Arthur Robinson from Indiana publicly held Raskob responsible for the stock crash by urging common people to buy stock at the market peak.[2] In 1992, 63 years later, *Forbes* magazine warned investors of the overvaluation of stocks in its issue headlined "Popular Delusions and the Madness of Crowds." In a review of the history of market cycles, *Forbes* fingered Raskob as the "worst offender" of those who viewed the stock market as a guaranteed engine of wealth.[3]

The conventional wisdom is that Raskob's foolhardy advice epitomizes the mania that periodically overruns Wall Street. But is that verdict fair? The answer is decidedly no. If you calculate the value of the portfolio of an investor who followed Raskob's advice, patiently putting $15 a month into stocks, you find that his accumulation exceeded that of someone who placed the same money in Treasury bills after less than four years! After 20 years, his stock portfolio would have accumulated almost $9,000 and after 30 years over $60,000. Although not as high as Raskob had projected, $60,000 still represents a fantastic 13 percent return on invested capital, far exceeding the returns earned by conservative investors who switched their money to Treasury bonds or bills at the market peak. Those who never bought stock, citing the Great Crash as the vindication of their caution, eventually found themselves far behind investors who had patiently accumulated equity.[4]

---

2 Irving Fisher, *The Stock Market Crash and After*, New York: Macmillan, 1930, p. xi.
3 "The Crazy Things People Say to Rationalize Stock Prices," *Forbes*, April 27, 1992, p. 150.
4 Raskob succumbed to investors in the 1920s who wanted to get rich quickly by devising a scheme by which investors borrowed $300, adding $200 of personal capital, to invest $500 in stocks. Although in 1929 this was certainly not as good as putting money gradually in the market, even this plan beat investment in Treasury bills after 20 years.

John Raskob's infamous prediction is indeed illustrative of an important theme in the history of Wall Street. But this theme is not the prevalence of foolish optimism at market peaks; rather, it is that over the last century, accumulations in stocks have always outperformed other financial assets for the patient investor. Even such calamitous events as the Great 1929 Stock Crash did not negate the superiority of stocks as long-term investments.

## FINANCIAL MARKET RETURNS FROM 1802

This chapter analyzes the returns on stocks and bonds over long periods of time in both the United States and other countries. This two-century history is divided into three subperiods. In the first subperiod, from 1802 through 1871, the U.S. made a transition from an agrarian to an industrialized economy, much like the "emerging markets" of Latin America and Asia today.[5] In the second subperiod, from 1871 through 1925, the U.S. was transformed into the foremost political and economic power in the world.[6] The third subperiod, from 1926 to the present, contains the 1929-32 stock collapse, the Great Depression, and postwar expansion. The data from this period have been analyzed extensively by academics and professional money managers, and have served as a benchmark for historical returns.[7] Figure 1-1 tells the story. It depicts the total return indexes for stocks, long- and short-term bonds, gold, and commodities from 1802 through 1997. *Total returns* means that all returns, such as interest and dividends and capital gains, are automatically reinvested in the asset and allowed to accumulate over time.

It can be easily seen that the total return on equities dominates all other assets. Even the cataclysmic stock crash of 1929, which caused a generation of investors to shun stocks, appears as a mere blip in the stock return index. Bear markets, which so frighten investors, pale in the context of the upward thrust of total stock returns. One dollar invested

---

5 A brief description of the early stock market is found in the appendix. The stock data during this period are taken from Schwert (1990), though I have substituted my own dividend series. G. William Schwert, "Indexes of United States Stock Prices from 1802 to 1987," *Journal of Business*, 63 (1990), pp. 399-426.
6 The stock series used in this period are taken from Cowles indexes as reprinted in Shiller (1989): Robert Shiller, *Market Volatility*, Cambridge, Mass.: M.I.T. Press, 1989. The Cowles indexes are capitalization-weighted indexes of all New York Stock Exchange stocks and include dividends.
7 The data from the third period are taken from the Center for the Research in Stock Prices (CRSP) capitalization-weighted indexes of all New York stocks, and starting in 1962, American and NASDAQ stocks.

**FIGURE 1–1**

Total Nominal Return Indexes, 1802–1997

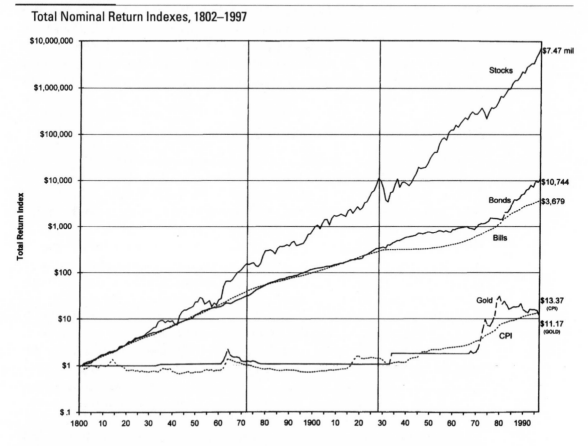

and reinvested in stocks since 1802 would have accumulated to nearly $7,500,000 by the end of 1997. Hypothetically, this means that $1 million, invested and reinvested during these 195 years, would have grown to the incredible sum of nearly $7.5 trillion in 1997, over one-half the entire capitalization of the U.S. stock market!

One million dollars in 1802 is equivalent to over $13 million in today's purchasing power. This was certainly a large, though not overwhelming, sum of money to the industrialists and landholders of the early 19th century.[8] But total wealth in the stock market, or in the economy for that matter, does not accumulate as fast as the total return in-

8 Blodget, an early 19th-century economist, estimated the wealth of the United States at that time to be nearly $2.5 billion so that $1 million would be only about 0.04 percent of the total wealth: S. Blodget, Jr., Economica, "A Statistical Manual for the United States of America," 1806 edition, p. 68.

dex. This is because investors consume most of their dividends and capital gains, enjoying the fruits of their past saving.

It is rare for anyone to accumulate wealth for long periods of time without consuming part of his or her return. The longest period of time investors typically plan to hold assets without touching principal and income is when they are accumulating wealth in pension plans for their retirement or in insurance policies that are passed on to their heirs. Even those who bequeath fortunes untouched during their lifetimes must realize that these accumulations are often dissipated in the next generation. The stock market has the power to turn a single dollar into millions by the forbearance of generations—but few will have the patience or desire to let this happen.

## HISTORICAL SERIES ON BONDS

Bonds are the most important financial assets competing with stocks. Bonds promise a fixed monetary payment over time. In contrast to equity, the cash flows from bonds have a maximum monetary value set by the terms of the contract and, except in the case of default, do not vary with the profitability of the firm.

The bond series shown in Figure 1-1 are based on long- and short-term government bonds, when available; if not, similar highly rated securities were used. Default premiums were removed from all interest rates in order to obtain a comparable series over the entire period.[9]

Figure 1-2 displays the interest rates on long-term bonds and short-term bonds, called *bills*, over the two-hundred-year period. The behavior of both long- and short-term interest rates changed dramatically from 1926 to the present. Interest rate fluctuations during the 19th and 20th centuries remained within a narrow range. But during the Great Depression of the 1930s, short-term interest rates fell nearly to zero and yields on long-term government bonds fell to a record-low 2 percent. Government policy maintained low rates during World War II and the early postwar years, and strict limits (known as Regulation Q[10]) were imposed on bank deposit rates through the 1950s and 1960s.

---

9 See Siegel, "The Real Rate of Interest from 1800-1990: A study of the U.S. and UK," *Journal of Monetary Economics*, 29 (1992), pp. 227-52, for a detailed description of process by which a historical yield series was constructed.

10 Regulation Q was a provision in the Banking Act of 1933 that imposed ceilings on interest rates and time deposits.

**F I G U R E   1–2**

U.S. Interest Rates, 1800–1997

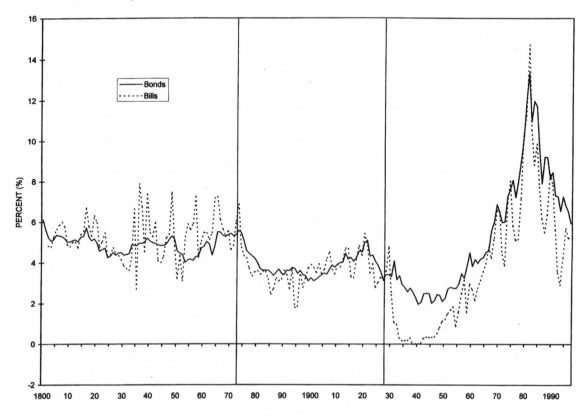

The 1970s marked an unprecedented change in interest rate behavior. Inflation reached double-digit levels, and interest rates soared to heights that had not been seen since the debasing of continental currency in the early years of the republic. Never before had inflation been so high for so long.

The public clamored for the government to act to slow rising prices. Finally, by 1982, the restrictive monetary policy of Paul Volcker, chairman of the Federal Reserve System since 1979, brought inflation and interest rates down to more moderate levels. The volatility of inflation, whose cause is discussed later in this chapter, should make one wary of using the period since 1926 as a benchmark for determining future bond returns.

## THE PRICE LEVEL AND GOLD

Figure 1-3 depicts consumer prices in the U.S. and the United Kingdom over the past 200 years. In each country, the price level was essentially the same at the end of World War II as it was 150 years earlier. But since World War II, the nature of inflation has changed dramatically. The price level has risen almost continuously over the past 50 years, often gradually, but sometimes at double-digit rates as in the 1970s. Excluding wartime, the 1970s witnessed the first rapid and sustained inflation ever experienced in U.S. history.

Economists understand what caused the inflationary process to change so dramatically. During the nineteenth and early twentieth century, the U.S., U.K., and the rest of the industrialized world were on a

**F I G U R E   1–3**

U.S. and U.K. Price Indexes, 1800–1997

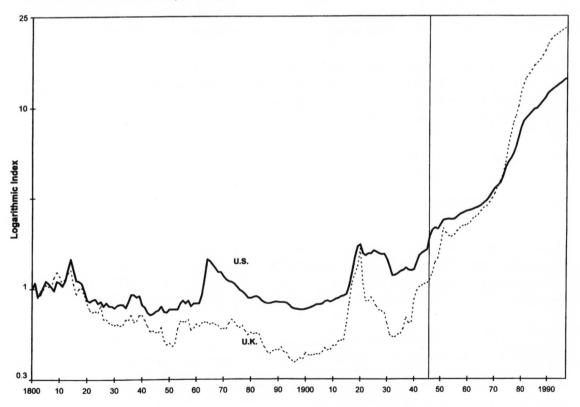

*gold standard*. As described in detail in Chapter 10, a gold standard restricts the supply of money and hence the inflation rate. But from the Great Depression through World War II, the world shifted to a *paper money standard*. Under a paper money standard there is no legal constraint on the issuance of money, so inflation is subject to political as well as economic forces. Price stability depends on the ability of the central banks to limit the supply of money and control the inflationary policies of the federal government.

The chronic inflation that the U.S. and other developed economies have experienced since World War II does not mean that the gold standard was superior to the current paper money standard. The gold standard was abandoned because of its inflexibility in the face of economic crises, particularly the banking collapse of the 1930s. The paper money standard, if properly administered, can avoid the banking panics and severe depressions that plagued the gold standard. But the cost of this stability is a bias towards chronic inflation.

It is not surprising that the price of gold has closely followed the trend of overall inflation over the past two centuries. Its price soared to $850 per ounce in January 1980, following the rapid inflation of the preceding decade. When inflation was brought under control, its price fell. One dollar of gold bullion purchased in 1802 was worth $11.17 at the end of 1997. That is actually less than the change in the overall price level! In the long run, gold offers investors some protection against inflation, but little else. Whatever hedging property precious metals possess, these assets will exert a considerable drag on the return of a long-term investor's portfolio.[11]

## TOTAL REAL RETURNS

The focus of every long-term investor should be the growth of purchasing power—monetary wealth adjusted for the effect of inflation. Figure 1-4 shows the growth of purchasing power, or total *real* returns, in the same assets that were graphed in Figure 1-1: stocks, bonds, bills, and gold. These data are constructed by taking the dollar returns and

---

11 Ironically, despite the inflationary bias of a paper money system, well-preserved *paper* money from the early 19th century is worth many times its face value on the collectors' market, far surpassing gold bullion as a long-term investment. An old mattress found containing 19th century paper money is a better find for the antique hunter than an equivalent sum hoarded in gold bars!

## FIGURE 1–4

Total Real Return Indexes, 1802–1997

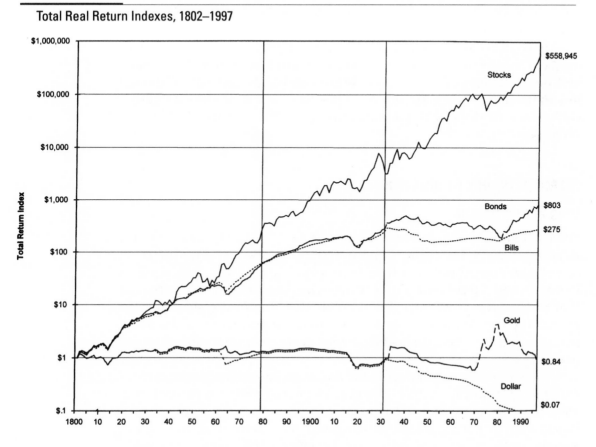

correcting them by the changes in the price level, shown in Figure 1-3.[12]

It is clear that the growth of purchasing power in equities not only dominates all other assets but is remarkable for its long-term stability. Despite extraordinary changes in the economic, social, and political environment over the past two centuries, stocks have yielded between 6.6 and 7.2 percent per year after inflation in all major subperiods.

The wiggles on the stock return line represent the bull and bear markets that equities have suffered throughout history. The long-term

---

12 Total returns are graphed on a ratio, or logarithmic scale. Economists use this scale to graph virtually all long-term data since equal vertical distances anywhere in the chart represent equal percentage changes in return. As a result, a constant slope represents a constant after-inflation rate of return.

perspective radically changes one's view of the risk of stocks. The short-term fluctuations in market, which loom so large to investors, have little to do with the long-term accumulation of wealth.

In contrast to the remarkable stability of stock returns, real returns on fixed income assets have declined markedly over time. In the first, and even second subperiods, the returns on bonds and bills, although less than equities, were significantly positive. But since 1926, and especially since World War II, fixed income assets have returned little after inflation.

## INTERPRETATION OF RETURNS

### Long Period Returns

Table 1-1 summarizes the annual returns on U.S. stocks over the past two centuries.[13] The shaded column represents the real after-inflation, compound annual rate of return on stocks. The real return on equities has averaged 7.0 percent per year over the past 195 years. This means that purchasing power has, on average, doubled in the stock market every 10 years. With an inflation of 3 percent per year, a 7.0 percent real return translates into a 10.2 percent average annual money return in equities.

Note the extraordinary stability of the real return on stocks over all major subperiods: 7.0 percent per year from 1802-1870, 6.6 percent from 1871 through 1925, and 7.2 percent per year since 1926. Even since World War II, during which all the inflation that the U.S. has experienced over the past two hundred years occurred, the average real rate of return on stocks has been 7.5 percent per year. This is virtually identical to the previous 125 years, which saw no overall inflation. This remarkable stability of long-term real returns is a characteristic of *mean reversion*, a property of a variable to offset its short-term fluctuations so as to produce far more stable long-term returns.

---

13 The dividend yield for the first subperiod has been estimated by statistically fitting the relation of long-term interest rates to dividend yields in the second subperiod, yielding results that are closer to other information we have about dividends during the period. See Walter Werner and Steven Smith, *Wall Street*, New York: Columbia University Press, 1991, for a description of some early dividend yields. See also a recent paper by William Goetzmann and Phillipe Jorion, "A Longer Look at Dividend Yields," *Journal of Business*, 1995, vol. 68 (4), pp. 483-508 and William Goetzmann, "Patterns in Three Centuries of Stock Market Prices," *Journal of Business*, 1993, vol. 66 (2), pp. 249-270.

**TABLE 1–1**

Annual Stock Market Returns 1802–1997

Comp = compound annual return
Arith = arithmetic average of annual returns
Risk = standard deviation of arithmetic returns

| | | Total Nominal Return % | | | % Nominal Capital Appreciation | | | Div | Total Real Return % | | | % Real Capital Appreciation | | | Real Gold Retn | Consumer Price Inflation |
|---|---|---|---|---|---|---|---|---|---|---|---|---|---|---|---|---|
| | | Comp | Arith | Risk | Comp | Arith | Risk | Yld | Comp | Arith | Risk | Comp | Arith | Risk | | |
| Periods | 1802-1997 | 8.4 | 9.8 | 17.5 | 3.0 | 4.4 | 17.5 | 5.4 | 7.0 | 8.5 | 18.1 | 1.6 | 3.2 | 17.9 | -0.1 | 1.3 |
| Periods | 1871-1997 | 9.1 | 10.7 | 18.5 | 4.2 | 5.9 | 18.3 | 4.9 | 7.0 | 8.7 | 18.9 | 2.1 | 3.9 | 18.6 | -0.2 | 2.0 |
| Major Sub-Periods | I 1802-1870 | 7.1 | 8.1 | 15.5 | 0.7 | 1.8 | 15.5 | 6.4 | 7.0 | 8.3 | 16.9 | 0.6 | 1.9 | 16.6 | 0.2 | 0.1 |
| Major Sub-Periods | II 1871-1925 | 7.2 | 8.4 | 15.7 | 1.9 | 3.1 | 16.1 | 5.2 | 6.6 | 7.9 | 16.8 | 1.3 | 2.7 | 17.1 | -0.8 | 0.6 |
| Major Sub-Periods | III 1926-1997 | 10.6 | 12.6 | 20.4 | 6.0 | 7.9 | 19.8 | 4.6 | 7.2 | 9.2 | 20.4 | 2.8 | 4.8 | 19.8 | 0.2 | 3.1 |
| Post-War Periods | 1946-1997 | 12.2 | 13.4 | 16.7 | 7.9 | 9.1 | 16.1 | 4.3 | 7.5 | 9.0 | 17.3 | 3.4 | 4.8 | 16.8 | -0.7 | 4.3 |
| Post-War Periods | 1966-1981 | 6.6 | 8.3 | 19.5 | 2.6 | 4.3 | 18.7 | 4.1 | -0.4 | 1.4 | 18.7 | -4.1 | -2.4 | 18.0 | 8.8 | 7.0 |
| Post-War Periods | 1966-1997 | 11.5 | 12.9 | 17.0 | 7.6 | 8.9 | 16.5 | 3.9 | 6.0 | 7.5 | 17.1 | 2.3 | 3.7 | 16.7 | 0.6 | 5.2 |
| Post-War Periods | 1982-1997 | 16.7 | 17.4 | 13.1 | 12.9 | 13.6 | 13.0 | 3.7 | 12.8 | 13.6 | 13.2 | 9.1 | 9.9 | 13.1 | -7.0 | 3.4 |

The long-term stability of these returns is all the more surprising when one reflects on the dramatic changes that have taken place in our society during the last two centuries. The U.S. evolved from an agricultural to an industrial, and now to a post-industrial, service- and technology-oriented economy. The world shifted from a gold-based standard to a paper money standard. And information, which once took weeks to cross the country, can now be instantaneously transmitted and simultaneously broadcast around the world. Yet despite mammoth changes in the basic factors generating wealth for shareholders, equity returns have shown an astounding persistence.

## Short Period Returns

The long-term stability of real equity returns does not deny that short-term returns can be quite variable. In fact, there are considerable periods of time when stock returns differ from their long-term average. Samples of such episodes after World War II are reported at the bottom of Table 1-1.

The bull market from 1982 through 1997 has given investors an after-inflation return of 12.8 percent per year, which is nearly six percentage points above the historical average. But the superior equity returns over this period has barely compensated investors for the dreadful stock returns realized in the previous 15 years, from 1966-1981, when the real rate of return was –0.4 percent. In fact, during the 15-year period that preceded the current bull market, stock returns were more *below* their historical average than they have been above their average during the past 16 years.

The bull market of the last 16 years has brought stocks back from the extremely undervalued state that they reached at the beginning of the 1980s. Certainly the superior performance of stocks over the recent past is unlikely to persist, but this does not necessarily imply that stock returns over the next decade must be below average in order to offset the bull market from 1982.

## REAL RETURNS ON FIXED-INCOME ASSETS

As stable as the long-term real returns have been for equities, the same cannot be said of fixed-income assets. Table 1-2 reports the nominal and real returns on both short-term and long-term bonds over the same time periods as in Table 1-1. The real returns on bills has dropped precipitously from 5.1 percent in the early part of the nineteenth century to a bare 0.6 percent since 1926, a return only slightly above inflation.

The real return on long-term bonds has shown a similar pattern. Bond returns fell from a generous 4.8 percent in the first subperiod to 3.7 percent in the second, and then to only 2.0 percent in the third. If the returns from the last 70 years are projected into the future, it would take nearly 40 years in order to double one's purchasing power in bonds, and 120 years to do so in treasury bills, in contrast to the ten years it takes in stocks.

The decline in the average real return on fixed-income securities is striking. In any 30-year period beginning with 1889, the average real rate of return on short-term government securities has exceeded 2 percent only three times. Since the late 19th century, the real return on bonds and bills over *any* 30-year horizon has seldom matched the average return of 4.5 to 5 percent reached during the first 70 years of our sample. From 1880, the real return on long-term bonds over every 30-year period has never reached 4 percent, and exceeded 3 percent during only 12 such periods.

**TABLE 1–2**

Fixed-Income Returns 1802–1997

Comp = compound annual return
Arith = arithmetic average of annual returns
Risk = standard deviation of arithmetic returns

| | | Long Term Governments | | | | | | Short Term Governments | | | | Consumer |
|---|---|---|---|---|---|---|---|---|---|---|---|---|
| | | Coupon Rate % | Nominal Return % | | | Real Return % | | | Nominal Rate % | Real Return % | | | Price Inflation |
| | | | Comp | Arith | Risk | Comp | Arith | Risk | | Comp | Arith | Risk | |
| Periods | 1802-1997 | 4.7 | 4.8 | 5.0 | 6.1 | 3.5 | 3.8 | 8.8 | 4.3 | 2.9 | 3.1 | 6.1 | 1.3 |
| Periods | 1871-1997 | 4.7 | 4.8 | 5.1 | 7.2 | 2.8 | 3.1 | 9.0 | 3.8 | 1.7 | 1.8 | 4.6 | 2.0 |
| Major Sub-Periods | I 1802-1870 | 4.9 | 4.9 | 4.9 | 2.8 | 4.8 | 5.1 | 8.3 | 5.2 | 5.1 | 5.4 | 7.7 | 0.1 |
| Major Sub-Periods | II 1871-1925 | 4.0 | 4.3 | 4.4 | 3.0 | 3.7 | 3.9 | 6.4 | 3.8 | 3.2 | 3.3 | 4.8 | 0.6 |
| Major Sub-Periods | III 1926-1997 | 5.2 | 5.2 | 5.6 | 9.3 | 2.0 | 2.6 | 10.6 | 3.8 | 0.6 | 0.7 | 4.2 | 3.1 |
| Post-War Periods | 1946-1997 | 6.1 | 5.4 | 5.9 | 10.5 | 1.1 | 1.6 | 11.3 | 4.9 | 0.5 | 0.6 | 3.4 | 4.3 |
| Post-War Periods | 1966-1981 | 7.2 | 2.5 | 2.8 | 7.1 | -4.2 | -3.9 | 8.1 | 6.9 | -0.2 | -0.1 | 2.1 | 7.0 |
| Post-War Periods | 1966-1997 | 7.9 | 7.8 | 8.4 | 12.2 | 2.5 | 3.3 | 13.2 | 6.7 | 1.4 | 1.4 | 2.5 | 5.2 |
| Post-War Periods | 1982-1997 | 8.7 | 13.4 | 14.1 | 13.7 | 9.6 | 10.4 | 13.6 | 6.5 | 2.9 | 2.9 | 1.9 | 3.4 |

You have to go back more than 1½ centuries to the period from 1831 through 1861 to find any 30-year period where the return on either long- or short-term bonds exceeded that on equities. The dominance of stocks over fixed-income securities is overwhelming for investors with long horizons.

## EXPLANATIONS FOR THE FALL IN FIXED-INCOME RETURNS

Although the returns on equities have fully compensated stock investors for the increased inflation since World War II, the returns on fixed-income securities have not. The change in the monetary standard from gold to paper had its greatest effect on the returns of fixed-income assets. It is clear in retrospect that the buyers of bonds in the 1940s, 1950s, and early 1960s did not recognize the consequences of the change in monetary regime. How else can you explain why investors voluntarily purchased long-term bonds with 3 and 4 percent coupons despite the

fact that government policy was determined to avoid the deflation that
so favors bonds?

But there must have been other reasons for the decline in real returns on fixed-income assets. Theoretically, the surprise inflation of the
postwar period should have had a significantly smaller effect on the real
return of *short-term* bonds, such as treasury bills. This is because short-
term rates are changed frequently to capture expected inflation. But, as
noted previously, the decline in the real return on short-term bonds actually exceeded the decline in the real return on long-term bonds.

Another explanation for the fall in bond returns is investors' reaction to the financial turmoil of the Great Depression. The stock collapse
of the early 1930s caused a whole generation of investors to shun equities and invest in government bonds and newly-insured bank deposits,
driving their return downward. Furthermore, the increase in the financial assets of the middle class, whose behavior towards risk was far
more conservative than that of the wealthy of the nineteenth century,
likely played a role in depressing bond and bill returns.

Moreover, during World War II and the early postwar years, interest rates were kept low by the stated bond support policy of the Federal
Reserve. Bondholders had bought these bonds because of the widespread predictions of depression after the war. This support policy was
abandoned in 1951 because the low interest rate fostered inflation. But
interest rate controls, particularly on deposits, lasted much longer. And
finally, one cannot ignore the transformation of a highly segmented market for short-term instruments in the nineteenth century into one of the
world's most liquid markets. Treasury bills satisfy certain fiduciary and
legal requirements not possessed by any other asset. But the premium
paid for these services has translated into a meager return for investors.

## EQUITY PREMIUM

Whatever the reasons for the decline in the return on fixed-income assets over the past century, it is almost certain that the real returns on
bonds will be higher in the future than they have been over the last 70
years. As a result of the inflation shock of the 1970s, bondholders
have incorporated a significant inflation premium in the coupon on
long-term bonds. In most major industrialized nations, if inflation
does not increase appreciably from current levels, real returns of
about 3 to 4 percent will be realized from bonds whose nominal rate
is between 6 and 8 percent. These projected real returns are remark-
ably similar to the 3.5 percent average compound real return on U.S.

long-term government bonds over the past 195 years and the yields of the newly floated 5- and 10-year inflation-linked bonds issued in 1997 by the U.S. treasury.

The excess return for holding equities over short-term bonds is referred to as the *equity risk premium*, or simply the *equity premium*, and is plotted in Figure 1-5.[14] The equity premium, calculated as the difference in compound annual real returns on stocks and bills, averaged 1.9 percent in the first subperiod, 3.4 percent in the second subperiod, and 6.6 percent since 1926.

**F I G U R E   1–5**

Equity Risk Premium (30-Year Compound Annual Moving Average), 1831–1997

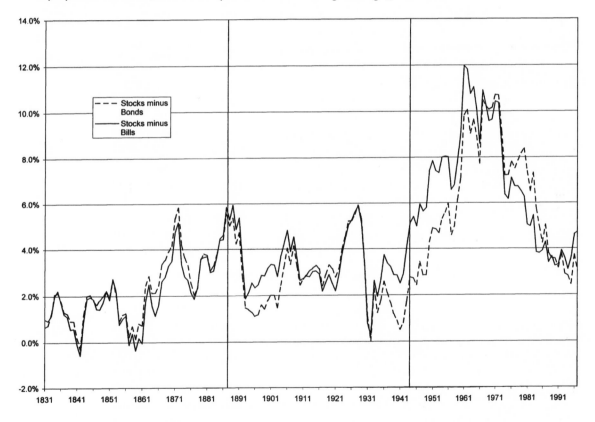

14 For a rigorous analysis of the equity premium, see Jeremy Siegel and Richard Thaler, "The Equity Premium Puzzle," *Journal of Economic Perspectives*, vol. 11, no. 1 (Winter 1997), pp. 191-200.

The high equity premium since World War II is certainly not sustainable. It is not a coincidence that the highest 30-year average equity return occurred in a period marked by very low real returns on bonds. Since firms finance a large part of their capital investment with bonds, the low cost of obtaining such funds increased returns to shareholders.

As real returns on fixed-income assets have risen in the last decade, the equity premium appears to be returning to the 2 to 3 percent norm that existed before the postwar surge. In support of this contention is the fact that the real return on the indexed linked bond is about three percentage points lower than the real long-term return on equity.

## INTERNATIONAL RETURNS

Some economists have maintained that the superior returns to equity are a consequence of choosing data from the United States, a country that has been transformed from a small British colony to the world's greatest economic power over the last 200 years.[15] But equity returns in other countries have also substantially outpaced those on fixed-income assets.

Figure 1-6 displays the total real stock return index for the United States, the United Kingdom, Germany, and Japan from 1926 to the present.[16] It is striking that the cumulative real returns on German and U.K. stocks over the 67-year period from 1926 through 1997 come so close to that of the United States. The compound annual real returns on stocks in each of these three countries are all within about one percentage point of each other.

The collapse of Japanese stocks during and after World War II was far greater than occurred in its defeated ally, Germany. The breakup of the zaibatsu industrial cartels, the distribution of its shares to the workers, and the hyperinflation that followed the war caused a 98 percent fall in the real value of Japanese equities.[17]

Despite the collapse of the equity market, Japanese stocks regained almost all of the ground they lost to the Western countries by the end of the 1980s. From 1948 through the real return on the Japanese market has exceeded 10.4 percent per year, nearly 50 percent higher than the U.S.

---

15 See Brown, S. J., Goetzmann, W. N., and Ross, S. A., "Survival," *Journal of Finance*, 50 (1995), p. 853-873.

16 The German returns are obtained from Gregor Gielen, *Können Aktienkurse Noch Steigen? Langfristige Trendanalyse des deutschen Aktienmarktes*, Gabler, 1994, Germany. British returns are from Shiller (1989) and updated from various sources.

17 T. F. M. Adams and Iwao Hoshii, *A Financial History of the New Japan*, Tokyo: Kodansha International Ltd., 1972, p. 39

International Real Stock Returns in the U.S., Germany, the U.K., and Japan, 1926–1997

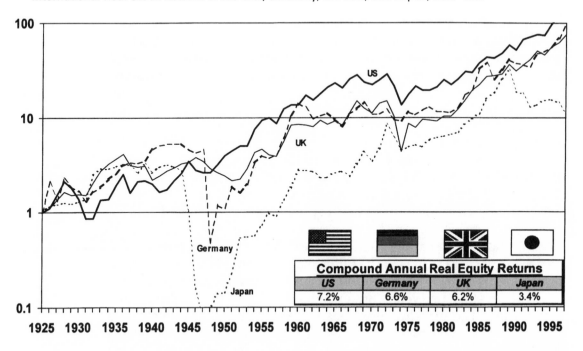

| Compound Annual Real Equity Returns | | | |
|---|---|---|---|
| *US* | *Germany* | *UK* | *Japan* |
| 7.2% | 6.6% | 6.2% | 3.4% |

market. Even including its recent bear market, Japan's real equity returns since 1926 have been 3.4 percent per year. And because the yen has appreciated in real terms relative to the dollar, the average annual real *dollar* returns in the Japanese market have been 4.3 percent per year. Measured in any common currency, the real returns in *every one* of these major countries from 1926–1997 have exceeded the real returns on fixed income assets in *any* of these countries.

## Germany

Despite the fact that the Second World War resulted in a 90 percent drop in real German equity prices, investors were not wiped out. Those who patiently held equity were rewarded with the tremendous returns in the postwar period.[18] By 1958, the total return for German stocks had

---

18 Of course, not everyone in Germany was able to realize the German postwar miracle. The stock holdings of many who resided in the eastern sector, controlled by the Soviet Union, were totally confiscated. Despite the reunification with the West, many of these claims were never recovered.

surpassed its prewar level. In the 12 years from 1948 to 1960, German stocks rose by over 30 percent per year in real terms. Indeed, from 1939, when the Germans invaded Poland, through 1960, the real return on German stocks nearly matched those in the United States and exceeded those in the United Kingdom. Despite the devastation of the war, the recovery of German markets powerfully attests to the resilience of stocks in the face of seemingly destructive political, social, and economic changes.

## United Kingdom

Over the long run, the returns in British equities are just as impressive as in the American market. In contrast to the U.S. experience, the greatest stock decline in Great Britain occurred in 1973 and 1974, not the early 1930s. The 1973–74 collapse, caused by rampant inflation as well as political and labor turmoil, brought the capitalization of the British market down to a mere $50 billion. This was less than the yearly profits of the OPEC oil-producing nations, whose increase in oil prices contributed to the decline in share values.[19] The OPEC nations could have purchased a controlling interest in every publicly traded British corporation at the time with less than one year's oil revenues! It is lucky for the British that they did not. The British market has increased dramatically since the 1974 crash and outstripped the dollar gains in all other major world markets. Again, those rewards went to those who held on to British stocks through this crisis.

## Japan

The postwar rise in the Japanese market is now legendary. The Nikkei Dow Jones stock average, patterned after the U.S. Dow Jones averages and containing 225 stocks, was first published on May 16, 1949. The day marked the reopening of the Tokyo Stock Exchange, which had been officially closed since August of 1945. On the opening day, the value of the Nikkei was 176.21—virtually identical to the U.S. Dow-Jones Industrials at that time. By June 1997, the Nikkei was over 20,000, after reaching nearly twice that value at the end of 1989.

But the gain in the Japanese market measured in dollars far exceeds that measured in yen. The yen was set at 360 to the dollar three weeks before the opening of the Tokyo Stock Exchange—a rate that was to hold for

---

19 "The défi Opec" (no author), *The Economist*, December 7, 1974, p. 85. OPEC stands for "Organization of Oil Exporting Countries," an oil cartel that regulated supply.

more than 20 years. Since then, the dollar has fallen to about 120 yen. So in dollar terms, the Nikkei climbed to over 60,000. Despite the Japanese bear market of the 1990s, the Nikkei, measured in terms dollars, has increased nearly 10 times its American counterpart over the past 50 years.

### Foreign Bonds

Figure 1-7 summarizes the return on foreign bonds as well as stocks. The postwar hyperinflation, when the yen was devalued from 4 to the dollar to 360 to the dollar, wasted Japanese bondholders. But nothing compares with the devastation experienced by the German bondholder during the 1922-23 hyperinflation, when the Reichsmark was devalued by more than one trillion to one. All German fixed-income assets were rendered worthless, yet stocks, which represented claims on real land and capital, weathered the crisis.

**FIGURE 1–7**

International Total Real Return Indexes, 1801–1997

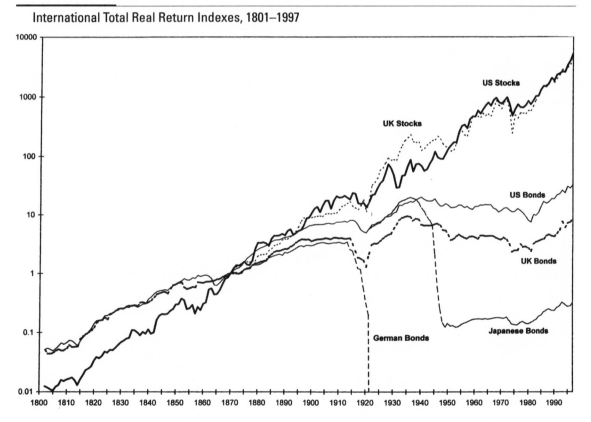

## CONCLUSION

The superiority of stocks to fixed-income investments over the long run is indisputable. Over the past 200 years the compound annual real return on stocks is nearly seven percent in the U.S., and has displayed a remarkable constancy over time. Furthermore, real stock returns in other major countries have matched those in the U.S.

The reasons for the persistence and long-term stability of stock returns are not well understood. Certainly the returns on stocks are dependent on economic growth, productivity, and the return to risk taking. But the ability to create value also springs from skillful management, a stable political system that respects property rights, and the need to provide value to consumers in a competitive environment. Political or economic crises can throw stocks off their long-term path, but the resilience of the market system enables them to regain their long-term trend. Perhaps that is why stock returns transcend the radical political, economic, and social changes that have impacted the world over the past two centuries.

The superior returns to equity over the past two centuries might be explained by the growing dominance of nations committed to free-market economics. Who might have expected the triumph of market-oriented economies 50 or even 30 years ago? The robustness of world equity prices in recent years might reflect the emergence of the golden age of capitalism—a system in ascendancy today but whose fortunes could decline in the next century. Yet even if capitalism declines, it is unclear which assets, if any, will retain value. In fact, if history is any guide, government bonds in our paper money world will fare far worse than stocks in any political or economic upheaval.

## APPENDIX 1: STOCKS FROM 1802 TO 1871

The first actively traded U.S. stocks, floated in 1791, were two banks: The Bank of New York and the Bank of the United States.* Both offerings were enormously successful and were quickly bid to a premium. But they collapsed the following year when Alexander Hamilton's assistant

---

* The oldest continuously operating firm is Dexter Corp., founded in 1767, a Connecticut maker of special materials; the second is Bowne & Co. (1775), which specializes in printing; the third is CoreStates Financial Corp., founded in 1782 as the First National Bank of Pennsylvania; and the fourth is the Bank of New York Corp., founded in 1782, which was involved in the successful 1791 stock offering with the Bank of the United States that was eventually involved in the crash of 1792.

at the Treasury, William Duer, attempted to manipulate the market and precipitated a crash. It was from this crisis that the antecedents of the New York Stock Exchange were born on May 17, 1792.

Joseph David, a historian of the 18th-century corporation, claimed that equity capital was readily forthcoming not only for every undertaking likely to be profitable, but, in his words, "for innumerable undertakings in which the risk was very great and the chances of success were remote."[**] Although over 300 business corporations were chartered by the states before 1801, fewer than 10 had securities that traded on a regular basis. Two thirds of those chartered before 1801 were connected with transportation: wharves, canals, turnpikes, and bridges. But the important stocks of the early 19th century were financial institutions: banks and, later, insurance companies. Bank and insurance companies held loans and equity in many of the manufacturing firms that, at that time, did not have the financial standing to issue equity. The fluctuations in the stock prices of financial firms in the 19th century reflected the health of the general economy and the profitability of the firms to whom they lent. The first large nonfinancial venture was the Delaware and Hudson Canal, issued in 1825, which also became an original member of the Dow-Jones Industrial average 60 years later. In 1830, the first railroad, the Mohawk and Hudson, was listed and for the next 50 years railroads dominated trading on the major exchanges.

## APPENDIX 2: ARITHMETIC AND GEOMETRIC RETURNS

The average *arithmetic return*, $r_A$, is the average of each yearly return. If $r_1$ to $r_n$ are the $n$ yearly returns, $r_A = (r_1 + r_2 \ldots + r_n)/n$. The average *geometric*, or *compound return*, $r_G$, is the $n^{\text{th}}$ root of the product of one-year total returns minus one. Mathematically this is expressed as $r_G = [(1 + r_1)(1 + r_2) \ldots (1 + r_n)]^{1/n} - 1$. An asset that achieves a geometric return of $r_G$ will accumulate to $(1 + r_G)^n$ times the initial investment over $n$ years. The geometric return is approximately equal to the arithmetic return minus one-half the variance, $\sigma^2$, of yearly returns, or $r_G \approx r_A - \frac{1}{2}\sigma^2$.

Investors can be expected to realize geometric returns only over long periods of time. The average geometric return is *always* less than the average arithmetic return except when all yearly returns are exactly equal. This difference is related to the volatility of yearly returns.

---

[**] Werner and Smith, *Wall Street*, p. 82.

A simple example demonstrates the difference. If a portfolio falls by 50 percent in the first year and then doubles (up 100 percent) in the second year, "buy-and-hold" investors are back to where they started, with a total return of zero. The compound or geometric return, $r_G$, defined above as $(1 - .5)(1 + 1) - 1$, accurately indicates the zero total return of this investment over the two years.

The average annual arithmetic return, $r_A$, is +25 percent = (–50 percent + 100 percent)/2. Over two years, this average return can be turned into a compound or total return only by successfully "timing" the market, specifically increasing the funds invested in the second year, hoping for a recovery in stock prices. Had the market dropped again in the second year, this strategy would have been unsuccessful and resulted in lower total returns than achieved by the buy-and-hold investor.

# 2

## CHAPTER

# RISK, RETURN AND THE COMING AGE WAVE

*"As a matter of fact, what investment can we find which offer real fixity or certainty income?. . . . As every reader of this book will clearly see, the man or woman who invests in bonds is speculating in the general level of prices, or the purchasing power of money.*

—Irving Fisher, 1912[1]

### MEASURING RISK AND RETURN

Risk and return are the building blocks of finance and portfolio management. Once the risk and expected return of each asset are specified, modern financial theory can determine the best portfolio for the investor. But the risk and return on stocks and bonds are not physical constants, like the speed of light or gravitational force, waiting to be discovered in the natural world. Historical values must be tempered with an appreciation of how investors, attempting to take advantage of the returns from the past, can alter those very returns in the future.

In finance, the problems estimating risk and return do not come from a lack of sufficient data. Daily prices on stocks and bonds go back more than 100 years, and monthly data on some agricultural and industrial prices go back centuries. But the overwhelming data does not guarantee accuracy in estimating these parameters, because you can never be

---

1 Irving Fisher et al., *How to Invest When Prices are Rising*, Scranton, Pa.: G. Lynn Sumner & Co., 1912, p. 6.

certain that the underlying factors that generate asset prices have remained unchanged. You cannot, as in the physical sciences, run controlled experiments, holding all other factors constant while changing the value of the variable in question. As Nobel laureate Paul Samuelson is fond of saying, "We have but one sample of history."

But you must start with the past in order to understand the future. The first chapter demonstrated that over the long run, not only have the returns on fixed-income assets lagged substantially behind equities, but, because of the uncertainty of inflation, fixed-income returns can be quite risky. In this chapter you shall see that this uncertainty makes portfolio allocations crucially dependent on the investor's planning horizon.

## RISK AND HOLDING PERIOD

For many investors, the most meaningful way to describe risk is by portraying a "worst case" scenario. Figure 2-1 displays the best and worst real returns for stocks, bonds, and bills from 1802 over holding periods ranging from 1 to 30 years. Note how dramatically the height of the bars, which measures the difference between best and worst returns, declines so rapidly for equities compared to fixed-income securities when the holding period increases.

Stocks are unquestionably riskier than bonds or bills in the short run. In every five-year period since 1802, however, the worst performance in stocks, at −11 percent per year, has been only slightly worse than the worst performance in bonds or bills. For ten-year holding periods, the worst stock performance has been *better than* that for bonds or bills.

For 20-year holding periods, stocks have never fallen behind inflation, while bonds and bills have fallen 3 percent per year behind the rate of inflation over this time period. A 3 percent annual loss over 20 years will wipe out one-half the purchasing power of a portfolio. For 30-year periods, the *worst* annual stock performance remained comfortably ahead of inflation by 2.6 percent per year, which is just below the *average* 30-year return on fixed-income assets.

The fact that stocks, in contrast to bonds or bills, have never offered investors a negative real holding period return yield over periods of 17 years or more is extremely significant. Although it might appear to be riskier to hold stocks than bonds, precisely the opposite is true: the safest long-term investment for the preservation of purchasing power has clearly been stocks, not bonds.

FIGURE  2–1

Maximum and Minimum Real Holding Period Returns, 1802–1997

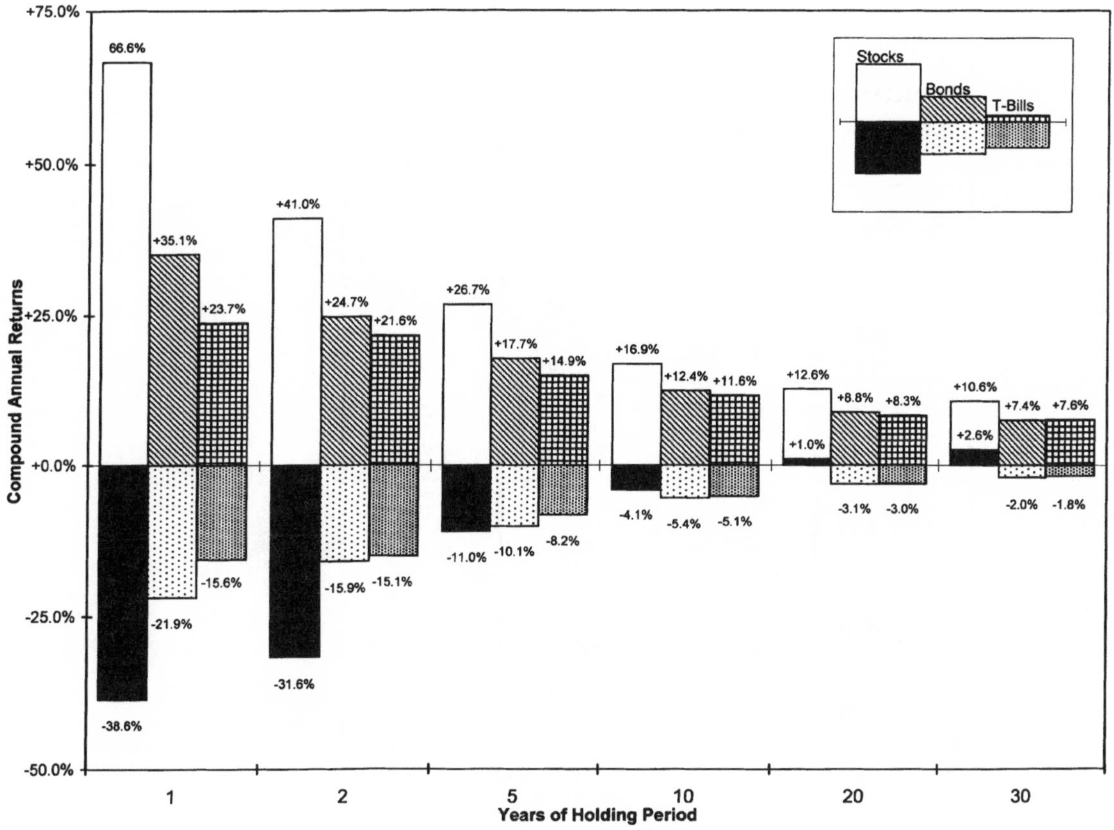

Table 2-1 shows the percentage of times that stock returns outper-form bond or bill returns over various holding periods. As the holding period increases, the probability that stocks will underperform fixed-income assets drops dramatically. For 10- year horizons, stocks beat bonds and bills about 80 percent of the time; for 20-year horizons, it is over 90 percent of the time; and over 30-year horizons, it is virtually 100 percent of the time. The last 30-year period in which bonds beat stocks ended in 1861, at the onset of the U.S. Civil War.

Although the dominance of stocks over bonds is readily apparent in the long run, it is more important to note that over one, and even two-year periods, stocks outperform bonds or bills *only* about three out

**TABLE 2–1**

Holding Period Comparisons: Percentage of Periods
When Stocks Outperform Bonds and Bills

| Holding Period | Time Period | Stocks outperform Bonds | Stocks outperform T-bills |
|---|---|---|---|
| 1 Year | 1802-1996 | 60.5 | 61.5 |
|        | 1871-1996 | 59.5 | 64.3 |
| 2 Year | 1802-1996 | 64.9 | 65.5 |
|        | 1871-1996 | 64.8 | 69.6 |
| 5 Year | 1802-1996 | 70.2 | 73.3 |
|        | 1871-1996 | 72.1 | 75.4 |
| 10 Year | 1802-1996 | 79.6 | 79.6 |
|         | 1871-1996 | 82.1 | 84.6 |
| 20 Year | 1802-1996 | 91.5 | 94.3 |
|         | 1871-1996 | 94.4 | 99.1 |
| 30 Year | 1802-1996 | 99.4 | 97.0 |
|         | 1871-1996 | 100.0 | 100.0 |

of every five years. This means that nearly two out of every five years a stockholder will fall behind the return on treasury bills or bank certificates. The high risk of underperforming fixed-income assets in the short run is the primary reason why it is so hard for many investors to stay in stocks.

## INVESTOR HOLDING PERIODS

Some investors might question whether holding periods of 10 or 20 or more years are relevant to their planning horizon. Yet these long horizons are far more relevant than most investors recognize. One of the greatest mistakes that investors make is to *underestimate* their holding period. This is because many investors think about the holding periods of a *particular* stock or bond. But the holding period that is relevant for portfolio allocation is the length of time the investors hold *any* stocks or bonds, no matter how many changes are made among the individual issues in their portfolio.

Figure 2-2 shows the average length of time that investors hold financial assets based on age and gender. It is assumed that individuals accumulate savings during their working years in order to build sufficient assets to fund their retirement, which normally occurs at age 65. After age 65, retirees live off the funds derived from both the returns and sale of their assets. It is assumed that investors either plan to exhaust all their assets by the end of their expected lifespan, or plan to retain one-half of their retirement assets at the end of their expected lifespan as a safety margin or for a possible bequest.

Under either assumption, Figure 2-2 shows that holding periods of 20 or 30 years or longer are not at all uncommon, even for investors relatively near retirement. It should be noted that the life expectancy of males at age 65 is now more than 16 years and for females is more than 20 years. Many retirees will be holding assets for 20 years or longer. And if the investor works beyond age 65, which is increasingly common, or plans to leave a large bequest, the average holding period is even longer than those indicated in Figure 2-2.

## INVESTOR RETURNS FROM MARKET PEAKS

Many investors, although convinced of the long-term superiority of equity, believe that they should not invest in stocks when stock prices appear at a peak. But this is not true for the long-term investor. Figure 2-3 shows the after-inflation total return over 30-year holding periods after major stock market peaks of the last century. Had you put $100 in stocks, bonds, or bills at those times and waited 30 years, you would still be significantly better off in stocks than any other investment.

From the 1929 peak, the total real return on stocks would have been $565 versus $141 in bonds or $79 in bills. From the January 1966 peak, stocks would have still garnered an advantage of greater than 2 to 1. On average, over the six major stock market peaks reached since 1900, stocks beat bonds and bills handily. The upward movement of

**FIGURE  2–2**

Average Holding Period Based on Retirement at Age 65 (M = Male, F = Female)

Life Expectancies Based on 1990 Data

stock values over time overwhelms the short-term fluctuations in the
market. There is no compelling reason for long-term investors to significantly reduce their stockholdings, no matter how high the market
seems.

Of course, if investors can identify peaks and troughs in the market, they can outperform the "buy-and-hold" investor. But, needless to
say, few investors can do this. And even if an investor sells stocks at the
peak, this does not guarantee superior returns. As difficult as it is to sell
when stock prices are high and everyone is optimistic, it is more difficult
to buy at market bottoms, when pessimism is widespread and few have
the confidence to venture back into stocks.

A number of "market timers" boasted how they yanked all their
money out of stocks before the 1987 stock crash. But many did not get

## FIGURE 2–3

Thirty-Year Real Returns After Market Peaks, With a $100 Initial Investment

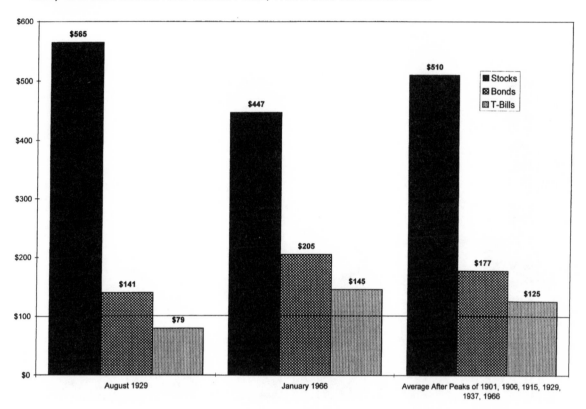

back into the market until it had already passed its previous highs. Despite the satisfaction of having sold before the crash, many of these "market seers" realized returns inferior to those investors who never tried to time the market cycles.

## STANDARD MEASURES OF RISK

The risk of holding stocks and bonds depends crucially on the holding period. Figure 2-4 displays the risk—defined as the standard deviation of *average* real annual returns—for stocks, bonds, and bills based on the historical sample of 195 years.

**FIGURE  2–4**

Holding Period Risk for Annual Real Returns, 1802–1996: Historical Data and Random Walk (Dashed Line)

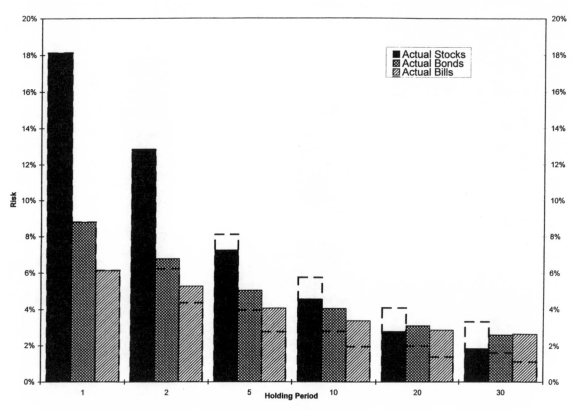

As was noted previously, stocks are riskier than fixed-income investments over short-term holding periods. But once the holding period increases to between 15 and 20 years, the *standard deviation* of average annual returns, which is the measure of the dispersions of returns used in portfolio theory, become *lower* than the standard deviation of average bond or bill returns. Over 30-year periods, equity risk falls to only two-thirds that of bonds or bills. As the holding period increases, the standard deviation of average stock returns falls nearly twice as fast as that of fixed-income assets.

It has been determined mathematically how fast the risk of average annual returns should decline as the holding period lengthens if asset returns follow a *random walk*.[2] A random walk is a process where future returns have no relation to, and are completely independent of, past returns. The dotted bars in Figure 2-4 show the decline in risk predicted under the random walk assumption. But data show that the random walk hypothesis cannot be maintained and that the risk of stocks declines far faster when the holding period increases more than predicted. This is a manifestation of the *mean reversion* of equity returns described in Chapter 1.

The risk of fixed-income assets, on the other hand, does not fall as fast as the random walk theory predicts. This slow decline of the standard deviation of average annual returns in the bond market is a manifestation of *mean aversion* of bond returns. Mean aversion means that once an asset's return deviates from its long-run average, there is increased chance that it will deviate further, rather than return to more normal levels. Mean aversion was certainly characteristic of both the Japanese and German bond returns depicted in Figure 1-6. Once inflation begins to accelerate, the process becomes cumulative, and bondholders have no chance of making up losses to their purchasing power. Stockholders, holding claims on real assets, rarely suffer a permanent loss due to inflation.

## CORRELATION BETWEEN STOCK AND BOND RETURNS

Even though the average return on bonds falls short of the return on stocks, bonds might still serve to diversify a portfolio and lower overall risk. This will be particularly true if bond and stock returns are negatively correlated. The *correlation coefficient*, which ranges between −1 and +1, measures the degree to which asset returns are correlated to the portfolio; the lower the correlation coefficient, the better the asset is for portfolio diversification. As the correlation coefficient between the asset and the portfolio increases, the diversifying quality of the asset declines.

Figure 2-5 shows the correlation coefficient between annual stock and bond returns for three subperiods between 1926 to 1996. From 1926 through 1969 the correlation was slightly negative, indicating that bonds were good diversifiers. From 1970 through 1989 the correlation

---

2 In particular, the standard deviation of average returns falls as the square root of the length of the holding period.

FIGURE 2–5

Correlation Coefficient Between Annual Stock and Bond Returns

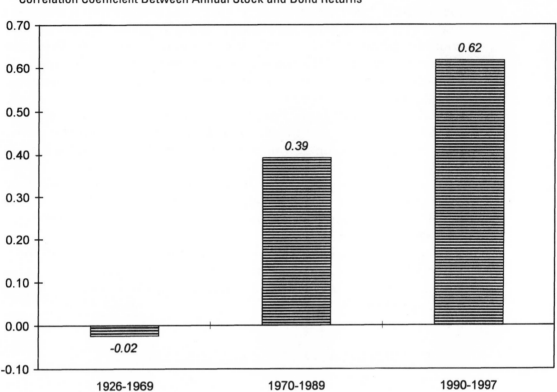

coefficient jumped to +0.46, and in the 1990s the correlation increased further to +0.62. This means that the diversifying qualities of bonds have diminished markedly over time.

There are good economic reasons why the correlation has become more positive. Under a gold-based monetary standard, bad economic times were associated with falling commodity prices. Therefore, the real value of government bonds rose and the stock market declined, as occurred during the Great Depression of the 1930s.

Under a paper-based monetary standard, bad economic times are more likely to be associated with *inflation*, not deflation. This is because the government often attempts to offset economic downturns with expansionary monetary policy, such as occurred during the 1970s. Such discretionary monetary expansion is impossible under a gold-based standard.

A second reason for the increase in correlation between stock and bond returns is the strategy that portfolio managers follow to allocate assets. Most tactical allocation models, which money managers use to minimize the risk and maximize the return of a portfolio, dictate that the share of a portfolio that is allocated to stocks be a function of the expected return on stocks relative to that on bonds. As interest rates rise, causing stock prices to fall, prospective bond returns become more attractive, motivating these managers to sell stocks. As a result, stock and bond prices move together. This is an example of how the actions by portfolio managers trying to take advantage of the *historical* correlation between stocks and bonds changes their future correlation.

## EFFICIENT FRONTIERS[3]

Modern portfolio theory describes how to alter the risk and return of a portfolio by changing the mix between assets. Figure 2-6, based on the nearly 200-year history of stock and bond returns, displays the risks and returns that result from varying the proportion of stocks and bonds in a portfolio.

The square at the bottom of each curve represents the risk and return of an all-bond portfolio, while the cross at the top of the curve represents the risk and return of an all-stock portfolio. The circle indicates the minimum risk achievable by combining stocks and bonds. The curve that connects these points represents the risk and return of all blends of portfolios from 100 percent bonds to 100 percent stocks. This curve, called the *efficient frontier*, is at the heart of modern portfolio analysis and the foundation of asset allocation models.

Investors can achieve any combination of risk and return along the curve by changing the proportion of stocks and bonds. Moving up the curve means increasing the proportion in stocks and correspondingly reducing the proportion in bonds. For short-term holding periods, moving up the curve increases both the return and the risk of the portfolio. The slope of any point on the efficient frontier indicates the risk-return trade-off for that allocation. By finding the points on the longer-term efficient frontiers that equal the slope on the one-year frontier, one can determine the allocations that represent the same risk-return trade-offs for all holding periods.

---

3 This section, which contains some advanced material, can be skipped without loss of continuity.

**FIGURE 2–6**

Risk-Return Trade-Offs for Various Holding Periods, 1802–1996

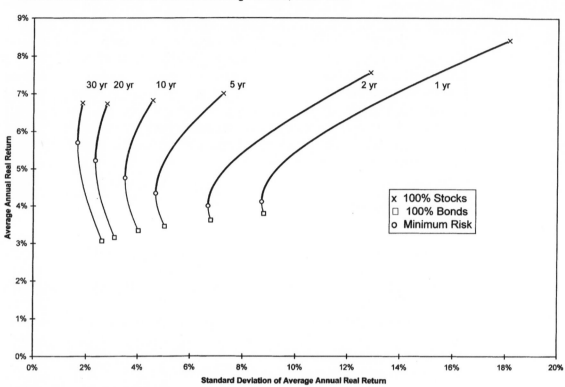

## RECOMMENDED PORTFOLIO ALLOCATIONS

Table 2-2 indicates the percentage of an investor's portfolio that should be invested in stocks based on both the risk tolerance and the holding period of the investor.[4] Four classes of investors are analyzed: the ultra-conservative investor who demands maximum safety no matter the return, the conservative investor who accepts small risks to achieve extra return, the moderate risk-taking investor, and the aggressive investor who is willing to accept substantial risks in search of extra returns.

The recommended equity allocation increases dramatically as the holding period lengthens. The analysis indicates that, based on the histor-

---

4 The one-year proportions (except minimum risk point) are arbitrary, and are used as benchmarks for other holding periods. Choosing different proportions as benchmarks does not qualitatively change the following results.

**TABLE 2–2**

Portfolio Allocation: Percentage of Portfolio in Stocks Based on All Historical Data

| Risk Tolerance | Holding Period | | | |
|---|---|---|---|---|
| | **1 year** | **5 years** | **10 years** | **30 years** |
| **Ultra-conservative (Minimum Risk)** | 7.0% | 25.0% | 40.6% | 71.3% |
| **Conservative** | 25.0% | 42.4% | 61.3% | 89.7% |
| **Moderate** | 50.0% | 62.7% | 86.0% | 112.9% |
| **Risk-taking** | 75.0% | 77.0% | 104.3% | 131.5% |

ical returns on stocks and bonds, ultra-conservative investors should hold nearly three-quarters of their portfolio in stocks over 30-year holding periods. This allocation is justified since stocks are safer than bonds in terms of purchasing power over long periods of time. Conservative investors should have nearly 90% of their portfolio in stocks, while moderate and aggressive investors should have over 100 percent in equity. This allocation can be achieved by borrowing or leveraging an all-stock portfolio.

Given these striking results, it might seem puzzling why the holding period has almost never been considered in portfolio theory. This is because modern portfolio theory was established when the academic profession believed in the random walk theory of security prices. As noted earlier, under a random walk, the relative risk of securities does not change for different time frames, so portfolio allocations do not depend on the holding period. The holding period becomes a crucial issue in portfolio theory when data reveal the mean reversion of the stock returns.[5]

---

5 For a similar conclusion, see Nicholas Barberis, "Investing for the Long Run When Returns Are Predictable," working paper, University of Chicago, July 1997. Paul Samuelson has shown that mean reversion will increase equity holdings if investors have a risk aversion coefficient greater than unity, which most researchers find is the case. See Samuelson, "Long-Run Risk Tolerance When Equity Returns Are Mean Regressing: Pseudoparadoxes and Vindication of 'Businessmen's Risk'" in W.C. Brainard, W.D. Nordhaus, and H.W. Watts, eds., *Money, Macroeconomics, and Public Policy*, Cambridge, Mass.: The MIT Press, 1991, pp. 181–200. See also Zvi Bodie, Robert Merton, and William Samuelson, "Labor Supply Flexibility and Portfolio Choice in a Lifecycle Model," *Journal of Economic Dynamics and Control*, vol. 16, no. 3 (July/October 1992), pp. 427–450. Bodie, et al. have shown that equity holdings can vary with age because stock returns can be correlated with labor income.

## INFLATION-INDEXED BONDS[6]

Until recently, there was no asset in the U.S. whose return was guaranteed against changes in the price level. Both stocks and bonds are risky when uncertain inflation is taken into account. But in January 1997, the U.S. Treasury issued the first government-guaranteed inflation-indexed bond. The coupons and principal repayment of this inflation-protected bond are automatically increased when the price level rises, so bondholders suffer no loss of purchasing power when they receive the coupons or final principal. Since any and all inflation is compensated, the interest rate on this bond is a *real*, or inflation-adjusted, interest rate.

In the summer of 1997, the interest rate on the inflation-indexed bond was 3.6 percent. Although this is about one-half the historical return on equity, these bonds are a very attractive alternative for investors who do not want to assume the risks inherent in stocks, but fear loss of purchasing power through inflation. In fact, for one-quarter of all ten-year periods from 1926, a 3.6 percent real return has matched or surpassed the performance of stocks.

Figure 2-7 replicates the efficient frontier for the ten-year holding period, and includes the risk and return possibilities achieved by adding inflation-indexed securities. Investors can attain any risk and return tradeoff along the straight line connecting the risk-free asset (indicated with a triangle) and the tangency to the efficient frontier. The point of tangency is the optimal mix of the risky assets in the portfolio.

The addition of inflation-indexed securities makes standard nominal bonds even less attractive. Based on historical data, the optimal portfolio of risky assets is 195 percent stocks and –95 percent bonds! This means you should sell (or "short") substantial bonds, using the proceeds to buy stocks or the indexed-linked bond. Historical data indicate that standard nominal bonds are completely dominated by stocks and inflation-indexed bonds. The failure of nominal bonds to provide long-term protection against uncertain inflation effectively excludes them from a long-term portfolio on the basis of historical risk and return data.

## THE COMING AGE WAVE

All estimates of risk and return must take account of the broad mix of economic, political, and social factors that impact the market. The next millennium reveals factors that are unlike anything we have witnessed for many generations. Population trends are likely to be the dominant

---

6 The material in this section can be skipped without loss of continuity.

**FIGURE 2–7**

Risk-Return Trade-Off for a Ten-Year Holding Period, 1802–1996

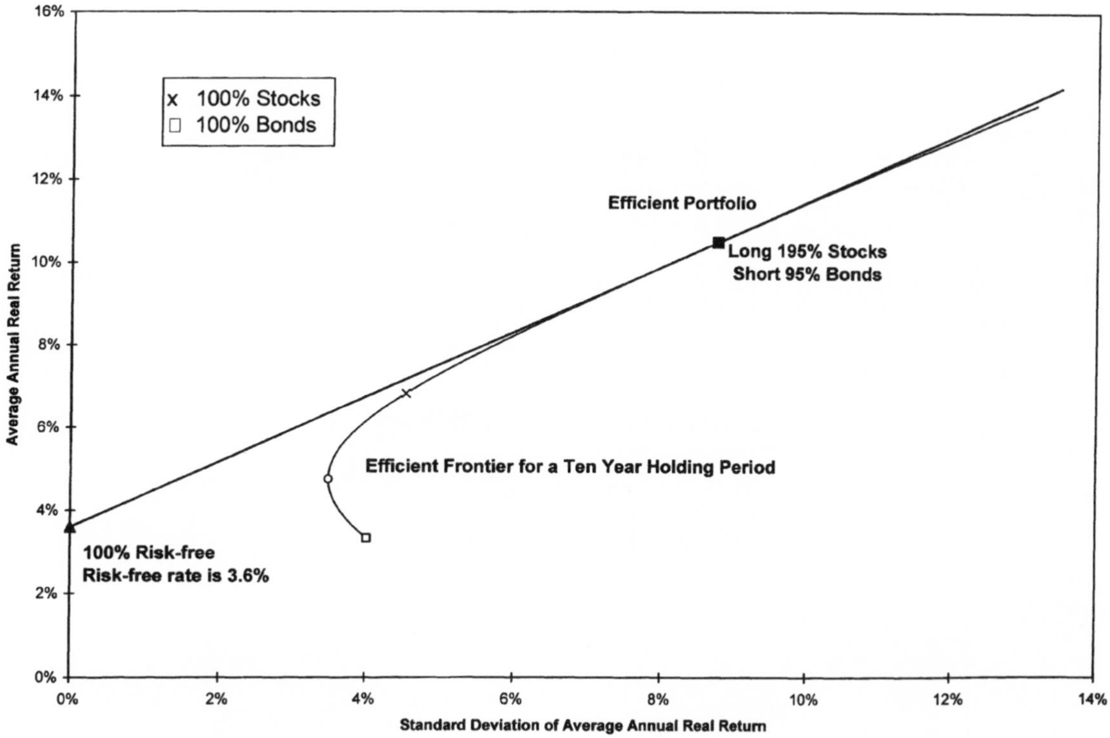

force guiding the accumulation and distribution of capital into the next century.

The "baby boomers," those born between 1946 and 1964, are rapidly accumulating assets in anticipation of their retirement needs. Their highest saving years occur when they are in their 40s and 50s, with the mortgage paid off (or nearly so) and children well on their way to finishing college. Many are hoping to prepare for their retirement by accelerating their tax-exempt contributions to IRAs, 401(k), and Keogh plans.

So far, the markets have been good to the boomers. Stock and bond returns in the 1980s and 1990s have been far above the norm and have left many with substantial assets. With their retirement nest eggs in place, many are projecting a life of leisure.

The only problem is that when it comes time to cash in your assets, you cannot eat your stock or bond certificates. Assets can be turned into purchasing power only if someone *else* is willing to give up his or her consumption so you can enjoy yours. Throughout history the younger generation, when they reach middle age, has had sufficient purchasing power to buy their parents' assets. But this time it is different. There are not nearly enough Generation Xers (the generation born in the late 1960s and 1970s) with sufficient wealth to absorb the boomer's substantial portfolio of stocks and bonds. The "Age Wave" of baby boomers is depicted in Fgure 2-8.

The looming problem of the boomer population is reminiscent of an old Wall Street story. A broker recommends that his client buy a small speculative stock with good earning prospects. The investor purchases

## FIGURE 2–8

U.S. Population Trends and Pension Flows

### U.S. AGE DISTRIBUTION: 1995 and 2040

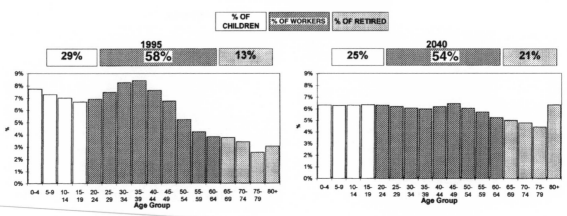

### PROJECTED INFLOWS AND OUTFLOWS IN U.S. PENSION FUNDS
(Real 1997$ Billion)

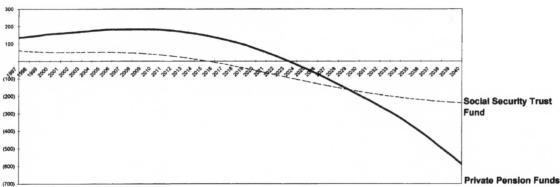

the stock, accumulating thousands of shares at ever-rising prices. Patting himself on the back, he phones his broker, instructing him to sell all his shares. His broker snaps back, "Sell? Sell to whom? You're the only one who has been buying the stock!"

The words "Sell? Sell to whom?" might haunt the baby boomers in the next century. Who are the buyers of the *trillions* of dollars of boomer assets? The generation that has swept politics, fashion, and the media in the last half of this century has produced an "Age Wave" that threatens to drown in financial assets. The consequences could be disastrous not only for the boomer's retirement but also for the economic health of the entire population.

John Shoven of Stanford University and Sylvester Scheiber of the Wyatt Company have projected the accumulation and distribution of boomer assets into the next century.[7] Their data as well as those of the Social Security Trust Fund are displayed in Figure 2-8. The net inflow of pension assets, which has contributed to the bull market of the 1990s, becomes a net outflow by 2015 in the Social Security Trust Fund and 10 years later for all private pension plans. The massive distribution of stocks and bonds portends soaring interest rates and falling security prices.

## SOLUTION TO THE "AGE WAVE CRISIS"

Is there a resolution to this "Age Wave Crisis? Yes, but it cannot be resolved by the United States, or for that matter by any country acting alone. A solution must involve the world economy. As Figure 2-9 indicates, the age wave is strictly a phenomenon of the *developed* world. The *developing* world, such as China, India, Indonesia, and Latin America has experienced ever-increasing population growth. Over the next half-century workers aged 20–65 will decline from 60% of the population to 54% in the developed world while in the faster-growing developing countries the percentage of workers will rise from 51% to 58%.[8]

The developing world emerges as the answer to the age mismatch of the industrialized economies. If their progress continues, they will sell goods to the baby boomers and thereby acquire the buying power to purchase their assets. In the 1990s the developed world is many times richer than the developing world and is providing them with capital to

---

7 John Shoven and Sylvester Scheiber, *The Consequences of Population Aging on Private Pension Fund Saving and Asset Markets*, Center for Economic Policy Research, pub. no. 363, September 1993.
8 The data come from United Nations, *The Sex and Age Distribution of the World Populations*, The 1994 Revision.

## FIGURE 2–9

Capital Flowing Between the Developed and Developing Worlds

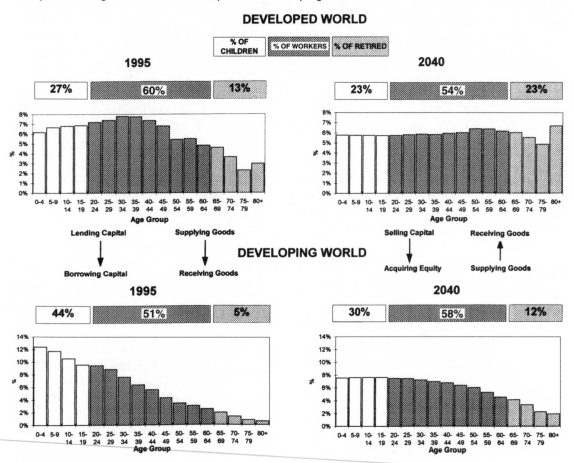

develop their factories and infrastructures. As these economies grow, the rest of the world will increase their standard of living and saving. First they will pay off their debts, then acquire ownership of their own capital and eventually buy the assets of the developed world.

The success of this scenario is critically dependent on the continued integration of the world economies and growth of the developing nations. Protectionism, import restrictions, or other impediments to the free flow of goods, services, and capital among countries would sharply curtail the ability of the world economy to effect these massive asset transfers. A permanent slowdown in growth of the developing economies will have sharply negative implications for all the world's capital markets.

# 3
CHAPTER

# PERSPECTIVES ON STOCKS AS INVESTMENTS

*It was only as the public came to realize, largely through the writings of Edgar Lawrence Smith, that stocks were to be preferred to bonds during a period of dollar depreciation, that the bull market began in good earnest to cause a proper valuation of common shares.*

—Irving Fisher, 1930[1]

*The "new-era" doctrine—that "good" stocks (or "blue chips") were sound investments regardless of how high the price paid for them—was at the bottom only a means of rationalizing under the title of "investment" the well-nigh universal capitulation to the gambling fever.*

—Benjamin Graham and David Dodd, 1934[2]

It was a seasonally cool Monday evening on October 14, 1929 when Irving Fisher arrived at the Builders' Exchange Club at 2 Park Avenue in New York City. Fisher, a professor of economics at Yale University and the most renowned economist of his time, was scheduled to address the monthly meeting of the Purchasing Agents Association.

---

1 Irving Fisher, *The Stock Market Crash and After*, New York: MacMillan Co., 1930, p. 99.
2 Benjamin Graham and David Dodd, *Security Analysis*, 1934, p. 11.

Irving Fisher, the founder of modern capital theory, was no mere academic. He actively analyzed and forecast financial market conditions, wrote dozens of newsletters on topics ranging from health to investments, and created a highly successful card indexing firm based on one of his own patented inventions. Despite hailing from a modest background, his personal wealth in the summer of 1929 exceeded $10 million.[3]

Members of the association and the press crowded into the meeting room. Fisher's speech was mainly designed to defend investment trusts, the forerunner of today's mutual funds. But the audience was most eager to hear his views on the stock market.

Investors had been nervous since early September when Roger Babson, businessman and market seer, predicted a "terrific" crash in stock prices.[4] Fisher had dismissed this pessimism, noting that Babson had been bearish for some time. But the public sought to be reassured by the great man who had championed stocks for so long.

The audience was not disappointed. After a few introductory remarks, Fisher uttered a sentence that, much to his regret, became one of the most quoted phrases in stock market history: "Stock prices have reached what looks like a permanently high plateau."[5]

On October 29, two weeks to the day after Fisher's speech, stocks crashed. Fisher's "high plateau" transformed into a bottomless abyss. The next three years witnessed the most devastating market collapse in history. Like Neville Chamberlain's proud claim that the "agreement" Adolph Hitler signed in Munich in September 1938 guaranteed "peace in our time," Fisher's prediction about the stock market stands as a memorial to the folly of great men who failed to envision impending disaster.

After the crash, Fisher's reputation as a forecaster was shattered. It made little difference that he was right in many of his other economic predictions. He had correctly forecast the rising bull market in the 1920s, rightly emphasized the importance of the Federal Reserve in creating a favorable economic climate, and properly defended investment trusts, the forerunners of today's mutual funds, as the best way that the public could participate in the stock market.

---

3 Robert Loring Allen, *Irving Fisher: A Biography*, Cambridge: Blackwell, 1993, p. 206.
4 *Commercial and Financial Chronicle*, September 7, 1929.
5 "Fisher See Stocks Permanently High," *New York Times*, October 16, 1929, p. 2.

Fisher was also right that October evening when he pointed out that the increase in stock prices at the time largely stemmed from a rise in earnings. Fisher noted, "Time will tell whether the increase will continue sufficiently to justify the present high level. I expect that it will."[6]

Time did eventually justify stock levels in 1929. But the time frame was far longer than Irving Fisher, or for that matter anyone else, believed. The truth that stocks were in fact better investments after their prices had *dropped* from their highs held no interest for investors. The proven long-term superiority of equity investing, which served as the rationale during the stock market advance, was roundly ignored as investors dumped stocks regardless of their intrinsic value.

## EARLY VIEWS OF STOCK INVESTING

Throughout the nineteenth century, stocks were deemed the province of speculators and insiders, but certainly not conservative investors. It was not until the early twentieth century that researchers came to realize that stocks, as a class, might be suitable investments under certain economic conditions. At that time, Irving Fisher himself maintained that stocks would indeed be superior to bonds during inflationary times, but that common shares would likely underperform bonds during periods of declining prices.[7] That stocks were better investments during inflation but inferior during deflation became the conventional wisdom of the early twentieth century.

This popular conception, however, was exploded by Edgar Lawrence Smith, a financial analyst and investment manager of the 1920s. Smith was the first to demonstrate that accumulations in a diversified portfolio of common stocks outperformed bonds not only in times of rising commodity prices, but also when prices were falling. Smith published his studies in 1924 in a book entitled *Common Stocks as Long-Term Investments*. In the introduction he stated:

> These studies are a record of a failure—the failure of facts to sustain a preconceived theory. [The theory] that high-grade bonds had proved to be better investments during periods of [falling commodity prices].[8]

---

6 *New York Times*, Ibid, p.2.
7 Irving Fisher, *How to Invest When Prices Are Rising*, Scranton, Pa.: G. Lynn Sumner & Co., 1912.
8 Edgar L. Smith, *Common Stocks as Long-Term Investments*, New York: Macmillan, 1925, p. v.

By examining stock returns back to the Civil War, Smith found that not only did stocks beat bonds whether prices were rising or falling, but there was a very small chance that you would have to wait a long time (which he put at 6 and, at most, 15 years) before having an opportunity to liquidate your stocks at a profit. He concluded:

> We have found that there is a force at work in our common stock holdings which tends ever toward increasing their principal value . . . unless we have had the extreme misfortune to invest at the very peak of a noteworthy rise, those periods in which the average market value of our holding remains less than the amount we paid for them are of comparatively short duration. Our hazard even in such extreme cases appears to be that of time alone.[9]

Smith's conclusion was right, not only historically, but also prospectively. It took just over 15 years to recover the money invested at the 1929 peak, following a crash far worse than Smith had ever examined. And since World War II, the recovery period for stocks has been better than Smith's wildest dreams. The *longest* it has even taken since 1945 to recover an original investment in the stock market (including reinvested dividends) was the 3½-year period from December 1972 to June 1976.

## INFLUENCE OF SMITH'S WORK

Smith wrote his book at the onset of one of the greatest bull markets in our history. Its conclusions caused a sensation in both academic and investing circles. The prestigious weekly, *The Economist*, stated, "Every intelligent investor and stockbroker should study Mr. Smith's most interesting little book, and examine the tests individually and their very surprising results."[10]

Irving Fisher saw Smith's study as a confirmation of his own long-held belief that bonds were overrated as safe investment in a world with uncertain inflation. Fisher summarized:

> It seems, then, that the market overrates the safety of "safe" securities and pays too much for them, that it underrates the risk of risky securities and pays too little for them, that it pays too much for immediate and too little for remote returns, and finally, that it mistakes the steadiness of money income from a bond for a steadiness of real income which it does

---

9 Edgar L. Smith, Ibid., p. 81.
10 "Ordinary Shares as Investments," *The Economist*, June 6, 1925, p. 1141.

not possess. In steadiness of real income, or purchasing power, a list of diversified common stocks surpasses bonds.[11]

Smith's ideas quickly crossed the Atlantic and were the subject of much discussion in Great Britain. John Maynard Keynes, the great British economist and originator of the business cycle theory that became the accepted paradigm for generations, reviewed Smith's book with much excitement. Keynes stated:

> The results are striking. Mr. Smith finds in almost every case, not only when prices were rising, but also when they were falling, that common stocks have turned out best in the long-run, indeed, markedly so . . . . This actual experience in the United States over the past fifty years affords *prima facie* evidence that the prejudice of investors and investing institutions in favor of bonds as being "safe" and against common stocks as having, even the best of them, a "speculative" flavor, has led to a relative over-valuation of bonds and under-valuation of common stocks.[12]

Money managers were quick to realize the impact of Smith's work. Hartley Withers wrote in *The London Investors Chronicle* and *Money Market Review*:

> Old-fashioned investors and their old-fashioned advisers have so long been in the habit of looking on all holdings of ordinary shares or common stocks as something rather naughty and speculative, that one feels a certain amount of hesitation in even ventilating the view that is now rapidly gaining acceptance that ordinary shares, under certain conditions, are really safer than [bonds], even though the latter may be of the variety which is commonly called "gilt-edged."[13]

Smith's writings were published in such prestigious journals as the *Review of Economic Statistics* and the *Journal of the American Statistical Association*.[14] Further research confirmed his results. Smith acquired

---

11 From foreword by Irving Fisher in Kenneth S. Van Strum, *Investing in Purchasing Power*, New York: Barrons, 1925, p. vii. Van Strum, a writer for Barron's weekly, followed up and confirmed Smith's research.
12 J. M. Keynes, "An American Study of Shares versus Bonds as Permanent Investments," *The Nation & The Athenaeum*, May 2, 1925, p. 157.
13 Quoted by Edgar Lawrence Smith in *Common Stocks and Business Cycles*, New York: The William-Frederick Press, 1959, p. 20.
14 Edgar Lawrence Smith, "Market Value of Industrial Equities," *Review of Economic Statistics*, IX, pp. 37–40, January, 1927 and "Tests Applied to an Index of the Price Level for Industrial Stocks," *Journal of the American Statistical Association*, supplement (March 1931), pp. 127–35.

an international following when Siegfried Stern published an extensive study of returns in common stock in 13 European countries from the onset of World War I through 1928. Stern's study showed that the advantage of investing in common stocks over bonds and other financial investments extended far beyond America's financial markets.[15]

## COMMON STOCK THEORY OF INVESTMENT

The research demonstrating the superiority of stocks became known as the "Common Stock Theory of Investment."[16] Smith himself was careful to not overstate his findings. He wrote:

> *Over a period of years* the principal value of a *well-diversified holding* of common stocks of *representative* corporations in *essential* industries tends to increase in accordance with the operation of compound interest. . . . Such stock holding may be relied upon *over a term of years* to pay an average income return on such increasing values of something more than the average current rate on commercial paper.[17]

Yet Chelcie C. Bosland, a professor of economics at Brown University in the 1930s, claimed that the common stock theory was often misused to justify any investment in stocks no matter what the price. Bosland stated:

> The purchase of common stocks after 1922 was more likely to result in profit than in loss. Even though this was largely a cyclical up-swing, many believed that it was a vindication of the theory that common stocks are good long-term investments. Participation in this profit-making procedure became widespread. The "boom psychology" was everywhere in evidence. No doubt the "common stock theory" gave even to the downright speculator the feeling that his actions were based upon the solid rock of scientific finding.[18]

---

15 S. Stern, *Fourteen Years of European Investments, 1914–1928*, The Bankers' Publishing Co., 1929.
16 Chelcie C. Bosland, *The Common Stock Theory of Investment, Its Development and Significance*, New York: The Ronald Press Co., 1937.
17 Edgar Lawrence Smith, op. cit., p. 79, emphasis added.
18 Chelcie C. Bosland, *The Common Stock Theory of Investment*, by Assoc. Prof. of Economics, Brown University, New York: The Ronald Press, 1937, p. 4.

## A RADICAL SHIFT IN SENTIMENT

But the glorious days for common stocks did not last. The crash pushed the image of stocks as good investments into the doghouse, and with it the credibility of Smith's contention that stocks were the best long-term investments. Lawrence Chamberlain, an author and well-known investment banker, stated, *"Common stocks, as such, are not superior to bonds as long-term investments, because primarily they are not investments at all. They are speculations."*[19]

The common-stock theory of investment was attacked from all angles. In 1934 Benjamin Graham, an investment fund manager, and David Dodd, a finance professor at Columbia University, wrote *Security Analysis*, which became the bible of the value-oriented approach to analyzing stocks and bonds. Through its many editions, the book has had a lasting impact on students and market professionals alike.

Graham and Dodd clearly blamed Smith's book for feeding the bull market mania of the 1920s by proposing plausible sounding but fallacious theories to justify the purchase of stocks. They wrote:

> The self-deception of the mass speculator must, however, have its element of justification. . . . In the new-era bull market, the "rational" basis was the record of long-term improvement shown by diversified common-stock holdings. [There is] a small and rather sketchy volume from which the new-era theory may be said to have sprung. The book is entitled *Common Stocks as Long-Term Investments* by Edgar Lawrence Smith, published in 1924.[20]

## POST-CRASH VIEW OF STOCK RETURNS

The crash left the impression that stocks could not be worthy long-term investments. So much had been written about so many who had been wiped out by the market that the notion that stocks could still beat other financial assets was regarded as ludicrous.

In the late 1930s, Alfred Cowles III, founder of the Cowles Commission for economic research, constructed capitalization-weighted stock indexes back to 1871 of all stocks traded on the New

---

19 Lawrence Chamberlain and William W. Hay, *Investment and Speculations*, New York: Henry Holt & Co., 1931, p. 55. Emphasis his.
20 Benjamin Graham and David Dodd, *Security Analysis*, 2nd edition, New York: McGraw-Hill, 1940, p. 357.

York Stock Exchange. Cowles examined stock returns including reinvested dividends and concluded:

> During that period [1871–1926] there is considerable evidence to support the conclusion that stocks in general sold at about three-quarters of their true value as measured by the return to the investor.[21]

Yet Cowles placed the blame for the crash of 1929 squarely on the shoulder of the government, claiming that increased taxation and government controls drove stock prices downward.

As stocks slowly recovered from the depression, their returns seemed to warrant a new look. In 1953, two professors from the University of Michigan, Wilford Eiteman and Frank P. Smith, published a study of the investment returns on all industrial companies with trading volume over one million shares in 1936. By regularly purchasing these 92 stocks without any regard to the stock market cycle (a strategy called "dollar cost averaging"), they found that the returns over the next 14 years, at 12.2 percent per year, far exceeded those in fixed-income investments. Twelve years later they repeated the study, using the same stocks they used in their previous study. This time the returns were even higher, despite the fact they made no adjustment for any of the new firms or new industries that had surfaced in the interim. They wrote:

> If a portfolio of common stocks selected by such obviously foolish methods as were employed in this study will show an annual compound rate of return as high as 14.2 percent, then a small investor with limited knowledge of market conditions can place his savings in a diversified list of common stocks with some assurance that, given time, his holding will provide him with safety of principal and an adequate annual yield.[22]

Many dismissed the Eiteman and Smith study because it did not include the great crash of 1929–32. But in 1964, two professors from the University of Chicago, Lawrence Fisher and James H. Lorie, examined stock returns through the stock crash of 1929, the Great Depression, and World War II.[23] Fisher and Lorie concluded that stocks offered significantly higher returns (which they reported at 9.0 percent per year) than

---

21 Alfred Cowles III and associates, *Common Stock Indexes 1871–1937*, Bloomington, Indiana: Pricipia Press, 1938, p. 50.

22 Wilford J. Eiteman and Frank P. Smith, *Common Stock Values and Yields*, Ann Arbor, Michigan: University of Michigan Press, 1962. p. 40.

23 "Rates of Return on Investment in Common Stocks," *Journal of Business*, 37 (January 1964), pp. 1–21.

any other investment media during the entire 35-year period, 1926 through 1960. They even factored taxes and transaction costs into their return calculations and concluded:

> It will perhaps be surprising to many that the returns have consistently been so high. . . . The fact that many persons choose investments with a substantially lower average rate of return than that available on common stocks suggests the essentially conservative nature of those investors and the extent of their concern about the risk of loss inherent in common stocks.[24]

Ten years later, Roger Ibbotson and Rex Sinquefield published an even more extensive review of returns in an article entitled, "Stocks, Bonds, Bills, and Inflation: Year-by-Year Historical Returns (1926–74)."[25] They acknowledged their indebtedness to the Lorie and Fisher study and confirmed the superiority of stocks as long-term investments. Their summary statistics, which are published annually in yearbooks, are frequently quoted and have often served as the return benchmarks for the securities industry.[26]

## INVESTMENT PHILOSOPHY AND THE VALUATION OF EQUITY

The high prices that stocks reach during bull markets, which historians often characterize as filled with "undue" or "unwarranted" optimism, are in fact often justified on the basis of the *long-term record* of corporate earnings and dividend growth. Unfortunately, this long perspective does not interest most players in the market. Most investors roundly ignore forecasters who analyze the long run, but do not predict the direction of the market in the short run.

Over 60 years ago, John Maynard Keynes lamented the lack of long-term investors in the securities market. He ascribed it to human psychology, stating:

> Life is not long enough; human nature desires quick results, there is a peculiar zest in making money quickly, and remoter gains are discounted by the average man at a very high rate.[27]

---

24 Ibid., p. 20.
25 *Journal of Business*, 49 (January 1976), pp. 11–43.
26 *Stocks, Bonds, Bills, and Inflation Yearbooks, 1983–1997*, Ibbotson and Associates, Chicago, Illinois.
27 John Maynard Keynes, *The General Theory of Employment, Interest and Money* (originally published in 1936), New York: Harcourt Brace and World, 1965 edition, p. 157.

Yet these "remote gains," which accrue so assuredly to the long-run stockholder, must be the center of most people's investment strategy. The doctrine that common stocks provide the best way to accumulate long-term wealth, first expounded by Edgar Lawrence Smith nearly 75 years ago, has been reconfirmed in all subsequent research.

PART TWO

# STOCK RETURNS

# CHAPTER 4

# STOCKS, STOCK AVERAGES, AND THE DOW STRATEGY

*It has been said that figures rule the world.*

—Johann Wolfgang Goethe, 1830

## MARKET AVERAGES

### The Dow-Jones

"How's the market doing?" one stock investor asks another.
"It's having a good day—it's up over 70 points."

Exchanges like this are made thousands of times a day throughout the United States. No one asks, "What's up 70 points?" Everyone knows the answer: the Dow-Jones Industrial Average, the most quoted stock average in the world. This index, popularly called the "Dow," is so renowned that the news media often call the Dow "the stock market." No matter how imperfectly the index describes the movement of share prices—and virtually no money manager pegs his or her performance to it—it is the way most investors think of the stock market.

Charles Dow, one of the founders of Dow Jones & Co., which also publishes *The Wall Street Journal*, created the Dow-Jones averages in the late 19th century. On February 16, 1885, he began publishing a daily average of 12 stocks (10 rails and 2 industrials) that represented active and highly capitalized stocks. Four years later, Dow published a daily average based on 20 stocks—18 rails and 2 industrials.

As industrial and manufacturing firms succeeded railroads in importance, the Dow Industrial average was created on May 26, 1896 from the 12 stocks shown in Table 4-1. The old index created in 1889 was re-constituted and renamed the *Rail Average* on October 26, 1896. In 1916, the Industrial average was increased to 20 stocks, and in 1928 the number was expanded to 30. The Rail Average, whose name was changed in 1970 to the *Transportation Average*, is comprised of 20 stocks, as it has been for over a century.

**TABLE 4–1**

The Dow Jones Industrial Average

| 1896 | 1916 | 1928 | 1997 | | |
|------|------|------|------|------|------|
| | | | Dow Companies | Price Wght | Mkt Value Wght |
| American Cotton Oil | American Beet Sugar | Allied Chemical | Allied-Signal | 4.11% | 1.33% |
| | American Can | American Can | Aluminum Co. of America | 3.97% | 0.79% |
| American Sugar | | American Smelting | American Express | 3.80% | 2.05% |
| | American Car & foundry | American Sugar | American Tel & Tel | 1.90% | 3.53% |
| | American Locomotive | American Tobacco | Boeing | 2.62% | 3.02% |
| American Tobacco | | Atlantic Refining | Caterpillar | 2.70% | 1.17% |
| | American Smelting | Bethlehem Steel | Chevron | 3.72% | 2.79% |
| Chicago Gas | | Chrysler | Coca-Cola | 2.85% | 8.09% |
| | American Sugar | General Electric | Du Pont | 2.94% | 3.81% |
| | American Tel & Tel | General Motors | Eastman Kodak | 3.27% | 1.22% |
| Distilling & Cattle | | General Railway Signal | Exxon | 3.04% | 8.63% |
| | Anaconda Copper | Goodrich | General Electric | 3.15% | 11.78% |
| Feeding | Baldwin Locomotive | International Harvester | General Motors | 3.15% | 2.59% |
| | | International Nickel | Goodyear | 2.95% | 0.53% |
| | Central Leather | Mack Trucks | Hewlett-Packard | 3.09% | 3.60% |
| General Electric | | Nash Motors | IBM | 4.92% | 5.54% |
| | General Electric | North American | International Paper | 2.57% | 0.89% |
| Laclede Gas | Goodrich | Paramount Publix | J.P. Morgan | 5.27% | 1.08% |
| | | Postum, Inc. | Johnson & Johnson | 2.76% | 4.21% |
| | Republic Iron & Steel | Radio Corp. | McDonald's | 2.21% | 1.74% |
| National Lead | Studebaker | Sears, Roebuck | Merck | 4.54% | 6.28% |
| | | Standard Oil (N.J.) | Minn. Mining | 4.37% | 2.08% |
| North American | Texas Co. | Texas Corp. | Philip Morris | 2.11% | 5.85% |
| | U.S. Rubber | Texas Gulf Sulphur | Procter & Gamble | 6.34% | 4.91% |
| | | Union Carbide | Sears Roebuck | 2.68% | 1.20% |
| Tennessee Coal & Iron | U.S. Steel | U.S. Steel | Travelers Group | 3.21% | 2.36% |
| | Utah Copper | Victor Talking Machine | Union Carbide | 2.46% | 0.35% |
| U.S. Leather pfd. | | Westinghouse Electric | United Technologies | 3.78% | 1.02% |
| | Westinghouse | Woolworth | WalMart | 1.80% | 4.66% |
| U.S. Rubber | Western Union | Wright Aeronautical | Walt Disney | 3.72% | 2.88% |

The early Dow stocks were centered on commodities: cotton, sugar, tobacco, lead, leather, rubber, etc. Six of the 12 companies have survived in much the same form, but only one—General Electric, which boasts the world's highest market value—has both retained its membership in the Dow Industrials and not changed its name.[1]

Almost all of the original Dow stocks thrived as large and successful firms, even if they did not remain in the index (see Appendix A for details). The only exception was U.S. Leather Corp., which was liquidated in the 1950s. Shareholders received $1.50 plus one share of Keta Oil & Gas, a firm acquired earlier. But in 1955, Keta's assets were looted by the president, Lowell Birrell, who later fled to Brazil to escape U.S. authorities. Shares in U.S. Leather, which in 1909 was the seventh-largest corporation in the United States, became worthless.

## Computation of the Dow Index

The original Dow-Jones averages were simply the sum of the prices of the component shares divided by the number of stocks in the index. But this divisor had to be adjusted over time because of changes in the companies that constituted the average and stock splits. In January 1998, the divisor was about 0.25, so that a one-point rise in any Dow stock caused the average to increase about 4 points.[2]

The Dow Industrials is a price-weighted index, which means that the prices of the component stocks are added together and then divided by the number of firms in the index. As a result, proportional movements of high-priced stocks in the Dow averages have a much greater impact than movements of lower-priced stocks, regardless of the size of the company. A price-weighted index has the property that when a component stock splits, the split stock has a reduced impact on the average, and all the other stocks a slightly increased impact.[3]

---

1 Chicago Gas Company, an original member of the 12 Dow stocks, became People's Energy Inc. and was a member of the Dow Utilities Average until May 1997.
2 The procedure for computing the Dow-Jones averages when a new (or split) stock is substituted is as follows: the component stock prices are added up before and after the change, and a new divisor is determined that yields the same average as before the change. Because of stock splits, the divisor generally moves downward over time, but the divisor could increase if a higher-priced stock is substituted for a lower-priced one in the average.
3 Before 1914, the divisor was left unchanged when a stock split and the stock price was multiplied by the split ratio when computing the index. This led to rising stocks having greater weight in the average, something akin to value-weighted stock indexes today.

Price-weighted indexes are unusual since the impact of the firm's price on the index has nothing to do with the relative size of the company. This is in stark contrast to a capitalization-weighted index, such as Standard and Poor's 500 Index, which is described later in the chapter. As of September 1997, the 30 Dow stocks were valued at $1.8 trillion, which is about 20 percent of the capitalization of the entire U.S. market. Out of the 10 largest U.S.-based capitalization stocks, all but Microsoft and Intel are in the Dow Industrials. But not all the Dow stocks are large. Three Dow stocks are not in the top 100: Alcoa, Goodyear, and the smallest, Union Carbide, which is ranked 240th.

## Long-Term Trends in the Dow-Jones

Figure 4-1 plots the monthly high and low of the Dow-Jones Industrial average from its inception in 1885, corrected for changes in the price level. The inset shows the Dow Industrial average, uncorrected for inflation.

A trend line and a channel are created by statistically regressing the Dow on a time trend. The upper and lower bound are one standard deviation, or 50 percent, above and below the trend. The slope of the trend line, 1.70 percent per year, is the average compound rate at which the Dow stocks have appreciated after inflation since 1885. The Dow-Jones average, like most other popular averages, excludes dividends, so the change in the index greatly understates the total return on the Dow stocks. Since the average dividend yield on stocks was about 4.7 percent during this time, the total annual real compound return on the Dow stocks was 6.5 percent over this period, very close to the long-term real stock return reported in Chapter 1.

The inflation-corrected Dow Industrials have stayed within the channel about three-quarters of the time. When the Dow broke out of the channel to the upside, as it did in 1929 and again in the mid-1960s, stocks subsequently suffered poor short-term returns. On the other hand, when stocks penetrated the channel on the downside, they subsequently experienced superior short-term returns.

Yet penetration through the upper trend line does not mean that the long-term investor should abandon stocks. There were six bull markets when the Dow reached the trend line in the last 100 years. The 30-year returns on stocks purchased at those times still greatly exceeded the returns on either short or long bonds, as has been shown in Figure 2-3.

The Dow can stay above the upper trend line for long periods of time, as it did in the 1960s. The rapid inflation of the 1970s sent real

## FIGURE 4-1

The Real Dow Jones Industrial Average, February 1885 to July 1997 (in 1997 Dollars)

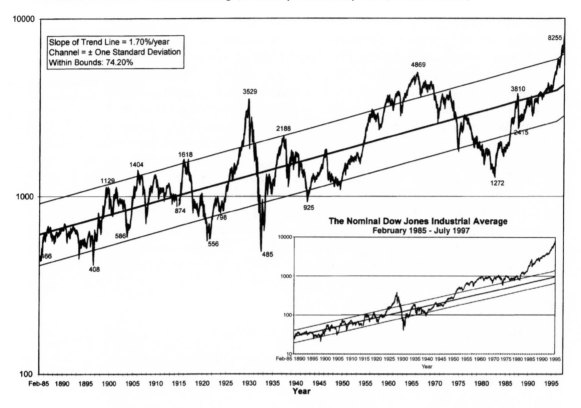

stock prices downward, but bonds and bills also suffered negative real returns during that decade. Only real assets, such as precious metals and real estate, were able to outperform inflation during the 1970s.

## Use of Trend Lines to Predict Trends

Using channels and trend lines to predict future returns, however tempting, can be misleading. Long-standing trends have been broken in the past. Uncorrected for inflation, the Dow industrials broke and stayed above the trend line in the mid-1950s, as shown in the inset of Figure 4-1. This is because inflation, caused by the shift to a paper money standard, propelled nominal stock prices justifiably above their previous, noninflationary trend. Those who use trend-line analysis and who failed to analyze stock prices in real, instead of nominal terms, would have sold in 1955 and never reentered the market.[4]

There could be another reason why the trend line on the long-term real Dow might be permanently penetrated in the future. Since stock indexes record only capital appreciation, they understate total returns, which also includes dividends. The magnitude of understatement has increased in recent years as firms have paid an extremely low fraction of their earnings as dividends. Instead, management has used retained earnings to buy back stock, retire debt, and expand and upgrade capital, all of which increase the price of the shares. This means that there has been an increase in capital gains, which is represented in stock indexes, and a decrease in dividend income, which is not.

If the low payout ratio and correspondingly low dividend yield continue, we should see the trend line shown in Figure 4-1 eventually broken on the upside. This does not mean that stocks will yield a higher future total return to investors, but merely that the *composition* of those returns has shifted toward capital appreciation and away from dividend income. We shall explore this in more detail in the next chapter.

## VALUE-WEIGHTED INDEXES

### The Cowles Index

Although the Dow Industrial Average was published in 1885, it was certainly not comprehensive, covering at most 30 stocks. In 1939, Alfred Cowles, founder of the Cowles Foundation for Economic Research, constructed a stock index back to 1871 that consisted of all stocks listed on the New York Stock Exchange. This index was the first to weight each stock's performance by its capitalization, or market value, a technique now recognized as giving the best indication of the direction of the overall market.

### Standard & Poor's Index

The Cowles index became the basis of what is currently the most important benchmark among portfolio analysts, the Standard & Poor's, or S & P 500 Index. This, like the Cowles index, is a capitalization-weighted index of the largest U.S. corporations.

---

4 For a related situation where a long-standing benchmark was broken because of inflation, see the first section in Chapter 5, *An Evil Omen Returns*.

The Standard & Poor's stock price index was inaugurated on March 4, 1957. At that time, the value of the S & P 500 Index comprised about 90 percent of all NYSE-listed stocks. The 500 stocks contained 425 industrials, 25 railroad, and 50 utility corporations. In 1988, the Standard & Poor's Corporation dropped any fixed weighting between different industries.

The S & P 500 Index was calculated back to 1926, although for many years before 1957 the index did not contain 500 stocks. A base value of 10 was chosen for the average index value from 1941 to 1943 so that when the index was first published in 1957, the average price of a share of stock (which stood between $45 and $50) was approximately equal to the value of the index. An investor at that time could easily identify with the changes in the S & P 500 Index, since a one-point change approximated the price change for an average stock.

The S & P 500 Index does not contain the 500 largest stocks, nor are all the stocks in the index United States-based corporations. For example, Warren Buffet's Berkshire Hathaway, which is considered a holding company, is not in the S & P 500 Index, while Royal Dutch Petroleum and Unilever, both large Dutch-based firms, are included. On the other hand, the S & P 500 Index has a few firms that are quite small, representing companies that have fallen in value and have yet to be replaced. As of May 1997, the value of S & P 500 companies was over $6 trillion, but this constituted about three-quarters of the value of all stocks traded in the United States, significantly less than the 90 percent from 40 years ago.

## Indexes of Large and Small U.S. Stocks

The largest comprehensive index of U.S. firms is the Wilshire 5000 Index, which, although created with 5000 stocks in 1974, now includes 7335 firms with readily available price data.[5] Figure 4-2 shows the size and total market cap of the stocks in this index. The top 500 firms, which closely match the S & P 500 Index,[6] constitute over 76 percent of the total value of the Wilshire 5000. The top 1000 firms, called the Russell 1000 and published by the Frank Russell Co., comprise 86 percent of total value of equities. The Russell 2000 contains the next 2000 largest com-

---

5 There are nearly 10,000 listed stocks on U.S. exchanges, excluding some 20,000 "penny stocks" that are infrequently traded.
6 Royal Dutch Petroleum and Unilever, which are in the S & P 500 Index, are not in the Wilshire or Russell indexes. Berkshire Hathaway is not in either.

**FIGURE  4–2**

The Wilshire 5000 Index: 7335 Stocks Valued at $9.193 Trillion as of June 30, 1997

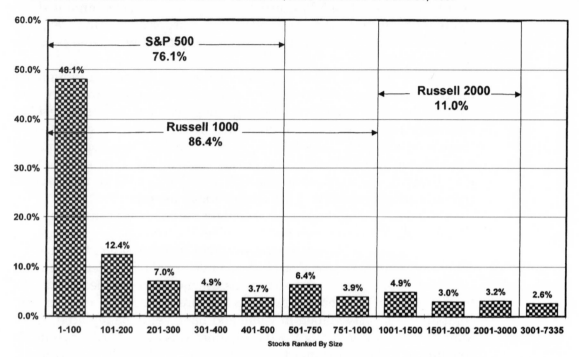

Stocks Ranked By Size

panies, and an additional 11 percent of the market value of the total index. The Russell 3000, the sum of the Russell 1000 and 2000 indexes, comprises almost the entire value of U.S. stocks. The remaining 4335 firms that are in the Wilshire Index but not in the Russell 3000 constitute less than 3 percent of the total value of U.S. equity.

## Market Capitalization of Individual Stocks

In July 1997, General Electric, at $240 billion, had the world's highest market capitalization. Microsoft, Coca-Cola, Exxon, and Intel follow. Nippon Telephone and Telegraph, which for years reigned supreme as the world's most valuable company since its privatization by the Japanese government in 1987, barely makes it into the world's top ten, having fallen victim to the Japanese bear market. AT&T, for many years the world's largest corporation, has fallen to 21st place on the U.S. list. But this is because of the court-ordered divestiture of the "Baby Bells" in 1993, and the spin-offs of Lucent Technologies and NCR in 1996. If we include these firms with AT&T, the total capitalization of "Ma Bell," as America's most popular and widely owned stock was once called, would be near $300 billion today, the world's largest.[7]

The history of large corporations reflects the history of industrial America. In 1909, U.S. Steel was by far the largest American corporation, with assets approaching $2 billion. It was followed by Standard Oil Company, which was only one-fifth the size of U.S. Steel, American Tobacco, International Mercantile Marine (later U.S. Lines), and International Harvester (now Navistar).

Table 4-2 lists the 20 largest corporations in terms of market value in the S & P 500 Index in 1964 and 1997. It is fascinating to see the change in composition of this benchmark index. Despite the perception that large companies are, through mergers and acquisitions, becoming ever more dominant in corporate America, the truth is quite the opposite. There is a clear tendency for the largest companies to represent a smaller fraction of the market value of all stocks. The top five firms constituted more than 28 percent of the market value of the index in 1964, but that had declined to less than 13 percent in 1997.

Only one company that made the top five in 1964, Standard Oil of New Jersey, is on the list today. In 1964, eight of the top 20 firms were oil companies; today there are only two (and only one—Exxon—if you count just U.S.-based firms). Three drug firms occupy the 1997 list, while in 1964 there were none. And the new technology giants Intel and Microsoft, which went public in 1971 and 1986, now are among the top five most valuable firms in the U.S. Furthermore, most stocks in the top 20 today are *growth* stocks, which is in sharp contrast to 1964. Chapter 6 will examine the characteristics of growth and value stocks in detail.

## Return Biases in Stock Indexes

Many of the companies that were in the S & P 500 Index in 1964 are not there today because they were either absorbed by merger, or declined in

---

7 The world's largest private corporation, in terms of sales, is General Motors, which is not even in the top 20 in terms of market capitalization.

**T A B L E  4–2**

The Top 20 Companies in the S & P 500 Index

| 1964 | | | 1997 | | |
|---|---|---|---|---|---|
| *Company* | *% of Mkt Cap* | *Cum %* | *Company* | *% of Mkt Cap* | *Cum %* |
| AT&T | 9.1 | 9.1 | **General  Electric** | 3.03 | 3.03 |
| General Motors | 7.3 | 16.4 | Exxon | 2.72 | 5.75 |
| Standard Oil of NJ | 5.0 | 21.4 | **Coca-Cola** | 2.58 | 8.33 |
| **IBM** | 3.7 | 25.1 | **Microsoft** | 2.22 | 10.55 |
| Texaco | 3.1 | 28.2 | **Intel** | 2.07 | 12.62 |
| Du Pont | 2.9 | 31.1 | **Merck** | 1.72 | 14.34 |
| Sears Roebuck | 2.5 | 33.6 | **Philip Morris** | 1.62 | 15.96 |
| **General Electric** | 2.2 | 35.8 | Royal Dutch | 1.59 | 17.55 |
| Gulf | 1.6 | 37.4 | **Procter & Gamble** | 1.42 | 18.97 |
| **Eastman Kodak** | 1.4 | 38.8 | IBM | 1.37 | 20.34 |
| Std Oil of California | 1.4 | 40.2 | **Johnson & Johnson** | 1.28 | 21.62 |
| Socony Mobil | 1.2 | 41.4 | **Bristol-Myers** | 1.06 | 22.68 |
| Royal Dutch | 1.1 | 42.6 | **Wal-Mart** | 1.05 | 23.73 |
| Union C&C | 1.0 | 43.6 | **Pfizer** | 1.00 | 24.73 |
| Shell | 0.9 | 44.5 | AIG | 0.96 | 25.69 |
| **Proctor & Gamble** | 0.9 | 45.4 | Du Pont | 0.96 | 26.65 |
| General T&T | 0.8 | 46.3 | **PepsiCo** | 0.90 | 27.55 |
| Std Oil of Indiana | 0.8 | 47.1 | **Disney** | 0.88 | 28.43 |
| **MMM** | 0.8 | 47.8 | **Hewlett Packard** | 0.87 | 29.30 |
| Ford Motor | 0.7 | 48.6 | Citicorp | 0.86 | 30.16 |

*Cum = Cumulative*
**Boldface denotes growth stocks**

value and were removed. Some of the firms in the small stock indexes, such as those in the Russell 2000, either graduate into large cap indexes, are absorbed by other firms, or decline and fall from even this small stock index.

Some investors believe there are biases in these popular size-based indexes, so that over time investors can expect the return from indexes of these stocks to be either higher or lower than the overall market. But this is not the case. It is true that the strongest stocks will stay in the S & P 500 Stock Index, but this index misses the powerful upside move of many small and mid-sized issues. For example, Microsoft was not added to the S & P 500 Stock Index until June 1994, eight years after going public. While small stock indexes are the incubators of some of the greatest growth stocks, they also contain those "fallen angels" that dropped out of the large cap indexes and are headed downward.

An index is not biased if it can be *replicated* or matched by an investor. To replicate an index, the date that additions and deletions are made to the index must be announced in advance so the new stocks can be bought and the removed stocks sold. This is particularly important for issues that enter into bankruptcy: the postbankrupt price (which might be zero) must be factored into the index. It should be noted that all the major stock indexes, such as Standard and Poor's, Dow-Jones, and Russell, can be replicated by investors.[8] For this reason there is no statistical reason for size-based indexes to be biased.

## DOW 10 STRATEGY

The Dow 10 strategy, which calls for investors to buy the ten highest-yielding stocks in the Dow-Jones Industrial Average, has been regarded as one of the most successful investment strategies of all time. James Glassman of the *Washington Post* claimed that John Slatter, a Cleveland investment adviser and writer, invented the Dow 10 system in the 1980s.[9] Harvey C. Knowles III and Damon H. Petty analyzed and praised the system in their book, the *Dividend Investor*, written in 1992, as did Michael O'Higgins and John Downes in *Beating the Dow*.

The basic theory behind the Dow 10 strategy is grounded in "value investing." Value investors are contrarians who believe that the swings of optimism and pessimism about the market and individual stocks are frequently unjustified, so buying out-of-favor stocks is a winning strategy. Since firms reduce cash dividend payouts infrequently, stocks with a high dividend yield are often those that have fallen in price and are out of favor with investors. For this reason the Dow 10 strategy is often called the "dogs of the Dow."

Table 4-3 shows the compound annual returns from investing in the Dow 10, as compared to the Dow Jones average and the S & P 500 Index. The Dow 10 theory has worked. Since 1928, the average compound return on the Dow 10 of 13.21 percent per year has exceeded the equally weighted Dow 30 by 1.81 percent annually, and the S & P 500 Index by 2.57 percent per year over the whole period.

---

8 The original Value Line Index of 1700 stocks, which was based on a geometric average of the changes in the individual stocks, was biased downward. This eventually led Value Line to abandon the geometric average in favor of the arithmetic one, which could be replicated.
9 John R. Dorfman, "Study of Industrial Averages Finds Stocks with High Dividends are Big Winners," *Wall Street Journal*, August 11, 1988, p. C2.

**T A B L E  4–3**

The Dow 10 Strategy vs. Standard Benchmarks (Compound Returns, with Standard Deviations in Parentheses)

*Strategy: One buys the 10 highest yielding Dow stocks on the close of the last trading day of the year.*

|  | Dow 10 | Dow | S&P 500 |
|---|---|---|---|
| **1928-97** | 13.21%<br><br>(22.2%) | 11.40%<br><br>(22.7%) | 10.64%<br><br>(20.4%) |
| **1940-97** | 15.91%<br><br>(18.3%) | 12.71%<br><br>(16.4%) | 12.46%<br><br>(16.7%) |
| **1970-97** | 18.04%<br><br>(15.8%) | 13.75%<br><br>(16.2%) | 12.83%<br><br>(16.2%) |
| **1930s** | -1.04% | 2.23% | -0.05% |
| **1940s** | 12.62% | 9.73% | 9.17% |
| **1950s** | 20.38% | 19.24% | 19.35% |
| **1960s** | 9.18% | 6.66% | 7.81% |
| **1970s** | 13.32% | 6.79% | 5.86% |
| **1980s** | 21.78% | 18.59% | 17.55% |
| **1990-97** | 19.45% | 16.83% | 16.57% |

The Dow 10 strategy has outperformed both the overall Dow and the S & P 500 Index in every decade except the 1930s, besting the Dow 30 by an average of 3.26 percent per year and the S & P 500 Stock Index by an even larger 3.7 percent per year since 1939. Since the 1930s, the

Dow 10 strategy has outperformed the Dow in 43 of the 58 years. And in the 15 years the Dow 10 failed to match the Dow 30, in nine of those years it did so by less than two percentage points. In only three years did it underperform the Dow by more than five percentage points, with its poorest performance being in 1953 when it fell 11 percent behind the Dow. In contrast, the Dow 10 outperformed the Dow by more than ten percentage points in eight years.

You might think that these spectacular returns were achieved with higher risk, but that is not the case. The standard deviation of annual returns on the Dow 10 strategy was actually lower than the Dow 30 and only slightly more than the S & P 500 Stock Index. And the Dow 10 was spectacular during the 1973–74 bear market. During those two years when the Dow 30 was down by 26.5 percent and the S & P 500 Index was down 37.3 percent, the Dow 10 strategy actually gained 2.9 percent!

Why has the Dow 10 strategy worked? There are two reasons: first, and most important, a value-based strategy based on a group of superior "survivor" firms; second, a high-dividend strategy.

It can be shown mathematically that a contrarian strategy of choosing stocks that have fallen in value works much better with firms that are likely to be "survivors" than with firms that are not. Playing a contrarian strategy does not work if the firm you have chosen to buy is actually heading for oblivion. But this almost never happens to companies that make up the Dow, which are chosen on the basis of being premier firms.

The editors at Dow Jones who select the firms that comprise the Dow-Jones Industrial average do seem to have superior stock-picking abilities.[10] The Dow Industrials have even better returns than the hard-to-beat S & P 500 Index. Earlier in this chapter it was noted that all but one of the original Dow 12 of 1896 stocks have survived to this day. Furthermore, the stocks that have been removed from the Dow Industrials have generally underperformed those that replaced them.

Table 4-4 displays the performance of several stock portfolios related to the Dow 10 since 1970. A portfolio of the ten Dow stocks with the greatest losses over the previous four years, a time period shown by researchers to reveal the best contrarian reversal strategies, yields a 16.6

---

10 The managing editor of the *Wall Street Journal* is primarily responsible for selecting the Dow stocks.

**T A B L E  4–4**

Analysis of Dow 10 Returns from 1970–1997

| Portfolio | Historical Return | Excess Return Over Dow 30 |
|---|---|---|
| *Equally-Weighted Dow 30* | 13.7% | N/A |
| *Equally-Weighted Dow 10* | 18.0% | 4.3% |
| *Standard & Poor 500* | 12.8% | -0.9% |
| *The "Dogs" of the Dow (Previous 1-year losers)* | 13.7% | 0.0% |
| *The "Dogs" of the Dow (Previous 4-year losers)* | 16.6% | 2.9% |
| *DJIA w/ Dow 10 January Returns* | 15.4% | 1.7% |
| *Top 50 Dividend Yielding Large ($1B) Stocks (excl. utils.)* | 14.9% | 1.2% |

percent annual return.[11] But just choosing the previous year's losers does not work. Over time the returns of the Dow stocks with the greatest *previous-year* losses just match the Dow 30.

The second reason the Dow 10 strategy works is that large high-dividend stocks do yield somewhat higher returns than large low-dividend stocks. James O'Shaughnessy has shown that the top 50 dividend-yielding stocks (excluding utilities) have yielded 14.9 percent per year since 1970,[12] a little more than one percentage point above the Dow 30 stocks. One reason that high-dividend stocks have higher returns is that the tax rate on dividend income is higher than capital gains (see Chapter 5). The high dividend yield, however, explains only a small fraction of the Dow 10's superior returns.

## How to Play the Dow 10 Strategy

There are basically two ways to play the Dow 10 strategy. You can either purchase the highest-yielding Dow stocks individually or buy them through a unit investment trust, which is sold by brokerage firms. The

---

11 DeBondt, W., and Thaler, R., 1985, "Does the Stock Market Overreact?" in Journal of Finance, 40, pp. 793–805 and "Further Evidence on Investor Overreactions and Stock Market Seasonality," Journal of Finance, 42, pp. 557–581

12 Data taken from James P. O'Shaughnessy, *What Works on Wall Street*, New York: McGraw-Hill, 1997. Data from 1997 estimated.

latter is more convenient, but the fees, which sometimes amount to 2 percent or more of assets, can eat up most if not all of the historical advantage of the strategy.[13]

An important caveat: The Dow 10 strategy performs best in January. Just by holding the Dow 10 stocks in that month can raise your return by 1.7 percent per year over the Dow 30 stocks. Why there is outperformance in January is not clear, but in Chapter 6 I will show that large value stocks, which comprise most of the Dow 10, have large returns in January. Consequently, it would be wise to make Dow 10 purchases before the year end.

A final warning: There are billions of dollars already invested in the Dow 10 strategy and professionals expect billions more. The strategy is now being applied to foreign stock indexes. The flow of money could push the prices of these stocks up and significantly erode the advantage of the Dow 10 or similar strategies in the future. Remember that historical returns (as well as historical risks) can be altered as investors attempt to take advantage of them.

## APPENDIX A: WHAT HAPPENED TO THE ORIGINAL 12 DOW INDUSTRIALS?

Two stocks (General Electric and Laclede) retained their original name (and industry); five (American Cotton, American Tobacco, Chicago Gas, National Lead, and North American) became large public companies in their original industries; one (Tennessee Coal and Iron) was merged into the giant U.S. Steel; and two (American Sugar and U.S. Rubber) went private—both in the 1980s. Surprisingly, only one (Distilling and Cattle Feeding) changed its product line (from alcoholic beverages to petrochemicals, although it still manufactures ethanol), and only one (U.S. Leather) liquidated. Here is a rundown of the original 12 stocks:

*American Cotton Oil* Became Best Food in 1923, Corn Products Refining in 1958, and finally CPC International in 1969—a major food company with operations in 58 countries. The current market value is $12.2 billion.

*American Sugar* Became Amstar in 1970, went private in 1984, and now manufactures, markets, and distributes portable electric power tools.

---

13 There is no mutual fund for the Dow 10 since the SEC requires more than ten stocks in open-ended (redeemable) mutual funds. There are some mutual funds available containing the S & P 500 stocks plus the Dow 10.

*American Tobacco* Changed its name to American Brands (AMB) in 1969, a global consumer products holding company, with core business in tobacco, liquor, office products, and home improvements. The current market value is $9.2 billion.

*Chicago Gas* Became People's Gas Light and Coke Co. in 1897, and then People's Energy Corp., a utility holding company in 1980. People's Energy Corp (PGL) has a market value of $1.2 billion and was a member of the Dow-Jones Utility Average until May 1997.

*Distilling and Cattle Feeding* Became American Spirits Manufacturing and then Distiller's Securities Corp. Two months after the passage of Prohibition, the company changed its charter and became U.S. Food Products Corp. and then National Distiller's and Chemical. The company became Quantum Chemical Corp. in 1989, a leading producer of petrochemicals and propane. Nearing bankruptcy, it was purchased for $3.4 billion by Hanson PLC, an Anglo-American conglomerate. It was spun off as Millenium Chemicals (MCH) in October 1996. The current market value is $1.4 billion.

*General Electric (GE)* Founded in 1892, it is the only stock still in the Dow Industrials. GE is a huge manufacturing and broadcasting conglomerate that owns NBC. The 1997 market value is $240 billion, the highest in the world.

*Laclede Gas (LG)* Retained its original name and is a retail distributor of natural gas in the St. Louis area. The market value is $390 million.

*National Lead (NL)* Changed its name to NL Industries in 1971, and manufactures titanium dioxide and specialty chemicals. The market value is $640 million.

*North American* Became Union Electric Co. (UEP) in 1956, providing electricity in Missouri and Illinois. The market value is $3.7 billion.

*Tennessee Coal and Iron* Bought out by U.S. Steel in 1907, now USX U.S. Steel Group (X), it has a market value of $2.6 billion.

*U.S. Leather* One of the largest makers of shoes in the early part of this century, the company liquidated in January 1952, paying its shareholders $1.50 plus stock in an oil and gas company that was to become worthless.

*U.S. Rubber* Became Uniroyal in 1961 and was taken private in August of 1985.

CHAPTER

# Dividends, Earnings, and Investor Sentiment

*Even when the underlying motive of purchase [of common stocks] is mere speculative greed, human nature desires to conceal this unlovely impulse behind a screen of apparent logic and good sense.*

—Benjamin Graham and David Dodd, 1940[1]

*"The market is most dangerous when it looks best; it is most inviting when it looks worst."*

—Frank J. Williams, 1930[2]

## AN EVIL OMEN RETURNS

In the summer of 1958, an event of great significance took place for those who followed long-standing indicators of stock market value. For the first time in history, the interest rate on long-term government bonds exceeded the dividend yield on common stocks.

*Business Week* noted this event in an August 1958 article entitled "An Evil Omen Returns," warning investors that when yields on stocks approached those on bonds, a major market decline was in the offing.[3] The stock market crash of 1929 occurred in a year when stock dividend yields fell to the level of bond yields. The stock crashes of 1907 and 1891

---

1 "The Theory of Common-Stock Investment," *Security Analysis*, 2nd edition, 1940, p. 343.
2 Frank J. Williams, *If You Must Speculate, Learn the Rules*, Burlington VT: Freiser Press, 1930.
3 *Business Week*, August 9, 1958, p. 81.

also followed episodes when the yield on bonds came within one percent of the dividend yield on stocks.

As Figure 5-1 indicates, prior to 1958, the dividend yield on stocks had always been higher than long-term interest rates, and most analysts thought that this was the way it was supposed to be. Stocks were riskier than bonds and therefore should command a higher yield in the market. Under this reasoning, whenever stock prices went too high and brought dividend yields down to that of bonds, it was time to sell.

But things did not work that way in 1958. Stocks returned over 30 percent in the 12 months after dividend yields fell below bond yields, and continued to soar into the early 1960s. There were good economic reasons why this famous benchmark fell by the wayside. Inflation increased the yield on bonds to compensate lenders for rising prices,

## FIGURE 5-1

Dividend and Nominal Bond Yields, 1871–1996

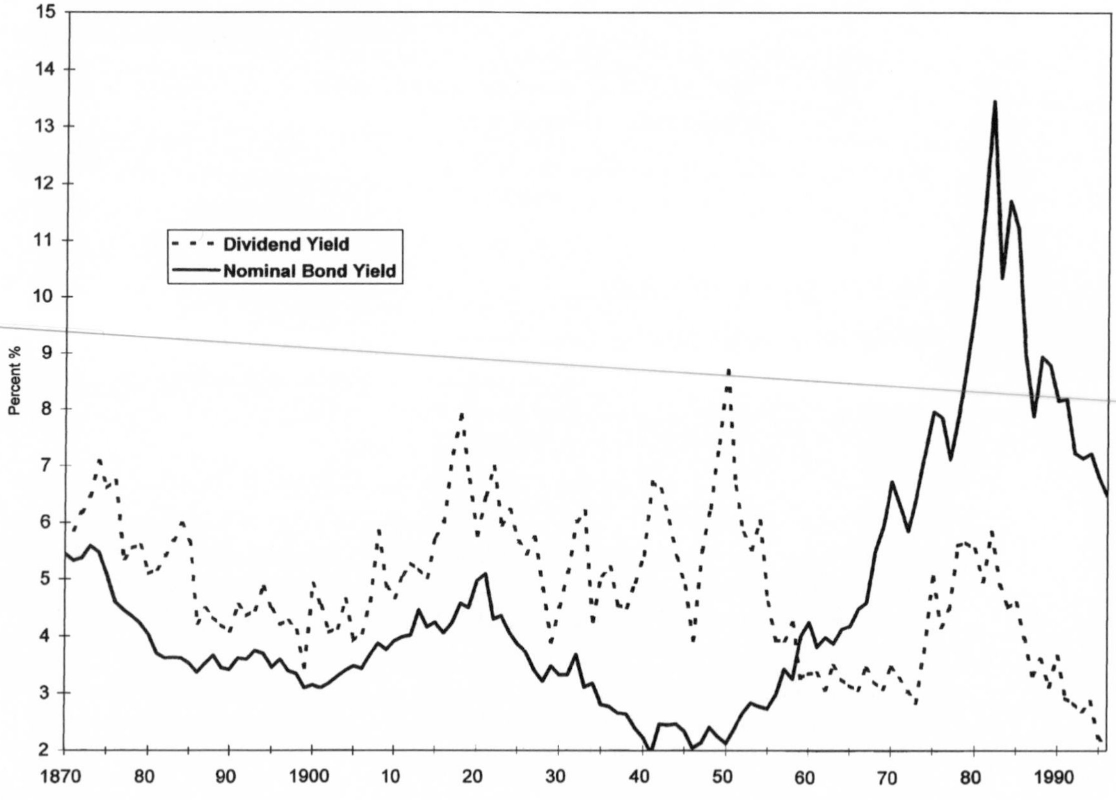

while investors regarded stocks as the best investment to protect against the eroding value of money. As early as September 1958, *Business Week* noted that "the relationship between stock and bond yields was clearly posting a warning signal, but investors still believe inflation is inevitable and stocks are the only hedge against it."[4]

Yet many on Wall Street were still puzzled by the "great yield reversal." Nicholas Molodovsky, Vice President of White, Weld & Co. and editor of the *Financial Analysts Journal*, observed:

> Some financial analysts called [the reversal of bond and stock yields] a financial revolution brought about by many complex causes. Others, on the contrary, made no attempt to explain the unexplainable. They showed readiness to accept it as a manifestation of providence in the financial universe.[5]

Imagine the value-oriented investor who pulled all his money out of the stock market in August of 1958 and put it into bonds, vowing never to buy stocks again unless dividend yields rose above those on high-quality bonds. Such an investor would still be waiting to get back into stocks. After 1958, stock dividend yields never again exceeded those of bonds. Yet, from August 1958 onward, overall stock returns overwhelmed the returns on fixed-income securities for *any* holding period.

Benchmarks for valuation are valid only as long as the economic institutions of the economy do not change. The chronic postwar inflation, resulting from a switch to a paper money standard, changed forever the way investors judged the yields on stocks and bonds.

## Valuation of Cash Flows from Stocks

The fundamental building blocks of stock valuation are the dividends and earnings of firms. In contrast to a work of art—which can be bought for its own enjoyment as well as an investment—stocks have value only because of the potential cash flows, coming primarily from dividends, which stockholders expect to receive from their share of the ownership of the firm.[6] It is by forecasting and valuing potential future dividends and earnings that you can judge the investment value of shares.

---

4 "In the Markets," *Business Week*, September 13, 1958, p. 91.
5 "The Many Aspects of Yields," *Financial Analysts Journal*, 18, no. 2 (March–April 1962), pp. 49–62.
6 There might be some psychic value to holding a controlling interest above and beyond the returns accrued. In that case, the owner values the stock more than minority shareholders.

The value of any asset is determined by the *discounted* value of all future expected cash flows. This means that future cash flows are not valued as highly as current flows. For stocks, cash flows come primarily in the form of dividends, but occasionally from other distributions resulting from the sale of assets or other transactions. For most assets— and especially for all stocks—the future cash flows are uncertain and depend on the financial circumstances of the firm.[7]

Future cash flows from assets are discounted because cash received in the future is not worth as much as cash received in the present. There are four reasons for this. The first three are: the innate *preferences* of most individuals to enjoy their consumption today rather than wait for tomorrow; *productivity*, which allows funds invested today to yield a higher return tomorrow; and *inflation*, which reduces the future purchasing power of cash received in the future. These factors apply to bonds with certain cash flows as well as stocks and are the foundation of the theory of interest rates. The fourth factor, the *uncertainty* associated with the magnitude of future cash flows, applies primarily to equities and constitutes the *equity risk premium*.

### Short and Long-Term Returns from Stocks

Estimates of all future cash flows are important for the valuation of equity—not only the ones received during the time the investor holds the asset. In contrast to the bondholder, the stockholder receives dividends from the earnings of the firm for as long as the firm is in operation, which could be indefinitely. However, for short-term investors, the return on an investment depends not only on the cash flows received during their ownership, but also on the *market's* assessment of the cash flows at the time they sell. This is because the largest part of the return for a short-term stockholder usually comes from the proceeds of the sale and not from the dividends received. Unless you intend to hold the stock forever, you must take into account how much other investors in the market will value the asset at the time of sale in order to estimate your return.

Most investors attempt to profit in the market by buying a stock with what they consider attractive future returns, hoping that other in-

---

7 Even the cash flows from corporate bonds are uncertain—either because of the potential default of the issuing firm or the premature payoff (called the *call*) of the bonds' principal value. The only assets with certain cash flows are noncallable federal government bonds.

vestors will come to agree with their judgment. If this comes to pass, the price of the stock will eventually rise. This is the strategy of value-based investors who buy stocks on the basis of earnings power that will, they hope, be recognized by other investors in the near future.

But the fastest way to make money in the market is to successfully forecast how *other* investors will value the stock in the near future. Accordingly, success for short-term investors comes primarily from predicting how the investing public changes its view of stocks in the future, and quite secondarily from the cash flows realized by the investment itself.

John Maynard Keynes likened short-term investment strategy to a newspaper competition where competitors have to pick the prettiest faces from hundreds of photographs, the prize being awarded to the competitor who most nearly matches the average preferences of all the other competitors. Keynes stated that to win the contest:

> It is not a case of choosing those which, to the best of one's judgment, are really the prettiest, nor even those which average opinion genuinely thinks the prettiest . . . we devote our intelligences to anticipating what average opinion expects the average opinion to be.[8]

Understanding average opinion, right or wrong, therefore becomes the key to short-term investment success. The right strategy for speculators is to be one step ahead of the market. If speculators know only what the market knows and fail to recognize that the market has already discounted the information they possess, they will not profit.

On the other hand, if speculators are too far ahead of the market, they will also be unsuccessful. In the short run, the market often makes mistakes. Although these are often corrected in the long run, being right in the long run will be of little use to speculators who must predict what information the market will understand and process quickly.

Keynes best described the tension between investing for the long run and speculating in the short run:

> Most of these [professional investors and speculators] are, in fact, largely concerned, not with making superior long-term forecasts of the probable yield of an investment over its whole life, but with foreseeing changes in the conventional basis of valuation a short time ahead of the public. They are concerned, not with what an investment is really worth to a man who buys it "for keeps," but with what the market will value it at, under the influence of mass psychology, three months or a year hence.[9]

---

8 John Maynard Keynes, *The General Theory of Employment, Interest, and Money*, 1936, op. cit., p. 155.
9 John Maynard Keynes, Ibid., p. 155.

The game of forecasting future investor sentiment is difficult and deters many from investing in stocks. But, as the last chapter indicated, you need not forecast market sentiment in order to profit in stocks. Although investment advice geared to the short run hinges on predicting the sentiment of other investors, in the long run you can ride out the waves of investor sentiment. Winning with stocks requires only patience, not foresight.

## Sources of Shareholder Value

The value of any asset is determined by the future cash flows to investors. The ultimate source of these cash flows is the *earnings* of firms. Earnings are the cash flows that remain after costs of production are subtracted from the revenues, which in turn are determined by the sales of the firm. The costs of production include labor and material costs, interest on debt, corporate taxes, and allowance for depreciation. Earnings can be paid out as dividends, or retained by firms to be put to work to provide greater cash flows to the investor in the future. Earnings that are not paid out as dividends are referred to as *retained earnings*.

Firms put earnings to work creating value to shareholders by engaging in one or more of the following activities:

- Payment of cash dividends
- Repurchase of shares
- Retirement of debt
- Reinvestment for future growth

If a firm repurchases its shares, it reduces the number of outstanding shares, so share repurchase increases future *per share* earnings even if the total earnings of the firm remain unchanged. If a firm retires its debt, it reduces its interest expense and therefore increases the cash flow available to shareholders. Finally, earnings can be invested in productive assets (financial or real) that will increase future profits. In summary, the firm increases future cash flows to shareholders by productively using earnings that are not paid as dividends today.

Some argue that, of the four sources of value listed above, the first factor, cash dividends, is valued most by shareholders. But this is not necessarily true. In fact, from a tax standpoint, share repurchase is superior to dividends. Cash dividends are taxed at the highest marginal tax rate of the investor. Share repurchase generates capital gains that can be realized at the shareholder's discretion and often at a lower capital gains tax rate.

Others might argue that debt repayment lowers shareholder value because the interest saved on the debt retired is generally less than the rate of return earned on equity capital. But debt entails a fixed commitment that must be met in good or bad times and, as such, increases the volatility of earnings that go to the shareholder. Reducing debt therefore lowers the fluctuations in future earnings and will not diminish shareholder value.

Many investors claim that the fourth factor, the reinvestment of earnings, is the most important source of value, but this is not always the case. If retained earnings are reinvested profitably, value will surely be created. But the availability of retained earnings might tempt managers to pursue goals, such as overbidding to acquire other firms, which do not increase the value to shareholders. Therefore, the market often views the buildup of cash reserves and marketable securities with suspicion and discounts their value.

If the fear of misusing retained earnings is particularly strong, it is possible that the market will value the firm at less than the value of its reserves. Great investors, such as Benjamin Graham, made some of their most profitable trades by purchasing shares in such companies and then convincing management (sometimes tactfully, sometimes with a threat of takeover) to disgorge its liquid assets.[10]

One might question why management would not employ assets in a way to maximize shareholder value. The reason is that there exists a conflict between the goal of the shareholders, which is to increase the price of the shares, and the goals of management, which are prestige, control of markets, and other objectives. Economists recognize the conflict between the goals of managers and shareholders as *agency costs*, and these costs are inherent in every corporate structure where ownership is separated from management. Payment of cash dividends or committed share repurchases often lowers management's temptation to pursue goals that do not maximize shareholder value.

On balance, I cannot say that a dollar of retained earnings generates more or less value to shareholders than a dollar of cash dividends. In many cases, share repurchase is often the most valuable to the shareholder, followed by cash dividends, debt retirement, and, lastly, reinvestment for growth. But this ordering will differ among firms. Younger, fast-growing companies often create more value by reinvesting retained earnings than by paying dividends, while in older, more

10 Benjamin Graham, *The Memoirs of the Dean of Wall Street*, New York: McGraw-Hill, 1946, Chapter 11.

mature industries, where agency costs are most severe, disbursing cash or repurchasing shares often maximizes the value to shareholders.

## Does the Value of Stocks Depend on Dividends or Earnings?

Dividend policy is set by management and is determined by many factors, including the tax differences between dividend income and capital gains, the need to generate internal funds to retire debt or invest, and the desire to keep dividends relatively constant in the face of fluctuating earnings. Since the price of a stock depends primarily on the present discounted value of all expected future *dividends*, it appears that dividend policy is crucial to determining the value of the stock.

But this is not generally true. If management (through share repurchase, debt retirement, or reinvestment) earns the same return on its retained earnings that shareholders demand on its stock (which is dependent on the perceived risk of the firm as well as market conditions), then, ignoring taxes, it makes absolutely no difference what dividend policy management chooses. The reason for this is that dividends not paid today are reinvested by the firm and paid as even larger dividends in the future. If the return to the firm is the same as to the shareholder, the present value of dividends, and hence the price of the stock, will be invariant with respect to the dividend policy.

Of course, the management's choice of *dividend payout ratio*, which is the ratio of cash dividends to total earnings, does influence the timing of the dividend payments. The lower the dividend payout ratio, the smaller the dividends will be in the near future. But over time, dividends will rise and eventually exceed the dividend path associated with a higher payout ratio. The present value of these dividend streams will be identical no matter what payout ratio is chosen.

Note that whether or not the firm earns the same return on retained earnings as the earnings yield on the stock, the price of the stock is always equal to the present value of all future *dividends* and not the present value of future earnings. Earnings not paid to investors can have value only if they are paid as dividends or other cash disbursements at a later date. Valuing stock as the present discounted value of future earnings is manifestly wrong and greatly overstates the value of a firm, unless all the earnings are always paid out as dividends.[11]

---

11 Firms that pay no dividends, such as Warren Buffett's Bershire Hathaway, have value since their assets, which earn cash returns, can be liquidated and disbursed to shareholders in the future.

John Burr Williams, one of the greatest investment analysts of the early part of this century and author of the classic *The Theory of Investment Value*, argued this point persuasively in 1938. He wrote:

> Most people will object at once to the foregoing formula for valuing stocks by saying that it should use the present worth of future earnings, not future dividends. But should not earnings and dividends both give the same answer under the implicit assumptions of our critics? If earnings not paid out in dividends are all successfully reinvested at compound interest for the benefit of the stockholder, as the critics imply, then these earnings should produce dividends later; if not, then they are money lost. Earnings are only a means to an end, and the means should not be mistaken for the end.[12]

## Total Returns to Stocks

Since earnings are the ultimate source of value, the *earnings yield*, which is the reciprocal of the price-earnings (or P-E) ratio, should be the best long-term guide to the real return that the market provides shareholders. This is because earnings are derived from real assets that in the long run will appreciate with inflation.

This observation is borne out by the data. Table 5-1 shows the summary statistics for dividends, earnings, and stock returns from 1871 through 1996. Over that period, the average real return on stocks has been 6.80 percent per year and the median earnings yields has been 7.30

**TABLE 5-1**

Earnings, Dividends, and Stock Returns (Compound Annual Returns)

| | real stock return | median earnings yield | median dividend yield | real earnings growth | div + real earnings growth | real dividend growth | dividend yield + growth | real capital gains | median p/e ratio | median payout ratio |
|---|---|---|---|---|---|---|---|---|---|---|
| *1871-1996* | 6.80% | 7.30% | 4.85% | 1.66% | 6.51% | 1.24% | 6.09% | 2.10% | 13.70 | 58.94% |
| *I. 1871-1945* | 6.57% | 7.35% | 5.16% | 0.72% | 5.88% | 0.79% | 5.95% | 1.04% | 13.61 | 66.67% |
| *II. 1946-1996* | 7.13% | 6.96% | 3.75% | 3.25% | 6.99% | 2.11% | 5.86% | 3.49% | 14.38 | 52.41% |

12 John Burr Williams, *The Theory of Investment Value*, Cambridge, Mass.: Harvard University Press, 1938, p. 30.

percent. For the last 50 years, the 6.96 percent median earnings yield almost matches the 7.13 percent real stock return.

Since the total return on stocks is the sum of the dividend yield (dividend divided by price) and the change in the price of the stock (capital appreciation), total return can be expressed in several different ways. If the earnings yield, or P-E ratio, remains constant, then the rate of price appreciation will equal the growth rate in per-share earnings. In this case, the total return on stock can be expressed as the sum of the dividend yield and the rate of growth of per-share earnings. As shown in Table 5-1, the sum of the dividend yield and the growth rate of real per-share earnings has approximated the real rate of return on equity.

If the dividend payout ratio (the ratio of dividends to earnings) is also constant, then dividends will grow at the same rate as earnings, and the total return to stock can also be expressed as the sum of the dividend yield and the rate of growth of dividends. Since the dividend yield has fallen markedly, the sum of the dividend yield and the rate of growth of per-share dividends is less than the total return to stocks.

Some analysts have viewed the recent decline in dividend yields with alarm. They believe the low dividend yield means that future stock returns will be low. But this fails to recognize that the current dividend yield and the future growth rate of per-share dividends are not independent. As long as the earnings yield does not decline, a reduction in the cash dividend means greater retained earnings, and hence a higher rate of growth of future earnings and dividends. This is confirmed in Table 5-1 by comparing the higher rate of growth in dividends in the period since World War II, when the payout ratio is low, to the prior period, when the payout ratio was higher.

Theoretically, for each percentage point reduction in the dividend yield, the growth rate of per-share dividends (and earnings) will increase by one percentage point, so the sum of the dividend growth and the dividend yield is unchanged. This is borne out by the data, as Table 5-1 indicates that the dividend yield since World War II has been 1.41 percent lower than before World War II, but the rate of growth of dividends has been 1.32 percent higher.

## Economic Growth, Earnings Growth, and P-E Ratios

I have shown that the real return on equity, the sum of the dividend yield, and price appreciation has averaged about 7.0 percent over long periods of time. For the 2 percent dividend yield prevailing in the late 1990s, this means that real share prices must appreciate at 5 percent per year to maintain a 7 percent real return. In order to keep the P-E ratio stable, this means that real earnings per share must grow by at least 5 percent per year.

One might wonder how the real growth of per-share earnings could exceed the long-run real growth of the entire economy, which is at most 3 percent per year. This is because *per-share* earnings are not the same as *total* earnings. With a 2 percent dividend yield, firms have sufficient cash flow to repurchase their shares. In fact, if all the increased cash flow caused by the reduction in the payout ratio were used for share repurchases, the number of shares would fall at 2 percent per year. In this case, aggregate real earnings can grow at 3 percent at the same time per-share earnings are growing at 5 percent.

It is true that *aggregate* earnings cannot grow forever at a rate faster than the growth rate of the economy. If that were the case, it would mean corporate profits would grow so large as to squeeze out all other forms of compensation, such as wages, salaries, and rents. Yet it is perfectly possible for *per-share* earnings to grow forever at a rate faster than the overall economy.

## HISTORICAL YARDSTICKS FOR VALUING THE MARKET

Many yardsticks have been used to evaluate whether stock prices are either overvalued or undervalued. These include price-to-earnings ratios, dividend yields, book-to-market ratios, and the total value of equity relative to some aggregate, such as gross domestic produce (GDP) or total replacement cost of the capital stock. To imply that these historical yardsticks constitute the "right" or "fair" value for stocks also implies that the historical *returns* to equity have also been "right" or "fair" to the shareholder. But since stock returns have far exceeded the returns on other financial assets, such a conclusion might not be justified. Higher valuations could occur as investors correctly recognize the superior returns on stocks.

### Price-Earnings Ratios and the Rule of 19

Figure 5-2 displays the inverse correlation between the price-to-earnings ratios and inflation rates over the past 40 years. High inflation rates are associated with low P-E ratios, and low inflation rates with higher P-E ratios. There is good reason for this correlation. Higher inflation lowers the *quality of reported earnings*. This refers to the ability of reported earnings to accurately reflect the true economic earnings of a firm. Because accounting is based on historical costs, periods of inflation lead to an overstatement of reported earnings compared to true economic earnings.

**FIGURE  5–2**

Valuation Rule of 19 (P-E = 19 – Inflation), 1956–1997

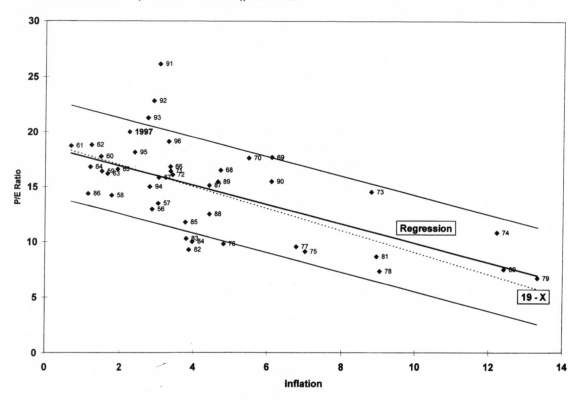

Furthermore, inflation increases the impact of corporate and capital gains taxes, which also lowers the valuation of earnings. All of these effects will be explained in more detail in Chapter 11.

The "Rule of 19" states that the market P-E ratio has approximated 19 minus the inflation rate in the recent past. Statistical regression analysis supports the historical validity of this valuation yardstick. Figure 5-2 displays the Rule of 19 and the regression line, as well as one standard deviation above and below this mean. At 3 percent inflation, the normal range for the P-E has ranged from 12 to 20, with 16 as the midpoint.

## Book Value, Market Value, and "Tobin's Q"

The *book value* of a firm is the value of a firm's assets minus its liabilities, evaluated at historical costs. Security analysts have long used book value to evaluate the fair market price of stocks. But the use of aggregate book value as a measure of the overall value of the market is severely limited because book value uses historical prices and thus ignores the effect of inflation on the value of the assets or liabilities. If a firm purchased a plot of land for $1 million that is now worth $10 million, examining the book value will not reveal this. Over time, the historical value of assets becomes less reliable as a measure of current market value.

To help correct these distortions, James Tobin, a professor at Yale University and a Nobel laureate, adjusted a book value for inflation and computed the "replacement cost" of the assets and liabilities on the balance sheet.[13] He developed a theory that indicated that the "equilibrium" or "correct" market price of a firm should equal its assets minus liabilities adjusted for inflation. If the aggregate market value of a firm exceeds the cost of capital, it would be profitable to create more capital, sell shares to finance it, and reap a profit. If the market value falls below the replacement cost, then it would be better for a firm to dismantle and sell its capital, or stop investment and cut production.

Tobin designated the ratio of the market value to the replacement cost with the letter Q, and indicated that its ratio should be unity if the stock market was properly valued. The historical values of "Tobin's Q," as the theory has become known, are shown in Figure 5-3a. The ratio has fluctuated between a high of 154 in 1996 to a low of 32 in 1980, with the average being 72.

Critics of Tobin's Q theory countered that Q should generally be less than unity because older capital is not as productive as newly installed capital, even when an adjustment is made for overall inflation.[14] This contention is supported by the actual data where the average value of Tobin Q is 0.72. But Tobin Q is hard to calculate since the mechanism for equating replacement cost with market value often fails. Capital equipment and structures lack a good secondary market and hence there is no realistic way to value much of the physical capital stock.

There is a more significant problem, however, with using Tobin's Q to value the market. Entrepreneurs do not create value solely by purchasing land or building plants and equipment. Value is created by the

---

13 "A General Equilibrium Approach to Monetary Theory," *Journal of Money, Credit, and Banking,* vol. 1 (February 1969), pp. 15–29.
14 This is also because in equilibrium the marginal productivity of capital should be equated to the cost of new capital, while the stock market measures the average productivity of both old and new capital.

## FIGURE 5-3

Market Values and Corporate Profitability, 1926–1996

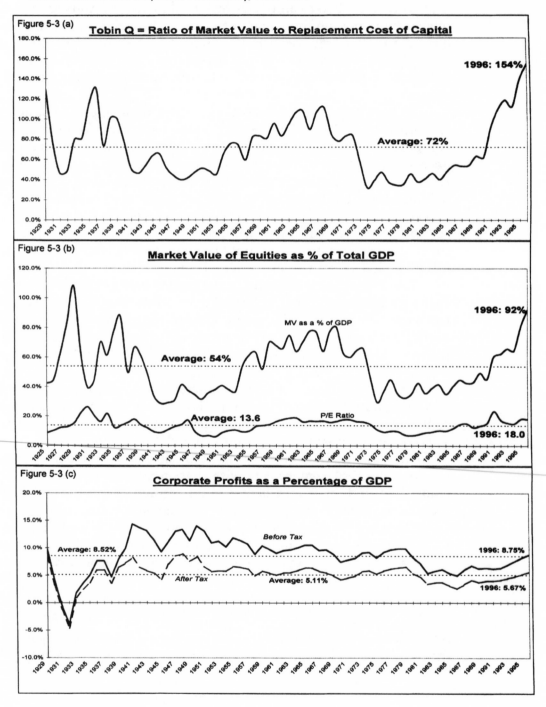

ability of management to organize these assets in such a way as to generate profits for shareholders. If productivity increases, or management better responds to consumer demand, or there is increased stability in the real economy, the value of firms can rise significantly above their historical costs, even if these costs are adjusted for past inflation. *Book value* is a construct of the past; *market value,* on the other hand, derives from prospective earnings and looks to the future.

## Corporate Profits and Market Value to GDP

Gross domestic product is a more familiar benchmark to compare to the aggregate market value of equity. GDP, despite its shortcomings, is universally regarded as the best measure of the overall output in the economy. It would be reasonable to assume that the market value of firms and the returns to corporate capital should bear some relation to that output. Figures 5-3b and 5-3c show the ratio of the market value of stocks to GDP and corporate profits to GDP since 1929.

The ratio of the value of equity to GDP can easily exceed one, and this is not alarming, as some financial writers have suggested.[15] Equity valuation is a balance-sheet item, while GDP is an annual flow. Many firms have capital that far exceeds their annual sales, so it not at all unusual for the value of an economy's capital to be greater than its output.

But more important, equity capital is only a part of total capital. Both debt and equity finance the capital stock, and the ratio between them changes over time. In the 1990s as interest rates fell, many firms retired bonds and reduced their leverage, a process called *deleveraging*. Deleveraging increases the value of equity and decrease the value of debt, but leaves the total value of the firms unchanged. In the same vein, corporate profits measure the part of the total return remitted to the shareholder, which also changes with leverage. Furthermore, the equity market values only publicly traded firms, excluding privately held corporations. As the market has risen, more firms have entered the public realm. This increases the market value of stock rise even though the total value of firms, public and private, may remain unchanged.

Moreover, the ratio of market capitalization to GDP differs widely among countries. Multinational firms might be headquartered in a particular country, but their sales span the globe. As international trade increases, it should not be surprising if market value shows less and less

---

15 See Alan Abelson, *Barron's,* May 5, 1997 (p. 3) about the ratio of stock values to GDP.

**TABLE 5–2**

Summary Market Statistics for Various Countries, May 1997: Market Value/GDP, Price-Earnings Ratio, and Dividend Yield (Market/GDP Data for March 31, 1997; P-E and Dividend Yield Based on Last 12 Months of Data)

| Country | US | Japan | Britain | Germany | Hong Kong | Switzerland | Italy |
|---------|------|-------|---------|---------|-----------|-------------|-------|
| Mkt/GDP | 101 | 58 | 154 | 31 | 221 | 150 | 21 |
| P-E | 21.1 | 88.4 | 17.4 | 25.6 | 16.1 | 68.5 | 20.4 |
| Div. Yld | 1.68 | 0.75 | 3.57 | 1.87 | 2.89 | 1.29 | 1.71 |

Source: *The Economist*, April 26, 1997, p. 109, and Bloomberg LP
* Data for Mkt/GDP for March 31, 1997.  P-E and Dividend Yield based on last 12 months data.

relation to the GDP of any one country. Table 5-2 shows that the market value of shares traded in Hong Kong are over 200 percent of its GDP, while in Italy the ratio is only 21 percent. Yet Hong Kong had the lowest average P-E ratio and the second highest dividend yield of these seven countries. The variation between countries results from large differences in the leverage and the fraction of firms that are publicly traded.[16]

## VALUATION: FUNDAMENTALS OR SENTIMENT?

Some investors believe that they can beat the market by basing their strategy on investor "sentiment" instead of fundamentals such as earnings and dividends. They contend that most investors are unduly optimistic when stock prices are high and unduly pessimistic when they are low.

It is difficult for even sophisticated investors to remain aloof of the prevailing sentiment. Rising prices breed excitement and those who have committed the most to the market realize the highest profits. When the market is falling, the opposite is true.

---

16 One ratio that has very little meaning is the ratio of a stock index such as the S & P 500 Stock Index or the Dow-Jones Industrials to GDP, or for that matter to any economy-wide variable. Stock indexes report the average prices of individual shares of common stock, not the value of such stock. Over time the number of shares can rise or fall depending on dividend and buy-back policies of firms.

But these emotions are counterproductive to being a successful trader. As Benjamin Graham and David Dodd stated nearly 65 years ago, ". . . the psychology of the speculator militates strongly against his success. For by relation of cause and effect, he is most optimistic when prices are high and most despondent when they are at bottom."[17]

As traders succumb to the prevailing psychology, market movements overshoot their fundamentals. Under these conditions, a *contrarian* strategy of buying stocks when the prevailing opinion is pessimistic about equity prospects, and selling when most are enthusiastic, will prove profitable to the long-run investor.

Contrarian strategy was first put forth by Humphrey B. Neill in a pamphlet called "It Pays to be Contrary," first circulated in 1951 and later turned into a book entitled *The Art of Contrary Thinking*. In it Neill declared: "When everyone thinks alike, everyone is likely to be wrong."[18] If this is true, determining the consensus forecast of market players might be a profitable way of timing the market.

## Contrarian Indicators

One of the most consistent indicators of investment sentiment has been published by Investor's Intelligence, a firm based in New Rochelle, New York. Over the past 35 years, president Michael Burke and his associates have evaluated scores of market newsletters, determining whether each letter is bullish, bearish, or neutral about the future direction of stocks.

From Investor Intelligence data, I computed an index of investor sentiment by finding the ratio of bullish newsletters to bullish plus bearish newsletters (omitting the neutral category). Then the returns on stocks subsequent to these sentiment readings are measured.

The results, shown in Table 5-3, indicate a strong predictive content to the sentiment index. Whenever the index of investor sentiment is high, subsequent returns on the market are poor, and when the index is low, subsequent returns are above average. The index is a particularly strong predictor of market return over the next 9 to 12 months.

This index shows strong predictive power in each decade. In the 1990s, largely due to an increase in the number of newsletters, the sentiment index has given few very high or very low readings and has

---

17 Benjamin Graham and David Dodd, *Security Analysis*, 1934, op. cit., p. 12.
18 Humphrey B. Neill, *The Art of Contrary Thinking*, Caldwell, Idaho: The Caxton Printers, Ltd., 1954, p. 1.

## TABLE 5–3

### Investor Confidence and Dow Price Returns, Sentiment = Bull/(Bull + Bear)

BULL and BEAR from Investors Intelligence Inc., New Rochelle, NY

| Sentiment | Frequency | Annualized Returns (January 2, 1970 - May 16, 1997) | | | |
|---|---|---|---|---|---|
| | | Three Month | Six Month | Nine Month | Twelve Month |
| 0.2 - 0.3 | 1.55% | 18.52% | 15.40% | 22.79% | 20.74% |
| 0.3 - 0.4 | 11.30% | 12.23% | 13.87% | 16.54% | 15.81% |
| 0.4 - 0.5 | 19.35% | 16.85% | 13.63% | 12.07% | 12.73% |
| 0.5 - 0.6 | 27.90% | 15.16% | 14.06% | 10.44% | 8.82% |
| 0.6 - 0.7 | 19.14% | 14.03% | 8.79% | 8.71% | 7.27% |
| 0.7 - 0.8 | 14.76% | 11.21% | 7.24% | 7.38% | 7.01% |
| 0.8 - 0.9 | 5.23% | -0.39% | 0.23% | -3.32% | -1.79% |
| 0.9 - 1.0 | 0.78% | 0.35% | -3.87% | -9.17% | -10.18% |
| Overall | 100.00% | 13.48% | 11.11% | 9.99% | 9.31% |

| 1970s | | Annualized Returns | | | |
|---|---|---|---|---|---|
| Sentiment | Frequency | Three Month | Six Month | Nine Month | Twelve Month |
| 0.2 - 0.3 | 2.30% | 14.36% | 3.49% | 16.58% | 12.96% |
| 0.3 - 0.4 | 11.88% | 2.12% | 8.96% | 15.14% | 11.81% |
| 0.4 - 0.5 | 16.28% | 0.93% | 0.92% | -0.35% | 1.66% |
| 0.5 - 0.6 | 20.50% | 11.04% | 7.25% | 3.22% | 3.55% |
| 0.6 - 0.7 | 16.67% | 8.97% | 6.21% | 3.12% | 3.09% |
| 0.7 - 0.8 | 20.88% | 12.08% | 3.81% | 3.02% | 2.28% |
| 0.8 - 0.9 | 9.39% | -7.44% | -6.57% | -6.28% | -7.47% |
| 0.9 - 1.0 | 2.11% | 0.35% | -3.87% | -9.17% | -10.18% |
| Overall | 100.00% | 6.32% | 3.91% | 3.15% | 2.77% |

| 1980s | | Annualized Returns | | | |
|---|---|---|---|---|---|
| Sentiment | Frequency | Three Month | Six Month | Nine Month | Twelve Month |
| 0.2 - 0.3 | 1.92% | 23.51% | 29.70% | 30.24% | 30.08% |
| 0.3 - 0.4 | 11.49% | 19.11% | 16.35% | 17.15% | 16.72% |
| 0.4 - 0.5 | 22.41% | 23.06% | 20.35% | 18.52% | 18.15% |
| 0.5 - 0.6 | 20.88% | 18.83% | 17.63% | 13.03% | 9.96% |
| 0.6 - 0.7 | 20.11% | 20.30% | 11.04% | 11.78% | 8.82% |
| 0.7 - 0.8 | 18.39% | 10.13% | 11.16% | 12.48% | 12.42% |
| 0.8 - 0.9 | 4.79% | 13.41% | 13.56% | 2.49% | 9.34% |
| 0.9 - 1.0 | 0.00% | No Data | No Data | No Data | No Data |
| Overall | 100.00% | 18.34% | 15.61% | 14.21% | 13.15% |

| 1990s | | Annualized Returns | | | |
|---|---|---|---|---|---|
| Sentiment | Frequency | Three Month | Six Month | Nine Month | Twelve Month |
| 0.30 - 0.35 | 2.96% | 20.43% | 15.83% | 15.51% | 20.66% |
| 0.35 - 0.40 | 7.26% | 16.82% | 18.85% | 18.79% | 20.99% |
| 0.40 - 0.45 | 8.87% | 19.85% | 19.39% | 19.63% | 21.45% |
| 0.45 - 0.50 | 10.48% | 30.39% | 16.33% | 13.38% | 13.40% |
| 0.50 - 0.55 | 27.42% | 18.49% | 17.79% | 15.63% | 14.39% |
| 0.55 - 0.60 | 20.70% | 11.29% | 13.41% | 12.43% | 10.84% |
| 0.60 - 0.65 | 16.13% | 11.62% | 10.67% | 13.81% | 13.80% |
| 0.65 - 0.70 | 5.11% | 10.15% | 6.18% | 6.08% | 8.90% |
| 0.70 - 0.75 | 0.81% | 14.11% | 8.01% | 5.22% | 7.85% |
| 0.75 - 0.80 | 0.27% | 11.84% | 3.30% | -1.04% | 0.74% |
| Overall | 100.00% | 16.72% | 15.04% | 13.94% | 13.55% |

proved less reliable for sentiment in the broad middle range. Nevertheless, it still appears to be a good short-term predictor of the market direction.

Richard Bernstein, Director of Quantitative and Equity Research at Merrill Lynch, developed a similar sentiment indicator based on the recommended portfolio allocations of market analysts and portfolio managers. Whenever their recommended allocation to stocks falls below 50 percent, indicating a high level of pessimism about the market's prospects, subsequent returns have been high. Bernstein calls this his single most powerful quantitative market-timing barometer. Over the past 12 years, one- year market returns have exceeded 20 percent whenever allocation percentages fall below 50 percent.

One might speculate what will happen if more and more investors follow the sentiment indicators and, in effect, become contrarians. This will have a stabilizing effect on the market, for if the prevailing sentiment becomes negative, there might be enough contrarians ready to buy and offset the sellers. Contrarians therefore counteract the normal impulse of investors (professional as well as amateurs) to "ride the trend" and invest with the prevailing sentiment. Breaking from the crowd is often the best way to enhance long-term returns.

## Current Trends and Conclusions

The extraordinary long-term returns to equity have been grounded in the earning power of firms that supply goods and services to the economy. The average historical earnings yield on stocks, defined as the earnings per share divided by the price, has been close to the average long-term real return on equities.

The bull market since 1982 has been fueled by investor recognition of the superior long-term returns that are found in equities. This has led to an increase of the price-to-earnings ratios and a consequent reduction in the earnings yield. The reduction in the earnings yield will, in the absence of other factors, lead to a lower long-term return on stocks.

The past decade has not been the only period when investors recognized the superiority of common stocks as long-term investments. In 1937, Professor Bosland of Brown University stated the consequences of the spread of knowledge of superior stock returns in the 1920s:

> Paradoxical though it may seem, there is considerable truth in the
> statement that widespread knowledge of the profitability of common
> stocks, gained from the studies that have been made, tends to diminish

the likelihood that correspondingly large profits can be gained from stocks in the future. The competitive bidding for stocks which results from this knowledge causes prices at the time of purchase to be high, with the attendant smaller possibilities of gain in the principal and high yield. The discount process may do away with a large share of the gains from common stock investment and returns to stockholders and investors in other securities may tend to become equalized.[19]

However, periods of high valuation for stocks, even if fully justified by the historical evidence, have not persisted. A wobble in earnings growth, an increase in interest rates, or an international disturbance causes many investors to rush for the safety of cash assets and send stock prices downward. Fear has a far greater grasp on human action than does the impressive weight of historical evidence.

Thus one should not be surprised if stock prices eventually settle back to levels relative to earnings that are closer to their historical norms. Although this will cause some short-term pain, it will ultimately benefit the long-term investor who can buy and accumulate equities at these discounted prices. And, as noted in Chapter 2, long-term stock returns, even when measured from market peaks, have exceeded those on all other financial assets. As the great investor, Warren Buffett said, "You pay a very high price in the stock market for a cheery consensus. Uncertainty actually is the friend of the buyer of long-term values."[20]

---

19 Chelcie C. Bosland, *The Common Stock Theory of Investment*, 1937, op. cit., p. 132.
20 Warren Buffett, "You Pay a Very High Price in the Stock Market for a Cheery Consensus," *Forbes*, August 6, 1979, p. 25.

# CHAPTER

# LARGE STOCKS, SMALL STOCKS, VALUE STOCKS, GROWTH STOCKS

*Security analysis cannot presume to lay down general rules as to the "proper value" of any given common stock. . . . The prices of common stocks are not carefully thought out computations, but the resultants of a welter of human reactions.*

—Benjamin Graham and David Dodd[1]

## OUTPERFORMING THE MARKET

What factors can investors use to choose individual stocks with superior returns? Earnings, dividends, cash flows, book values, capitalization, and past performance, among others have been suggested as important criteria to find stocks that will beat the market.

Yet finance theory has long maintained that if capital markets are efficient, in the sense that known valuation criteria are already factored into the stock prices, examining these fundamentals will not improve returns. The only factor yielding higher returns is higher risk,

---

1 "Price Earnings Ratios for Common Stocks" in *Security Analysis*, 2nd edition, New York: McGraw-Hill, 1940, p. 530.

and the correct measure of risk is the correlation of a stock's return to the overall market, which is known as *beta*.[2] Beta can be estimated from historical data and represents the risk to an asset's return that cannot be eliminated in a well-diversified portfolio. Risk that can be eliminated through diversification (called *diversifiable* or *residual* risk) does not warrant a higher return.

Unfortunately, beta has not been very successful at explaining the differences among the historical returns of individual stocks or groups of stocks. In 1981 Rolf Banz, a graduate student at the University of Chicago, investigated the returns on stocks using the database provided by the Center for the Research in Security Prices (CRSP). He found that small stocks systematically outperformed large stocks, even after adjusting for risk within the framework of the capital asset pricing models.[3]

## Risks and Returns in Small Stocks

Table 6-1 shows the compound annual return from 1926 on stocks listed on the New York Stock Exchange, sorted into deciles according to their market capitalization. The top two deciles, containing firms with over $3 billion in market value, are often called *large cap* and comprise most of the S & P 500 Stock Index. Deciles three through five, with market caps ranging between $750 million and $3 billion, are called *mid caps*; deciles six through eight ($200 million to $750 million) are called *low caps*; and the smallest 20 percent (below $200 million) are *micro caps*.[4]

The compound annual return on the smallest decile of stocks is about four percentage points above the largest decile, but the risk of

---

2 Greek letters have long been used in mathematics to designate the coefficients of regression equations. Beta, the second coefficient, is calculated from the correlation of an individual stock's return with the market. The first coefficient estimated is the average historical return on the stock and is termed *alpha*.

3 R. Banz, 1981, "The Relationship between Return and Market Value of Common Stock," *Journal of Financial Economics*, 9, pp. 3–18. Further research has shown that the excess returns on small stocks applies for foreign markets as well, especially Japan. For an excellent discussion of international returns, see Gabriel Hawawini and Don Keim, "The Cross Section of Common Stock Returns: A Review of the Evidence and Some New Findings," May 1997, working paper, Wharton School, University of Pennsylvania.

4 These dollar ranges are based on the September 1996 values and will vary with the level of the overall market.

**TABLE 6-1**

Long-Term Returns of NYSE Stocks Ranked by Size, 1926–1996 (B = Billion and M = Million)

| Size Decile | Compound Annual Return | Annual Risk | Largest Firm in Decile Sept. 1996 | Total Capitalization of Decile Sept. 1996 |
|---|---|---|---|---|
| Largest | 9.84% | 18.9% | $150.26 B | $3,829 B |
| 2 | 11.06% | 22.4% | $6.95 B | $842 B |
| 3 | 11.49% | 24.2% | $3.24 B | $439 B |
| 4 | 11.63% | 26.7% | $1.89 B | $264 B |
| 5 | 12.16% | 27.5% | $1.15 B | $166 B |
| 6 | 11.82% | 28.5% | $755 M | $112 B |
| 7 | 11.88% | 31.0% | $521 M | $75 B |
| 8 | 12.15% | 34.8% | $336 M | $46 B |
| 9 | 12.25% | 27.3% | $197 M | $25 B |
| Smallest | 13.83% | 46.5% | $94 M | $9 B |

these small stocks is also substantially higher. Some maintain that the superior historical returns on small stocks are compensation for the higher transaction costs of acquiring small stocks as well as their higher risk. It has been estimated that the average buy-sell or bid-ask spread for stocks in the S & P 500 Index is only 0.40 percent, while the spread on stocks in the Russell 2000 (the 2,000 smallest stocks among the top 3,000 traded) is 2.65 percent, more than six times as large.[5]

To take transaction costs into account, some of the small stock indexes currently use the actual return on the Dimensional Fund Advisors 9/10 Fund, an index fund that invests in micro caps. Costs of running this fund, which skillfully positions blocks of stock for purchase or sale, averages only 0.65 percent per year. Few money managers, not to say individual investors, can approach these low costs of transacting in the micro cap market.

---

5 Richard Bernstein and Satya Pradhuman, *Merrill Lynch Quantitative Viewpoint*, March 2, 1993. Updated May 1997.

## Trends in Small Stock Returns

Although the historical return on small stocks has outpaced large stocks since 1926, the magnitude of the small-stock premium waxes and wanes unpredictably over time. Figure 6-1 compares the returns on small stocks with those of the S & P 500 Stock Index over the past 70 years.[6]

Small stocks recovered smartly from their beating during the Great Depression, but still underperformed large stocks from the end of World War II until almost 1960. In fact, the cumulative total return on small stocks (measured by the bottom quintile of market capitalization)

### FIGURE 6–1

Total Returns to Small Stocks and Large Stocks, 1926–1997, Including and Excluding Years 1975–1983

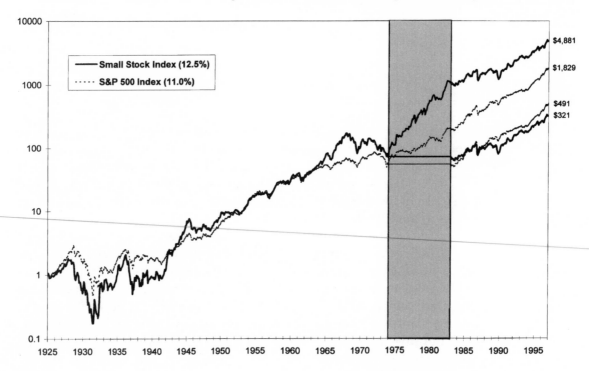

6 The small stock index is the bottom quintile (20 percent) size of the NYSE stocks until 1981, then the performance of Dimensional Fund Advisors (DFA) Small Company fund from 1982 through 1993, and the Russell 2000 index thereafter.

did not overtake large stocks once between 1926 and 1959. Even by the end of 1974, the average annual compound return on small stocks exceeded large stocks by only about 0.5 percent per year, not nearly enough to compensate most investors for their extra risk and trading costs.

But between 1975 and the end of 1983, small stocks exploded. During these years, small stocks averaged a 35.3 percent compound annual return, more than double the 15.7 percent return on large stocks. Total returns in small stocks during these nine years exceeded 1,400 percent.

After 1983, small stocks hit a long dry period and underperformed large stocks. In fact, Figure 6-1 shows that if the nine-year period from 1975 through 1983 is eliminated, the total accumulation in small stocks over the entire period from 1926 through 1997 falls nearly one-third *below* that in large stocks.

What caused the tremendous performance of small stocks during the 1975–83 period? First, at the beginning of the period the U.S. was recovering from the worst economic slowdown since the Great Depression, and small stock always do well coming out of recessions. Second, the OPEC oil price increases slammed many of the largest U.S. firms, such as the steel and motor companies, whose production process was not energy efficient. And finally, investors found themselves attracted to smaller stocks following the collapse of the "Nifty Fifty," large-cap growth stocks that were so popular in the preceding bull market.[7]

In 1975, money managers were able to find many undervalued stocks among these smaller issues. But by 1983, many of these stocks became overpriced and significantly underperformed large stock in subsequent years.

Some might object to drawing conclusions from return data where some of the best or worst years have been removed, since such a procedure can significantly distort returns. Yet that criticism is not applicable here. Computer simulations were performed that randomized the historical returns on small and large stocks, and then the nine best consecutive years were removed from the small stock series. Reversals of the magnitude that were found in the actual data were very rare and oc-

---

7 Some maintain that the fall in tax rates was partially responsible for the small stock surge. But tax rates on dividend income actually fell more than the capital gains tax rate, which should have favored the larger stocks that had a higher dividend yield.

curred in less than 10 percent of the cases analyzed. Even when the nine best consecutive years for large stocks (which ran from 1950–58) *and* the best nine consecutive years for small stocks have been removed, large stocks still outperformed small stocks over the past 70 years.

One may assert the small stocks should have higher returns because they have higher risk. Although the risk of individual small stocks is high, the standard deviation of the Russell 2000 small stock index returns has been declining over the past 20 years, and now is virtually the same as that of the S & P 500 Index.[8] A diversified portfolio of small stocks is no longer riskier than the S & P 500 Stock Index.

The streakiness of small stock returns does not mean that you should avoid these stocks. Large stocks, as measured by the S & P 500 Index, constitute about three quarters of the total stock market value. Therefore, mid caps and small caps should make up about one-quarter of your stock portfolio if only to reduce overall risk, even if they do not generate higher returns.

Small stock returns seem to be highly dependent on unique economic and market circumstances. In Chapter 17 it is shown that all the outperformance of small stocks has occurred, oddly enough, in the month of January. "Efficient markets" cannot explain this or the dramatic outperformance of small stocks during the 1975–83 period.

## VALUE CRITERIA

### Price-Earnings Ratios

Market capitalization is not the only factor influencing returns. In the late 1970s, Sanjoy Basu, building on the work of S. F. Nicholson in 1960, discovered that stocks with low price-to-earnings ratios have significantly higher returns than stocks with high price-to-earnings ratios.[9]

---

8 The beta of the Russell 2000 Index has been less than one during this period, meaning that most of the risk of small stocks is diversifiable and their return should be less than the S & P 500 Stock Index.
9 S. F. Nicholson, "Price-Earnings Ratios," *Financial Analysts Journal*, July/August 1960, pp. 43–50 and S. Basu, "Investment Performance of Common Stocks in Relation to their Price-Earnings Ratio: A Test of the Efficient Market Hypothesis," *Journal of Finance*, 32 (June 1977), pp. 663–82.

This would not have surprised Benjamin Graham and David Dodd who, in their classic 1934 text, *Security Analysis*, argued that a necessary condition for investing in common stock was a reasonable ratio of market price to average earnings. They stated:

> Hence we may submit, as a corollary of no small practical importance, *that people who habitually purchase common stocks at more than about 16 times their average earnings are likely to lose considerable money in the long run.*[10]

Yet even Benjamin Graham must have felt a need to be flexible on the issue of what constituted an "excessive" P-E ratio. In their second edition, written in 1940, the same sentence appears with the number *20* substituted for *16* as the upper limit of a reasonable P-E ratio.[11]

## Price-to-Book Ratios

Price-earnings ratios are not the only value-based criterion for buying stocks. A number of academic papers, beginning with Dennis Stattman's in 1980 and culminating in the paper by Eugene Fama and Ken French in 1992, have suggested that price-to-book ratios might be even more significant than price-to-earnings ratios in predicting future cross-sectional stock returns.[12]

Like price-earnings ratios, Graham and Dodd considered book value to be an important factor determining returns. They wrote, more than 60 years ago:

> [We] suggest rather forcibly that the book value deserves at least a fleeting glance by the public before it buys or sells shares in a business undertaking. . . . Let the stock buyer, if he lays any claim to intelligence, at least be able to tell himself, first, how much he is actually paying for the business, and secondly, what he is actually getting for his money in terms of tangible resources.[13]

---

10 Graham and Dodd, 1934, *Security Analysis*, p. 453. Emphasis theirs.
11 Graham and Dodd, Security Analysis, 1940 edition, p. 533.
12 D. Stattman, 1980 "Book Values and Expected Stock Returns," unpublished MBA honors paper, University of Chicago and E. Fama and K. French, 1992, "The Cross Section of Expected Stock Returns," *Journal of Finance*, 47, pp. 427–466.
13 Graham and Dodd, *Security Analysis*, 1934 edition, pp. 493–94.

## Value and Growth Stocks

Stocks that exhibit low price-to-book and low price-to-earnings ratios are often called *value stocks*, while those with high P-E and price-to-book ratios are called *growth stocks*. Value stocks are concentrated in oil, motor, finance, and most utilities, while growth stocks are concentrated in the high-technology industries such as drugs, telecommunications, and computers. Of the 10 largest U.S.-based corporations at the end of 1996, eight can be regarded as growth stocks (GE, Coca-Cola, Microsoft, Intel, Merck, Philip Morris, Proctor and Gamble, and Wal-Mart), while only two (Exxon and IBM) are value stocks.

Table 6-2 summarizes the compound annual returns on stocks from 1963 through 1996 ranked on the basis of both capitalization and book-to-market ratios. These tables appear to confirm Graham and Dodd's emphasis on value-based investing. Historical returns on value stocks have surpassed growth stocks, and this outperformance was especially true among smaller stocks: the smallest value stocks returned 19.51 percent per year, the highest of any of the 25 categories analyzed, while the smallest growth stocks returned only 6.67 percent, the lowest of any category. As firms become larger, the difference between the returns on value and growth stocks becomes much smaller. The largest value stocks returned 12.6 percent per year while the largest growth stocks returned about 10.2 percent.

One theory about why growth stocks have underperformed value stocks is that investors get overexcited about the growth prospects of firms with rapidly rising earnings and bid them up excessively. "Story stocks" such as Intel or Microsoft, which in the past provided fantastic returns, capture the fancy of investors, while those firms providing solid, although uneven earnings are neglected.

Yet upon closer examination of the data, the dominance of large value stocks is linked to the same nine-year period, from 1975–83, when small stocks outperformed large stocks. Figure 6-2 shows the total return on large value and growth stocks from 1963 to the present, including and excluding the years 1975–83. Once that nine-year period is excluded, large growth stocks actually beat large value stocks.

One of the reasons why value stocks did so well during this period is that the increase in oil prices caused the oil firms, which made up the largest group of value companies, to soar in value. Another surprising result, which will be discussed in Chapter 17, is that the entire difference between the returns on large value and growth stock returns takes place in January, even when the 1975–83 period is included.[14]

**TABLE 6–2**

Annual Compound Returns by Size and Book to Market Ratio

*July 1963 - June 1996*

| Entire Period | | Size Quintiles | | | | |
|---|---|---|---|---|---|---|
| | | **Small** | **2** | **3** | **4** | **Large** |
| Book to Market Quintiles | Value | **19.51** | 16.66 | 16.76 | 16.01 | **12.60** |
| | 2 | **19.07** | 16.63 | 14.51 | 13.32 | **10.67** |
| | 3 | **16.44** | 14.55 | 12.89 | 10.21 | **9.65** |
| | 4 | **12.65** | 11.85 | 11.70 | 9.74 | **9.29** |
| | Growth | **6.67** | 7.62 | 9.60 | 9.71 | **10.18** |

| Excluding 1975-83 | | Size Quintiles | | | | |
|---|---|---|---|---|---|---|
| | | **Small** | **2** | **3** | **4** | **Large** |
| Book to Market Quintiles | Value | **14.94** | 12.55 | 12.97 | 13.73 | **10.48** |
| | 2 | **14.18** | 12.95 | 11.87 | 11.07 | **9.57** |
| | 3 | **10.73** | 10.77 | 8.77 | 7.85 | **8.35** |
| | 4 | **6.65** | 7.28 | 8.01 | 6.82 | **9.10** |
| | Growth | **0.99** | 4.03 | 6.71 | 8.34 | **10.85** |

14 See Tim Loughran, "Book-to-market across firm size, exchange, and seasonality: Is there an effect?" in the *Journal of Financial and Quantitative Analysis*, 32 (September 1997), pp. 249–68.

FIGURE 6–2

Large Capitalization Growth and Value Stocks, July 1963 to December 1996, Including and Excluding Years 1975–1983

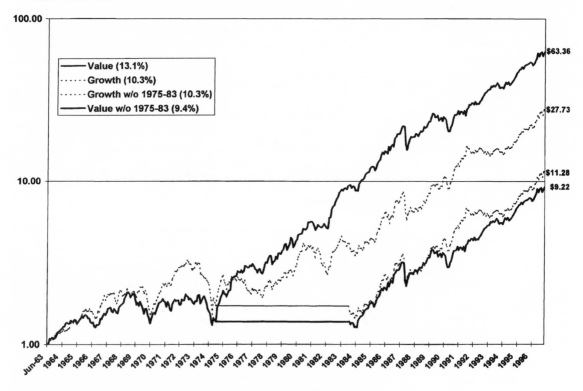

## Dividend Yields

Another favorite value-based criterion for choosing stocks is dividend yields. Chapter 3 confirmed that a strategy based on the highest yielding stocks in the Dow Jones Industrial Average outperformed the market. Research by Krishna Ramaswamy and Robert Litzenberger nearly 20 years ago established the correlation between dividend yield and subsequent returns.[15] More recent studies by James O'Shaughnessy

15 See Robert Litzenberger and Krishna Ramaswamy, "The Effects of Personal Taxes and Dividends on Capital Asset Prices: Theory and Empirical Evidence," *Journal of Financial Economics*, 1979, pp. 163–95.

have shown that from the period 1951 through 1994, the 50 highest dividend- yielding stocks had a 1.7 percent higher annual return among stocks with a capitalization of at least $1 billion.[16]

The correlation between the dividend yield and return can be partially explained by taxes. As will be discussed in detail in Chapter 8, dividends receive no tax preference, while capital gains offer investors favorable tax treatment. Thus stocks with higher dividend yields must offer higher before-tax returns to compensate shareholders for the tax differences. It should also be noted that most current studies, like O'Shaughnessy's, exclude utility stocks, which as a group have by far the highest dividend yield but have vastly underperformed the market over the past decade.

## Distressed Firms

Despite the higher returns provided by value-based firms, there is one class of stocks, *distressed firms*, that have among the highest returns of all. Many distressed firms have negative earnings, zero or negative book value, and pay no dividends. Research has shown that as the ratio of book value or earnings to price declines, so does the return. But when book value or earnings turn negative, the price of the stock becomes so depressed that the future returns soar.

This same discontinuity is also found with dividend yields. As noted above, the higher the dividend yield, the higher the subsequent return. But firms that pay no dividend at all have among the highest subsequent returns.

The superior returns to nondividend paying stocks were first recognized in a book entitled *Investing in Purchasing Power*, by Kenneth S. Van Strum, a financial writer of the 1920s. Van Strum set out to confirm Edgar Lawrence Smith's study of a year earlier, which proclaimed the superiority of stocks as long-term investments.

Expecting to find such superior performance only in "investment grade" stocks, Van Strum was surprised to find quite the opposite. In one of his studies, he analyzed what would happen if the common-stock investor purchased only stocks of companies that had no divi-

---

16 James O'Shaughnessy, *What Works on Wall Street*, McGraw-Hill, 1997, pp. 123–32.

dends and that were priced under $50 per share, which at that time were viewed as low-priced speculative stocks. He concluded:

> This group [no dividends and price under $50 per share] of low-priced common stocks not only permitted the stock investor to maintain his purchasing power intact, but also showed the best results of any investment made in the entire group of studies.[17]

In fact, Irving Fisher stated in the forward of Van Strum's book, "This result [the best performance of nondividend-paying stocks] is as surprising as any among the many surprising results of this investigation."[18] Recent analysis shows that Van Strum's findings persist today.

Most stocks that have negative earnings or negative book values have experienced very adverse financial developments and have become severely depressed. Many investors are quick to dump these stocks when the news gets very bad. This often drives the price down below the value justified by future prospects. Few investors seem able to see the light at the end of the tunnel, or cannot justify—to themselves or to their clients—the purchase of such stocks under such adverse circumstances.

## Initial Public Offerings

While many investors recall the newly-issued story stocks, such as Intel, Microsoft, and Wal-Mart, which have made investors rich, most forget about the many such firms that fail to fulfill their promise when they are issued. A study by Tim Loughran and Jay Ritter followed every operating company (almost 5,000) that went public between 1970 and 1990.[19] Those who bought at the market price on the first day of trading and held the stock for five years reaped an average annual return of only 5 percent. Those who invested in companies *of the same size* on the same days that the initial public offerings (IPOs) were purchased gave investors a 12 percent annual return.

One of the major reasons for the underperformance of smaller growth stocks is that they are frequently IPOs, often issued at huge

---

17 Kenneth S. Van Strum, *Investing in Purchasing Power*, New York: Barron's, 1925, p. 232.
18 Ibid., p. vii.
19 Jay Ritter, "The Long Run Performance of IPOs, *Journal of Finance*, vol. 46, no. 1, March 1991, pp. 3–27 and Tim Loughran and Jay Ritter, "The New Issue Puzzle," *Journal of Finance*, vol. 50. no. 1, March 1995, pp. 23–51.

price earning multipliers. The lessons from studying the IPO market are clear. If you can get an IPO at the offering price, it is often a great buy. But don't hold on! The subsequent performance almost always disappoints.

## Are Small Stocks Growth Stocks?

Many investors think of small stocks as potential "growth" stocks, hoping to catch one that will turn into a Microsoft or Intel. But most small stocks are not growth stocks. In fact, value stocks dominate the small stock indexes while, as we have seen in Chapter 4, the S & P 500 Index is now dominated by large growth stocks.

Even among the S & P 500 Index, value stocks tend to be smaller than growth stocks. BARRA, a California consulting management firm, and Standard & Poor's have ranked the firms in the S & P 500 Index by the book-to-market ratio and divided the index into two halves of approximately equal market value (with some of the stocks that fall in the middle put in both halves). The growth index needed only 195 firms, with a median market cap of $39 billion to constitute 50 percent of the S & P 500 Index value, while the value index needed 345 firms, with a median market cap of $14 billion.

The fundamental statistics on small stocks also reveal a value-stock bias. At the end of 1996, the average market-to-book ratio for the S & P 500 Index was 3.4, while for the Russell 2000 it was only 2.5. Even the average P-E ratio of the S & P 500 Index (19.6) was slightly higher than the 19.1 of the Russell 2000. The only value criteria suggesting that small stocks are primarily growth stocks is the dividend yield, which was very slightly higher on the S & P 500 Index than on small cap indices.

Furthermore, the industry composition of the Russell 2000 Index suggests that small stocks are not necessarily growth stocks. By far the largest sector of the Russell 2000 is financial, with almost one-quarter of the capitalization. This is almost twice its weighting in the S & P 500 Index. Although the technology sector is second with almost 18 percent (compared to only 12 percent for the S & P 500 Index), cyclical consumer stocks are more prominent in the small cap than large cap index.

## INVESTMENT STRATEGY

"Style investing," where money managers rotate between small and large and value and growth stocks, is all the rage on Wall Street.

Historical data seem to imply that small stocks outperform large stocks and value stocks outperform growth stocks.

Yet the historical returns on these investment styles might not represent their future returns at all. The superior performance of small stocks over large stocks and value stocks over growth stocks depends crucially on whether the 1975–83 period is included. And, as Chapter 17 will show, the outperformance of both small stocks and large value stocks occurs very early in the calendar year. These patterns are not well understood nor are they related to normal economic cycles.

All of this implies that the average investor will do best by diversifying among all classes of stocks. Trying to catch styles as they move in and out of favor is not only difficult, but also quite risky. As more money managers try to play the style game, their subsequent returns will certainly differ from their historical averages.

# 7

## CHAPTER

# THE NIFTY FIFTY REVISITED

*It was so easy to forget that probably no sizable company could possibly be worth over 50 times normal earnings. As the late Burton Crane once observed about Xerox, its multiple discounted not only the future but also the hereafter.*

—*Forbes*, 1977[1]

This chapter examines a group of high-flying growth stocks that soared in the early 1970s, only to come crashing to earth in the vicious 1973–74 bear market. These stocks were often held up as examples of speculation based on unwarranted optimism about the ability of growth stocks to continue to generate rapid and sustained earnings growth. And it was not just the public, but large institutions as well who poured tens of billions of dollars into these stocks. After the 1973–74 bear market slashed the value of most of the "Nifty Fifty," many investors vowed never again to pay over 30 times earnings for a stock.

But was the conventional wisdom justified that the bull market of the early 1970s markedly overvalued these stocks? Or is it possible that investors were right to predict that the growth of these firms would eventually justify their lofty prices? This chapter addresses the basic question: *What premium should an investor pay for large, well-established growth stocks?*

---

1 "The Nifty Fifty Revisited," *Forbes*, December 15, 1977, p. 72.

## THE NIFTY FIFTY

The Nifty Fifty were a group of premier growth stocks, such as Xerox, IBM, Polaroid, and Coca-Cola, which became institutional darlings in the early 1970s. All of these stocks had proven growth records, continual increases in dividends (virtually none had cut its dividend since World War II), and high market capitalization. This last characteristic enabled institutions to load up on these stocks without significantly influencing the price of their shares.

The Nifty Fifty were often called *one-decision* stocks: buy and never sell. Because their prospects were so bright, many analysts claimed that the only direction they could go was up. Since they had made so many rich, few if any investors could fault a money manager for buying them.

At the time, many investors did not seem to find 70, 80, even 100 times earnings at all an unreasonable price to pay for the world's preeminent growth companies. *Forbes* magazine retrospectively commented on the phenomenon as follows:

> What held the Nifty Fifty up? The same thing that held up tulip-bulb prices in long-ago Holland—popular delusions and the madness of crowds. The delusion was that these companies were so good it didn't matter what you paid for them; their inexorable growth would bail you out.
> Obviously the problem was not with the companies but with the temporary insanity of institutional money managers—proving again that stupidity well-packaged can sound like wisdom. It was so easy to forget that probably no sizable company could possibly be worth over 50 times normal earnings.[2]

## RETURNS OF THE NIFTY-FIFTY

Let's trace the performance of the Nifty Fifty stocks as identified by Morgan Guaranty Trust, one of the largest managers of equity trust assets.[3] These stocks are listed in Table 7-1, along with their 1972 price-to-earnings (P/E) ratios. The product lines of these stocks range from drugs, computers and electronics, photography, food, and tobacco to retailing, among others. Notably absent are the cyclical industries: auto, steel, transportation, capital goods, and oil.

2 Ibid., p. 52.
3 Noted by M. S. Forbes, Jr., in "When Wall Street Becomes Enamored," *Forbes*, December 15, 1977, p. 72.

**TABLE 7–1**

Nifty Fifty Returns from Market Peak, December 1972 to June 1997

| | Annualized Return (%) | 1972 Actual P/E Ratio | Warranted P/E Patio | EPS Growth (%) (through 1996) |
|---|---|---|---|---|
| Philip Morris Cos. Inc. | 19.9% | 24.0 | 78.2 | 17.9% |
| Gillette Co. | 18.3% | 24.3 | 54.5 | 10.4% |
| Coca-Cola Co. | 17.2% | 46.4 | 92.2 | 13.5% |
| Pfizer Inc. | 16.9% | 28.4 | 54.9 | 12.2% |
| Pepsico Inc. | 16.7% | 27.6 | 52.4 | 11.2% |
| Bristol-Myers | 16.7% | 24.9 | 46.4 | 12.7% |
| Merck & Co. Inc. | 16.1% | 43.0 | 74.4 | 15.1% |
| Heublein Inc. | 16.0% | 29.4 | 47.5 | n/a |
| General Electric Co. | 15.4% | 23.4 | 34.7 | 10.9% |
| Squibb Corp. | 15.3% | 30.1 | 45.1 | n/a |
| Lilly Eli & Co. | 13.8% | 40.6 | 46.7 | 10.9% |
| Procter & Gamble Co. | 13.7% | 29.8 | 33.6 | 13.9% |
| Schering Corp. | 13.7% | 48.1 | 54.4 | 12.9% |
| Revlon Inc. | 13.3% | 25.0 | 26.9 | n/a |
| American Home Products Corp. | 13.1% | 36.7 | 38.1 | 10.5% |
| Johnson and Johnson | 12.9% | 57.1 | 56.8 | 14.2% |
| Chesebrough Ponds Inc. | 12.4% | 39.1 | 36.2 | n/a |
| Anheuser-Busch Inc. | 12.3% | 31.5 | 28.7 | 12.3% |
| First National City Corp. | 12.3% | 20.5 | 18.9 | 9.3% |
| Schlumberger Ltd. | 12.2% | 45.6 | 40.3 | 11.5% |
| McDonald's Corp. | 12.0% | 71.0 | 59.2 | 17.5% |
| Disney Walt Co. | 11.7% | 71.2 | 56.4 | 14.6% |
| Dow Chemical Co. | 11.5% | 24.1 | 19.5 | 12.2% |
| American Express Co. | 11.1% | 37.7 | 28.4 | 9.6% |
| American Hospital Supply Corp. | 10.9% | 48.1 | 34.1 | n/a |
| Minnesota Mining & Manufacturing Co. | 10.5% | 39.0 | 27.2 | 8.7% |
| Upjohn Co. | 9.5% | 38.8 | 22.8 | 11.3% (a) |
| AMP Inc. | 9.3% | 42.9 | 22.5 | 9.5% |
| Lubrizol Corp. | 9.1% | 32.6 | 18.4 | 9.4% |
| Texas Instruments Inc. | 9.0% | 39.5 | 19.4 | 12.7% (b) |
| Int'l Telephone & Telegraph Corp. | 8.7% | 15.4 | 9.2 | 2.7% (a) |
| Sears Roebuck & Co. | 8.3% | 29.2 | 15.7 | 4.5% |
| Int'l Flavors & Fragrances | 8.3% | 69.1 | 33.2 | 9.4% |
| Halliburton Co. | 8.3% | 35.5 | 16.8 | 3.9% |
| Baxter Labs | 8.3% | 71.4 | 30.1 | 10.5% |
| Penney J.C. Inc. | 8.1% | 31.5 | 15.8 | 5.0% |
| International Business Machines | 7.1% | 35.5 | 15.4 | 6.6% |
| Schlitz Joe Brewing Co. | 6.6% | 39.6 | 15.0 | n/a |
| Xerox Corp. | 6.3% | 45.8 | 18.3 | 5.1% |
| Louisiana Land & Exploration Co. | 5.5% | 26.6 | 9.8 | 1.2% |
| Eastman Kodak Co. | 5.5% | 43.5 | 15.6 | 5.9% |
| Avon Products Inc. | 4.7% | 61.2 | 22.8 | 3.3% |
| Simplicity Patterns | 4.7% | 50.0 | 7.8 | n/a |
| Digital Equipment Corp. | 3.8% | 56.2 | 7.2 | -12.6% · |
| Black and Decker Corp. | 2.6% | 47.8 | 10.1 | 3.4% |
| Kresge (S. S.) Co. | 2.0% | 49.5 | 9.6 | 1.2% |
| Polaroid Corp. | 1.7% | 94.8 | 16.5 | -2.9% |
| Emery Air Freight Corp. | -1.0% | 55.3 | 8.8 | n/a |
| Burroughs Co. | -3.9% | 46.0 | 4.2 | -16.6% · |
| M. G. I. C. Investment Corp. | -8.6% | 68.5 | 4.8 | n/a |
| **Rebalanced Portfolio** | 12.7% | 41.9 | 40.5 | 11.0% |
| **Non-rebalanced Portfolio** | 12.4% | 41.9 | 38.6 | 11.0% |
| **S&P 500** | 12.9% | 18.9 | 18.9 | 8.0% |

\* *Companies had negative EPS in last year measured -- used $0.01 / share to calculate EPS growth.*

(a) *earnings growth through 1994;*  (b) *earnings growth through 1995;*

Many of the original Nifty Fifty stocks are still giants today. In 1997, 15 occupy the top 40 U.S. stocks in terms of market capitalization and six (General Electric, Coca-Cola, Merck, Philip Morris, Procter and Gamble, and IBM) are among the top 10. Corporate changes in the Nifty Fifty since the early 1970s are described in the appendix.

The Nifty Fifty did sell at hefty multiples. The average price-to-earnings ratio of these stocks was 41.9 in 1972, more than double that of the S & P 500 Index, while their 1.1 percent dividend yield was less than one-half that of other large stocks. Over one-fifth of these firms sported price-to-earnings ratios in excess of 50, and Polaroid was selling at over 90 times earnings.

Table 7-1 ranks these stocks according to their annual compound returns from December 1972 through June 1997.[4] December 1972 was chosen because an equally weighted portfolio of each of these stocks peaked in that month, which was considered the height of the Nifty Fifty mania.

Consumer brand-name stocks, such as Philip Morris, Gillette, Coca-Cola, and PepsiCo, were clearly the star performers after the 1972 peak. The drug stocks also performed extremely well. Merck, Bristol-Myers (which absorbed Squibb), Schering, Pfizer, Upjohn, and Johnson & Johnson all beat the S & P 500 Index. But the biggest winner was Philip Morris, which had an outstanding 19.9 percent annual return after December 1972.

Of course there were also some big losers. Technology issues as a whole did badly and three stocks, Emery Air Freight, Burroughs, and MGIC Investment Corp., had negative returns.

## Evaluation of Data

Did the Nifty Fifty stocks become overvalued during the buying spree of 1972? Yes—but by a very small margin. An equally weighted portfolio of Nifty Fifty stocks formed at the market peak in December 1972 and rebalanced monthly would have realized a 12.7 percent annual return to June 1997, just slightly below the 12.9 percent return on the S & P 500 Index.[5] The same portfolio would have returned 12.4 percent if it were never rebalanced over time.

---

4 I used the following procedure to compute total returns to the Nifty Fifty stocks over the entire period. If a stock merged with or was acquired by another firm, I combined the returns on the two stocks at the appropriate date of change. If the company went private, I spliced the return on the S & P 500 Index from that date forward.
5 The average annualized return of a portfolio of stocks is larger than the average annualized return of the individual stocks because of the mathematics of compound returns.

Figure 7-1 shows the degree of over- or undervaluation of an equally weighted portfolio of the Nifty Fifty from December 1972 to June 1997. A fairly valued portfolio would show the same return as the S & P 500 Index over this time period, an overvalued portfolio would underperform the Index, and an undervalued portfolio would outperform the Index. In December 1972, at the peak of the Nifty Fifty mania, these stocks were overvalued by only about 3.1 percent on the basis of their return over the next 25 years, but after 1976 they became greatly deeply undervalued.[6]

Since the average dividend yield on the Nifty Fifty was more than 1½ percentage points below the yield on the S & P 500 Index, most of their return came from lightly taxed capital gains. The after-tax yield on

**FIGURE  7–1**

Valuation of an Equally Weighted Nifty Fifty Portfolio Relative to the S & P 500, December 1970 to June 1997

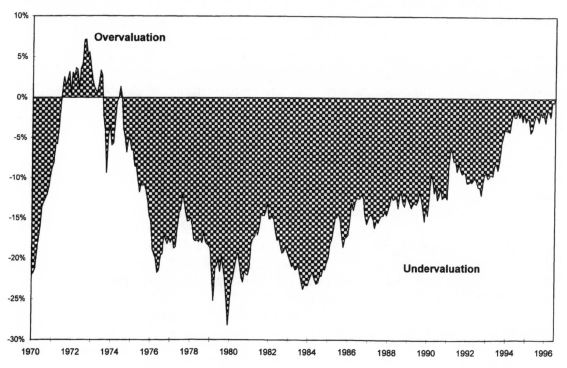

6 The Nifty Fifty became slightly more overvalued after the market began to decline in 1973, reaching a maximum overvaluation of 7.1 percent in August.

a portfolio of Nifty Fifty stocks, purchased at their market peak, would have surpassed the after-tax yield on the S & P 500 Index for an investor in or above the 28 percent tax bracket.

## WHAT IS THE RIGHT P/E RATIO TO PAY FOR A GROWTH STOCK?

If you could have presented long-term investors with a crystal ball in 1972 that revealed the 25 subsequent years of dividends, earnings, and 1997 prices of the Nifty Fifty stocks, what price would investors have paid for these stocks in December 1972? The answer is a price high or low enough so that, given their subsequent dividends and June 1997 price, their total returns over the past 25 years would match the overall market.[7] Table 7-1 reports these prices relative to their 1972 earnings. Since these prices are warranted by their future returns, these price-to-earnings ratios are called the *warranted P-E ratios*.

What is so surprising is that many of these stocks were worth far more than even the lofty heights that investors bid them. Investors should have paid 78.2 times the 1972 earnings for Philip Morris instead of the 24 they did pay, undervaluing the stock by more than 3 to 1. Coca-Cola was worth over 90 times its earnings and Merck should have sported a multiple of more than 70. Interestingly, the group that was the most undervalued, and subsequently most successful, catered to brand-name consumer foods, including McDonald's, PepsiCo, Coca-Cola, and even Phillip Morris.

In contrast to brand-name consumer stocks, the technology stocks failed badly. IBM, which commanded a 35 P-E ratio in the early 1970s, was actually worth only 15.4 times earnings despite its recent stellar comeback. And while investors paid 45.8 times earnings for Xerox, it was worth only 18.3 times earnings on the basis of its future growth. Polaroid sported the highest P-E, selling for a fantastic 94.8 times earnings, almost six times higher than was justified by its future returns. Despite its mix of winners and losers, an equally weighted portfolio of Nifty Fifty stocks was worth 40.5 times its 1972 earnings, marginally less than the 41.9 ratio that investors paid for them.

Of special interest is Coca-Cola Corporation. It carried a very pricey 46.4 multiple in 1972, which many analysts claimed was far too

---

7 Finance theory states that the required return on an individual stock is also related to its beta with the market. Making this correction does not materially change the estimates given in Table 7-1. See Jeremy Siegel, "The Nifty-Fifty Revisited: Do Growth Stock Ultimately Justify Their Price?" in the *Journal of Portfolio Management*, 21 (4), Summer 1995, pp. 8–20.

high. But on the basis of its future returns, Coke was worth over 90 times earnings. Who at that time would have thought in the 1970s that this soft-drink manufacturer would so thoroughly trounce technology giants such as IBM, Digital Equipment, Texas Instruments, Xerox, and Burroughs?

Burton Crane, a financial writer for the *New York Times*, did not know how right he was when he claimed that Xerox's multiple discounted the future and the hereafter. But had he said the same of Coca-Cola, which carried an even higher multiple, he would have learned that profits can really fall from soft-drink heaven.

## Earnings Growth and Valuation

Table 7-1 reports the rate of growth of per-share earnings of each Nifty Fifty firm over the subsequent 25 years. The average annual rate of growth of earnings was 11 percent, three percentage points higher than the earnings growth of the S & P 500 Stock Index. This contrasts sharply with the conclusion of some researchers who maintained that growth stocks had no better subsequent earnings growth than the average stock.[8]

The relation between the P-E ratios and the earnings growth of the Nifty Fifty showed that investors were not irrational to pay the premium they did for these stocks. In December 1972, the average P-E ratio of the S & P 500 Index was 18.9, which corresponds to an earnings yield of 5.3 percent (the reciprocal of the P-E ratio). The Nifty Fifty, with a P-E ratio of 41.9, had an earnings yield of 2.4 percent, about three percentage points lower than the S & P 500 Index. But the deficit in the earnings yield was almost exactly made up by the higher growth rate of future earnings, so their total return matched that of the S & P 500 Index. The Nifty Fifty investors, therefore, properly traded off a higher P-E ratio (and lower current yield) with higher subsequent earning growth.

A rule of thumb for stock valuation that is found on Wall Street is to calculate the sum of the growth rate of a stock's earnings plus its dividend yield and divide by its P-E ratio. The higher the ratio the better, and the famed money manager Peter Lynch recommends investors go for stocks with a ratio of two or higher, avoiding stocks with a ratio of one or less.[9]

---

8 See I. M. D. Little, "Higgledy-Piggeldy Growth," *Oxford Bulletin of Economics and Statistics*, vol. 24, 4, (1962) pp. 387–412
9 Peter Lynch, *One Up on Wall Street*, New York: Penguin Books, 1989, pp. 198–99. See also Nelson D. Schwartz, "Time to Cash In Your Blue Chips?" in *Fortune*, July 21, 1997, pp. 120–30.

Yet this procedure would have eliminated all of the best Nifty Fifty stocks. The top stocks had 25-year earnings growth between 10 and 15 percent per year, yet their warranted price-to-earnings ratios often exceeded 50. Stocks with persistent earnings growth are often worth far more than the multiple that Wall Street considered "reasonable."

But there is also a value-oriented theme hidden in the dazzle of these growth stocks. If you examine the actual P-E ratio of the Nifty Fifty stocks, the 25 stocks with the highest ratios (averaging 54) yielded only about half the subsequent return as the 25 stocks with the lowest low P-E ratios, whose P-E averaged 30. So although these growth stocks as a group were worth more than 40 times earnings, they should not be considered buys "at any price." Those stocks that sustain growth rates above the long-term average are worth their weight in gold, but few live up to their lofty expectations.[10]

## CONCLUSION

Examining the wreckage of the Nifty Fifty in the 1974 bear market, there are two possible explanations for what happened. The first is that a mania did sweep these stocks, sending them to levels that were totally unjustified on the basis of prospective earnings. The second explanation is that, on the whole, the Nifty Fifty were in fact properly valued at the peak, but a loss of confidence by investors sent them to dramatically undervalued levels.

In 1975 there was no way of knowing which explanation was correct. But 25 years later we can determine whether the Nifty Fifty stocks were overvalued in 1972. Examination of their subsequent returns shows that the second explanation, roundly rejected by Wall Street for years, is much closer to the truth. A portfolio of Nifty Fifty stocks purchased at the peak would have nearly matched the S & P 500 Index over

---

10 In response to the tremendous returns on some of the Nifty Fifty stocks, Tom McManus of Morgan Stanley (now of Natwest Securities) created a new list of 50 stocks in March 1995 called the Morgan Stanley Multinational Index. Nearly half of the original Nifty Fifty stocks indicated in Table 7-1 is on the new list, and they make up over 60 percent of the capitalization of the Index. Through June 1997, the Morgan Stanley Nifty Fifty outperformed the S & P 500 Index by over 7 percent per year, a period when very few money managers outperformed the S & P index.

the next 25 years.[11] Wall Street's misunderstanding led to a dramatic undervaluation of many of the large growth stocks throughout the 1980s and early 1990s. Stocks with steady growth records are worth 30, 40, and more times earnings.

Despite their dazzling performance, buying just a few of these growth stocks was quite dangerous. Among the many gems there were a number of bad apples. Even whole industries, like technology, which had enriched so many investors in the 1960s, vastly underperformed the market in the next 25 years. Diversification is a key to cutting risks and maintaining returns. No one stock or single industry is guaranteed to succeed. But good growth stocks, like good wines, are often worth the price you have to pay.

## APPENDIX: CORPORATE CHANGES IN THE NIFTY FIFTY STOCKS

There have been 11 corporate changes to the Nifty Fifty over the past several decades:

- American Hospital Supply merged with Baxter Travenol (later Baxter International) in November 1985.
- Burroughs changed its name to Unisys (UIS) in 1987.
- Chesebrough Ponds was merged in Unilever NV in February 1987.
- Emery Air Freight merged with Consolidated Freightways in April 1989 (now CNF Transportation).
- Heublein was merged into RJR Nabisco in October 1982, which became RJR Industries and was taken private on April 28, 1989.
- MGIC Investment merged with Baldwin United in March of 1982, which went bankrupt, and emerged from bankruptcy in November 1986 under the name PHL Corp. PHL was absorbed by Leucadia National Corp. in January 1993.
- Revlon was subject to a leveraged buy-out in July 1987.

---

11 In the early 1970s, some Nifty Fifty lists included Wal-Mart, which has a 26.07 percent annual return from December 1972 through June 1997, far eclipsing every stock on the Morgan Guaranty Trust list. If Wal-Mart had been included, the Nifty Fifty as a group would have undervalued at the market peak

- Schlitz merged in June 1982 with Stroh Brewing, a privately held firm.
- Simplicity Pattern became Maxxam in May 1984 and then Maxxam Group in May 1988.
- Squibb was purchased on October 4, 1989 by Bristol-Myers.
- Upjohn merged with Pharmacia AB (Sweden) in November 1995 and became Pharmacia & Upjohn, Inc.

# CHAPTER

# TAXES AND STOCK RETURNS

*In this world nothing is certain but death and taxes.*

—Benjamin Franklin[1]

*The power to tax involves the power to destroy.*

—John Marshall[2]

*For all long-term investors, there is only one objective—maximum total real return after taxes.*

—John Templeton[3]

John Templeton's objective, to maximize total real return after taxes, must be considered in all investment strategies. And stocks are very well suited to this purpose. In contrast to fixed-income investments, a significant portion of the return from stocks comes from capital appreciation, which is treated favorably by the tax code. Taxes are not paid until a gain is realized, and such gains have almost always been subject to a lower tax rate. So in addition to having superior before-tax returns, stocks also have a tax advantage over bonds.

## HISTORICAL TAXES ON INCOME AND CAPITAL GAINS

Figure 8-1a plots the marginal tax rate on dividend and interest income for investors at three income levels: the tax rate of an investor in the high-

---

1 Letter to M. Leroy, 1789.
2 *McCulloch v. Maryland*, 1819.
3 Excerpts from *The Templeton Touch* by William Proctor, quoted in *Classics*, ed. Charles D. Ellis, Homewood, Ill.: Dow Jones-Irwin, 1989, p. 738.

FIGURE  8–1

## FIGURE 8–1

Federal Tax Rates, 1913–1997

Figure (a)

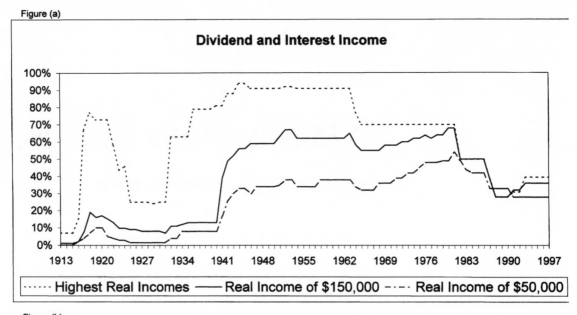

**Dividend and Interest Income**

Figure (b)

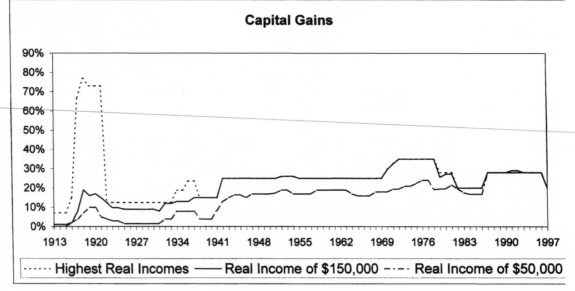

**Capital Gains**

est tax bracket, the tax rate for an investor with a real income of $150,000 in today's dollars, and the tax rate for an investor with a real income of $50,000. Figure 8-1b plots the tax rate on capital gains income. You can see the volatility in marginal tax rates for the high-income investor, while the tax rate on capital gains has remained far more stable. A history of the tax code applicable to stock investors is provided in the Appendix.

## A TOTAL AFTER-TAX RETURNS INDEX

In Chapter 1, I presented a total returns index for stocks, bonds, bills, and gold. In this chapter I will calculate a range of after-tax returns on these assets under various tax rates. Figure 8-2 presents the effect of taxes on total real returns. The upper line of the stock range represents the before-tax real stock return, identical to the one in Figure 1-4. This return would

**FIGURE  8–2**

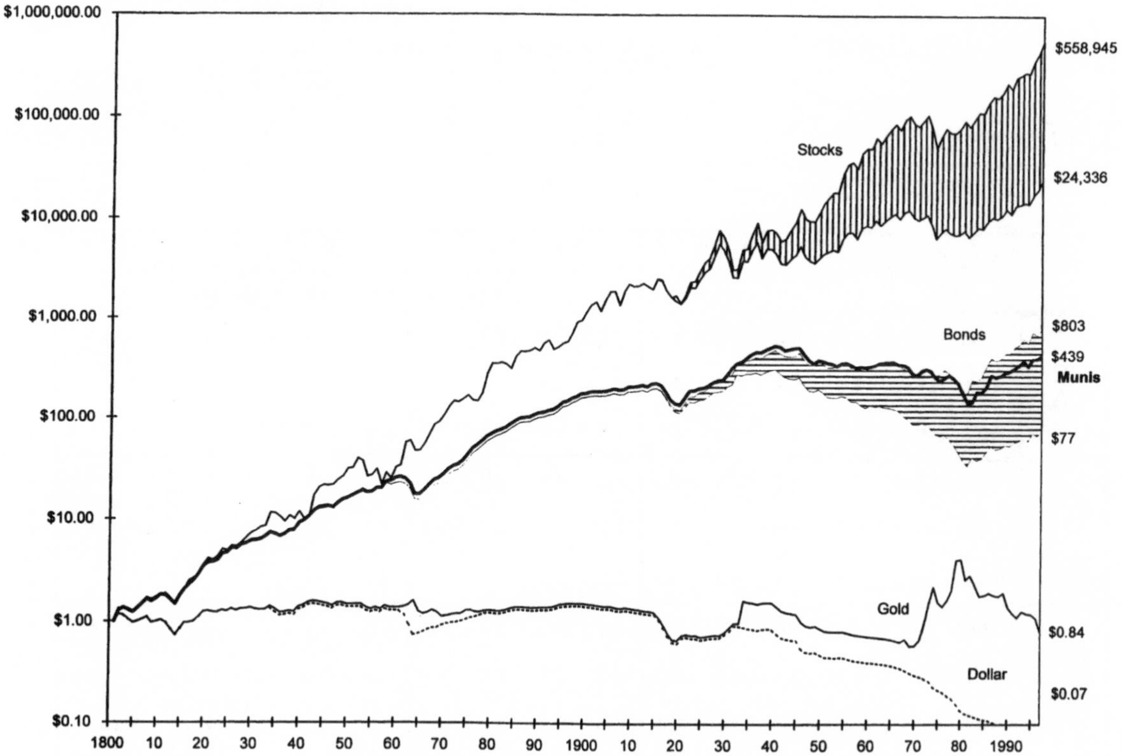

Total Real Return Indexes Before and After Federal Tax, 1802–1997

be applicable to tax-exempt individuals or institutions. The lower line of the stock range in Figure 8-2 assumes that investors pay the highest tax rate on dividend, interest, and capital gains income, with no deferral of capital gains taxes. The shaded range shows the range of total returns from zero to the highest marginal different tax rate. This chapter considers only federal taxes; no state, local, or estate taxes are included.

The difference between before- and after-tax total return is striking. Total before-tax real stock returns accumulate to nearly $560,000, while after-tax accumulations are about $24,000, less than ⅟20th the pretax accumulation. A return range is also displayed for the accumulations on treasury bonds as well as the total return from municipal bonds, which are exempt from federal taxes. Since municipal bond interest rates are generally lower than the interest paid by federal government bonds (called *treasuries*), the total return of municipal bonds is lower than that of treasuries for an untaxed investor, but higher than the return from treasuries for most taxable investors.

Table 8-1 displays the historical real after-tax returns for four tax brackets. Since 1913, when the federal income tax was instituted, the after-tax real return on stocks has ranged from 6.7 percent for untaxed investors to 2.8 percent for investors in the maximum bracket who do not defer their capital gains. For taxable bonds, the real annual return

## TABLE 8–1

Historical Asset Real Returns and Taxes (1802–1997)

|  |  | Stock Returns Tax Bracket | | | | Bond Returns Tax Bracket | | | | T-Bill Returns Tax Bracket | | | | Muni Bds | Gold | CPI |
|---|---|---|---|---|---|---|---|---|---|---|---|---|---|---|---|---|
|  |  | $0 | $50k | $150k | Max | $0 | $50k | $150k | Max | $0 | $50k | $150k | Max |  |  |  |
| Period | 1802-1997 | 7.0 | 6.2 | 5.8 | 5.3 | 3.5 | 2.8 | 2.6 | 2.2 | 2.9 | 2.4 | 2.2 | 2.0 | 3.2 | -0.1 | 1.3 |
|  | 1871-1997 | 7.0 | 5.7 | 5.2 | 4.4 | 2.8 | 1.7 | 1.4 | 0.9 | 1.7 | 0.9 | 0.6 | 0.3 | 2.2 | -0.2 | 2.0 |
|  | 1913-1997 | 6.7 | 4.9 | 4.1 | 2.8 | 1.7 | 0.2 | -0.4 | -1.1 | 0.4 | -0.7 | -1.1 | -1.6 | 0.8 | -0.5 | 3.3 |
| Major Sub-Periods | I 1802-1870 | 7.0 | 7.0 | 7.0 | 7.0 | 4.8 | 4.8 | 4.8 | 4.8 | 5.1 | 5.1 | 5.1 | 5.1 | 5.0 | 0.2 | 0.1 |
|  | II 1871-1925 | 6.6 | 6.6 | 6.4 | 6.2 | 3.7 | 3.7 | 3.6 | 3.4 | 3.2 | 3.1 | 3.1 | 2.7 | 3.6 | -0.8 | 0.6 |
|  | III 1926-1997 | 7.2 | 5.1 | 4.3 | 3.0 | 2.0 | 0.3 | -0.3 | -1.0 | 0.6 | -0.7 | -1.2 | -1.5 | 1.1 | 0.2 | 3.1 |
| Post-War Periods | 1946-1997 | 7.5 | 4.9 | 4.0 | 3.0 | 1.1 | -1.2 | -1.9 | -2.3 | 0.5 | -1.3 | -1.9 | -2.3 | -0.3 | -0.7 | 4.3 |
|  | 1966-1981 | -0.4 | -2.1 | -2.9 | -3.3 | -4.2 | -6.6 | -7.5 | -7.7 | -0.2 | -3.0 | -4.1 | -4.6 | -5.7 | 8.8 | 7.0 |
|  | 1966-1997 | 6.0 | 3.4 | 3.0 | 2.4 | 2.5 | -0.7 | -1.3 | -1.6 | 1.4 | -1.2 | -1.9 | -2.2 | 0.5 | 0.6 | 5.2 |
|  | 1982-1997 | 12.8 | 9.3 | 9.1 | 8.4 | 9.6 | 5.6 | 5.2 | 5.0 | 2.9 | 0.7 | 0.4 | 0.4 | 7.0 | -7.0 | 3.4 |

falls from 1.7 to –1.1 percent, and in bills from 0.4 to –1.6 percent. Municipal bonds have yielded a 0.8 percent annual real return since the income tax was instituted.

Despite the debilitating effect of taxes on equity accumulation, taxes cause the greatest damage to fixed-income investments. On an after-tax basis, an investor in the top tax bracket who put $1,000 in Treasury bills at the beginning of 1946 would have $299 after taxes and after inflation today, a loss in purchasing power of more than 70 percent. Such an investor could turn $1,000 into over $4,500 by buying stocks, a 350 percent increase in purchasing power.

In fact, for someone in the highest tax bracket, short-term treasury bills have yielded no after-tax real return since 1875, even longer if state and local taxes are taken into account. In contrast, top bracket investors would have increased their purchasing power in stocks 144-fold over the same period.

## THE BENEFITS OF DEFERRING CAPITAL GAINS TAXES

Many investors assume that capital gains are beneficial solely because of the favorable rates at which such gains have been taxed. But lower capital gains tax rates are not the only advantage of investing in appreciating assets. Taxes on capital gains are paid only when the asset is sold, not as the gain is accrued. The advantage of this tax deferral is that assets accumulate at the higher *before-tax* rates, rather than *after-tax* rates of return.

Table 8-2 documents the increase in the effective rate of return resulting from the deferral of the capital gains tax for an investor in the 31 percent marginal tax bracket. A 10 percent annual return is assumed, consisting of a 2 percent dividend yield and a 7.8 percent capital gain. The table assumes the 1997 tax legislation that indicates a 31 percent tax rate on gains held for less than one year (short term), a 28 percent capital gains tax rate for assets held more than 12 months but less than 18 months (intermediate term), and a 20 percent tax on capital gains held more than 18 months (long term).

Holding-period yields are calculated for six cases, so capital gains are realized on a short-term basis, on an intermediate-term basis, every two years, every five years, or at the end of the holding period. Lastly, capital gains can be untaxed. This last case would occur if the stock were left in a bequest or given to a charitable organization.

Table 8-2 shows that if capital gains are realized short term, the annual after-tax return is 6.9 percent. The total return is subject to the 31 percent marginal tax rate because the capital gain was realized too quickly to

**TABLE 8–2**

Holding Period Accumulations and Annual Returns: 10 Percent Total Stock Return, 2 Percent Dividend Yield, 7.8 Percent Capital Appreciation, 31 Percent Annual Tax on Dividends, 31 Percent Tax on Short-Term Capital Gains (Less Than 12 Months), 28 Percent Tax on Intermediate-Term Capital Gains (12–18 Months), 20 Percent Tax on Long-Term Capital Gains (Greater Than 18 Months), and an Initial Investment of $1,000

| Length of Hololding Period | Capital Gains Taxed at Short-Term Rate (31%) | Capital Gains Taxed at Intermediate-Term Rate (28%) | Capital Gains Taxed Every Two Years (20%) | Capital Gains Taxed Every Five Years (20%) | Capital Gains Taxed at the End (20%) | Capital Gains Not Taxed |
|---|---|---|---|---|---|---|
| 5 Years | $1,396 | $1,411 | $1,456 | $1,468 | $1,468 | $1,562 |
|  | 6.90% | 7.14% | 7.81% | 7.98% | 7.98% | 9.33% |
| 10 Years | $1,949 | $1,992 | $2,123 | $2,154 | $2,198 | $2,440 |
|  | 6.90% | 7.14% | 7.82% | 7.98% | 8.19% | 9.33% |
| 20 Years | $3,798 | $3,969 | $4,507 | $4,640 | $5,122 | $5,955 |
|  | 6.90% | 7.14% | 7.82% | 7.98% | 8.51% | 9.33% |
| 30 Years | $7,402 | $7,906 | $9,569 | $9,994 | $12,258 | $14,533 |
|  | 6.90% | 7.14% | 7.82% | 7.98% | 8.71% | 9.33% |
| 40 Years | $14,425 | $15,751 | $20,316 | $21,527 | $29,671 | $35,464 |
|  | 6.90% | 7.14% | 7.82% | 7.98% | 8.84% | 9.33% |
| 50 Years | $28,112 | $31,378 | $43,133 | $46,370 | $72,164 | $86,545 |
|  | 6.90% | 7.14% | 7.82% | 7.98% | 8.93% | 9.33% |

enjoy tax preference. If the gains are held between 12 and 18 months, the investor enjoys a reduction in tax rate on the capital gains, so the after-tax return rises to 7.14 percent. If gains are realized every two years, the after-tax return rises to 7.82 percent. This is due mostly to the lower 20 percent tax on capital gains but also to the deferral of taxes paid. If capital gains are realized every five years, the return rises to 7.98 percent per year. This 16-basis point gain is strictly due to the deferral of gains. If capital gains are taxed at the end of the holding period, the annual return rises to 8.19 percent in ten years, to 8.51 percent in 20 years, and to 8.71 percent in 30 years. For 50-year holding periods, the annual return rises to 8.93% and the total accumulation is almost three times those of investors who realize their gains on a short-term basis. If capital gains are untaxed, the return rises to 9.33 percent per year, as only the yearly dividend is taxed.

From a tax standpoint, there should be a clear preference for investors to receive capital gains over dividend income. But many investors still prefer to receive a steady (or increasing) flow of dividends rather than obtaining funds from selling stock. These investors show a desire to "preserve capital" and live off the dividends and interest. But under our current tax system, you pay a high price for this preference.

## Stocks or Bonds in Tax-Deferred Accounts?

The most important saving vehicle for many individuals is their tax-deferred accounts (TDA), such as Keogh, IRA, 401(k), or similar plans. Many investors hold most of their stock (if they hold any at all) in their tax-deferred account, while they hold primarily fixed-income assets in their taxable accounts.

Yet many financial advisors recommend that investors do exactly the opposite. They rightly claim that stocks will realize the capital gains tax advantage only if they are held in taxable accounts. This is because when a tax-deferred account is cashed in at retirement, you pay ordinary income tax on the *entire* withdrawal, regardless of how much has been received through capital gains and dividend income. As a result, these advisors assert that you should hold stocks in a taxable account where the lower capital gains tax can be enjoyed, and bonds in a tax-deferred account where interest can accumulate at before-tax rates. Because of the recent reduction in capital gains tax rates, advisors claim that these recommendations become even more imperative.

The above counsel, however, ignores several important factors. First, it is virtually impossible not to realize some capital gains through time in a taxable account. Even index funds must buy and sell stock to match the index and satisfy redemptions. So sheltering capital gains in a tax-deferred account is important. Second, although the government taxes your capital gain from stocks at ordinary rates in a TDA, the government also shares more of the downside risk. The government is a much larger (uninvited) partner in a tax-deferred account than in a taxable account, where the ability to deduct capital losses from taxable income is restricted. Consequently, investors can hold a larger amount of stock for the same total risk in a tax-deferred account compared to a taxable account.

When all the factors are considered, it is better for most investors to hold stocks in their tax-deferred account rather than in their taxable account. This is particularly true if they do not have sufficient savings to fund a TDA with bonds and hold stocks in a taxable account. It is important to fund your TDA to its maximum level, even if you have to borrow to do so. But it rarely pays to borrow just to hold stocks in your taxable account while you fund the TDA with bonds.[4]

If you buy more stock than the maximum allowed contribution to the tax-deferred account, then you should put the *higher-yielding* stock

4 For a more complete description of these criteria, see Jeremy Siegel, "Tax-Deferred Accounts: Should They be Funded with Stocks or Bonds?" a Wharton School working paper, April 1997.

in your TDA, where the dividend income is sheltered from taxes, and keep the low-dividend stock in your taxable account. Therefore, income-oriented funds, which tend to hold value stocks, should be put into a TDA, while growth-oriented funds should be placed in the taxable account. Individual stocks or specialized funds that have high-dividend yields, such as utilities and real estate investment trusts, make good candidates for TDAs. But do not over-buy these stocks just to shelter dividend income, since doing so would make your portfolio unbalanced. Make sure to diversify across the broadest base of stocks to maximize return for the lowest possible risk.

## SUMMARY

Tax planning is a significant factor in maximizing returns from financial assets. Because of favorable capital gains tax rates and the potential to defer those taxes, stocks hold a significant tax advantage over fixed-income assets. Nevertheless, because long-term returns on stocks are so much more favorable than those on bonds, it is advantageous to shelter the dividends and capital gains from taxes as long as possible. For that reason, equity accumulated in tax-deferred accounts often enables shareholders to maximize their long-term returns.

## APPENDIX: HISTORY OF THE TAX CODE

Federal income tax was first collected under the Revenue Act of 1913, when the 16th Amendment to the U.S. Constitution was ratified. Until 1921 there was no tax preference given to capital gains income. When tax rates were increased sharply during World War I, investors refrained from realizing gains and complained to Congress about the tax consequences of selling their assets. Congress was persuaded that such "frozen portfolios" were detrimental to the efficient allocation of capital, and so in 1922 a maximum tax rate of 12.5 percent was established on capital gains income. This rate became effective at a taxable income of $30,000, which is equivalent to about $240,000 in today's dollars.

In 1934, a new tax code was enacted that, for the first time, excluded a portion of capital gains from taxable income. This exclusion allowed middle-income groups, and not just the rich, to enjoy the tax benefits of capital gains income. The excluded portion of the gain depended on the length of time that the asset was held; there was no exclusion if the asset was held one year or less, but the exclusion was increased to 70 percent if the asset was held more than 10 years. Since marginal tax rates ranged up to 79 percent in 1936, the effective maximum tax on very-long-term gains was reduced to about 24 percent.

In 1938, the tax code was amended again to provide for a 50 percent exclusion of capital gains income if an asset was held more than 18 months, but in no case would the tax exceed 15 percent on such capital gains. The maximum rate on capital gains income was raised to 25 percent in 1942, but the holding period was reduced to six months. Except for a 1 percent surtax that raised the maximum rate to 26 percent during the Korean War, the 25 percent rate held until 1969.

In 1969, the maximum tax rate on capital gains in excess of $50,000 was phased out over a number of years, so ultimately the 50 percent exclusion applied to all tax rates. Since the maximum rate on ordinary income was 70 percent, this meant the maximum tax rate on capital gains rose to 35 percent by 1973. In 1978, the exclusion was raised to 60 percent, which lowered the effective maximum tax rate on capital gains to 28 percent. When the maximum tax rate on ordinary income was reduced to 50 percent in 1982, the maximum tax rate on capital gains was again reduced to 20 percent.

In 1986, the tax code was extensively altered to reduce and simplify the tax structure and ultimately eliminate the distinction between capital gains and ordinary income. By 1988, the tax rates for both capital gains and ordinary income were identical, at 33 percent. For the first time since 1922, there was no preference for capital gains income. In 1990, the top rate was lowered to 28 percent on both ordinary and capital gain income. In 1991, a slight wedge was reopened between capital gains and ordinary income: the top rate on the latter was raised to 31 percent, while the former remained at 28 percent. In 1993, President Clinton raised tax rates again, increasing the top rate on ordinary income to 39.6 percent while keeping the capital gains tax unchanged.* In 1997 Congress lowered the maximum capital gain tax to 20 percent for assets held more than 18 months.

---

* Because of the phase-outs of exemptions and deductions, the marginal tax rate is higher for certain middle-income ranges. This was exacerbated by the 1997 tax changes.

# 9

## GLOBAL INVESTING

*Today let's talk about a growth industry.*
*Because investing worldwide is a growth industry.*
*The great growth industry is international portfolio investing.*

—John Templeton[1]

In Chapter 1, I showed that the superior returns to equity were not unique to the United States. Investors in Britain, Germany, and even Japan have accumulated substantial wealth through investing in stocks. But for many years, foreign markets were almost exclusively the domain of native investors, considered too remote and risky to be entertained by outsiders.

But no longer. *Globalization* is the financial buzzword of the decade. The United States, once the unchallenged giant of capital markets, has become only one of many countries in which investors can accumulate wealth. At the end of World War II, U.S. stocks comprised almost 90 percent of the world's equity capitalization; by 1970 they still comprised two-thirds. But today they constitute less than half of the world's stock values. To invest only in the United States is to ignore most of the world's capital.

### FOREIGN STOCK RETURNS

Although over long periods of time equities yield a 6 or 7 percent rate of return after inflation, returns have varied widely over periods as long as

---

1 Transcript of address delivered to Annual Conference of the Financial Analysts Federation, May 2, 1984.

10 or 15 years. Comprehensive returns on markets in developed countries are available from 1970, but this 27-year stretch is not long enough to draw any definitive conclusions about the relative merits of U.S. and foreign equities.

The problem with projecting short-term historical returns into the future is best illustrated with the Japanese market. In the 1970s and 1980s, Japanese stocks experienced dollar returns that were more than 10 percentage points above the return in the U.S. market, and dominated those from every other industrialized country. In 1989, for the first time since the early part of this century, the American equity market was no longer the world's largest. Japan, a country whose economic base was totally destroyed by U.S. military action 44 years earlier and who possesses only half the population and 4 percent of the land mass of the United States, became the home to a stock market that exceeded the valuation of America or all of Europe.

The superior returns on the Japanese market attracted billions of dollars of foreign investment. Valuations on many Japanese stocks reached stratospheric levels. Nippon Telephone and Telegraph, or NTT, the Japanese version of America's AT&T, was priced at a P-E ratio above 300 and a market valuation of hundreds of billions of dollars. This value dwarfed the aggregate stock values of all but a handful of countries around the world.

While traveling in Japan in 1987, Leo Melamed, president of the Chicago Mercantile Exchange, questioned his Japanese hosts on how such high valuations could be placed on Japanese stocks. "You don't understand," they responded, "We've moved to an entirely new way of valuing stocks here in Japan." At that moment Melamed recalls feeling certain that the Japanese market was near the end of its great bull market.[2] For it is when investors cast aside the lessons of history that those lessons come back to haunt the market.

The Nikkei Dow-Jones, which had surpassed 39,000 at the end of 1989, fell to nearly 14,000 by August of 1992—a fall worse than any experienced by the U.S. markets since the great 1929–32 crash. The shares of NTT fell from 3.2 million yen to under 500,000. The mystique of the Japanese market was broken.

After the collapse of the Japanese market, the emphasis of global enthusiasts switched to emerging markets. (An *emerging market* is that of a developing or newly developed country.) Investors had already wit-

---

2 Martin Mayer, *Markets*, New York: W. W. Norton, 1988, p. 60.

nessed the stock booms of Taiwan, Korea, and Thailand. Now India, Indonesia, and even China were set to join the club.

And Asian countries were not the only markets put into play. Latin America, long a backwater of authoritarian, anti-free-market regimes (of both the right and left) had turned full circle and aggressively sought foreign investment. Equity gains have been impressive in such countries as Argentina and Mexico.

Even China, the last major country ruled by "communist" leaders, developed stock markets. The opening of the first Chinese stock market in Shenzhen was met with a riot as thousands stood days in lines waiting to be allocated shares in firms in the world's most populated country. And who would have imagined five years ago that one of the world's best performing stock markets would be Hong Kong, recently absorbed by communist China, once the sworn enemy of capitalism?

The term *emerging*, as applied to these markets, is evocative of a beautiful butterfly rising from its chrysalis, ready to soar to the heavens. But the enthusiasm that greeted these markets often far exceeded their ability to perform. Just as most butterflies are eaten by birds after they take their first flight, many of these newly emerging markets crash soon after reaching a peak.

Taiwan is a case in point. In 1986, the Taiwanese stock index stood at 848. By February 1990, less than four years later, it soared to 12,424, sporting an average price-to-earnings ratio in excess of 100. The market capitalization in Taiwan exceeded $300 billion, larger than Great Britain in 1985 and the entire world market outside the United States in 1969.

Financial analyst John S. Bolsover, chief executive officer of the London firm Baring Investment, believed that Taiwan was symptomatic of the over-optimistic attitudes towards emerging economies. In a speech delivered at the market peak, entitled "Alice in Taiwanderland," Bolsover warned, "Beware of the temptation to say, 'This time is different.'" He ended his speech with Santayana's famous words, "Those who ignore history are doomed to relive it."[3] By October 1990, the Taiwan stock market had collapsed nearly 80 percent.

## SUMMARY DATA ON GLOBAL MARKETS

Most financial advisers recommend foreign investments by projecting their past returns into the future. And many foreign stock markets

---

3 Quoted in *Classics II*, ed. Charles D. Ellis, Homewood, Ill.: Business One Irwin, 1991, pp. 20–522.

have indeed offered somewhat higher returns to dollar investors than U.S. stocks.

Table 9-1 displays the total returns in some of the world's stock markets from 1970 to the present,[4] while Table 9-2 shows the considerable variation in these returns over time. The dollar return from investing in foreign markets is the sum of the local return, which is calculated in terms of the local currency and the change in the exchange rate between the local currency and the dollar. Changes in the exchange rate can either enhance or diminish the local returns for the dollar investor.

**TABLE 9–1**

World Stock Returns: Annualized Geometric Returns, January 1970 to June 1997 (Standard Deviations in Parentheses)

| Country or Region | Local Returns | Exchange Rate Change | US Dollar Returns |
|---|---|---|---|
| Non-USA World Index | 10.97 (18.99) | 1.81 (9.70) | 12.99 (21.50) |
| Value Weighted World Index | 11.15 (16.18) | 0.95 (5.28) | 12.21 (16.54) |
| USA | 12.34 (16.20) | - - - | 12.34 (16.20) |
| Europe | 12.72 (20.10) | 0.34 (11.49) | 13.10 (21.21) |
| Japan | 10.43 (29.36) | 4.26 (13.17) | 15.14 (36.11) |

4 These summary data are taken from the Morgan Stanley Capital International database. These indexes cover about 60 percent of the capitalization in each country. In the United States, this amounts to over 500 stocks.

TABLE 9–2

Dollar Returns in World Stock Markets: Annualized Geometric Returns by Decades
(Standard Deviations in Parentheses)

| Country or Region | 1970 - 1979 | 1980 - 1989 | 1990 - 1997* |
|---|---|---|---|
| Non-USA World Index | 10.90 (21.91) | 21.51 (22.06) | 5.14 (17.96) |
| Value Weighted World Index | 6.96 (18.09) | 19.92 (14.59) | 9.45 (14.86) |
| USA | 4.61 (19.01) | 17.13 (12.52) | 16.87 (15.41) |
| Europe | 8.57 (20.97) | 18.49 (25.89) | 12.26 (13.54) |
| Japan | 17.37 (45.41) | 28.66 (28.57) | -3.22 (22.97) |

*Through June 1997

The average annual compound capitalization-weighted dollar return on all foreign markets has been almost 13 percent per year from January 1970 through June 1997. Over the same time period, the annual return from U.S. stocks has averaged 12.34 percent. It is of interest that the local stock returns in Europe and the United States are almost identical. Japan's stock market underperformed the other major world stock markets measured in their local currency, but outperformed them all in dollar terms. This is due to the more than 4 percent per year appreciation of the yen relative to the dollar, the world's strongest post-war currency.

Figure 9-1 displays the monthly dollar return index for the United States, the United Kingdom, Japan, and Germany since January 1970.

**FIGURE 9–1**

Total Dollar Returns in Major Markets, January 1970 Through June 1997

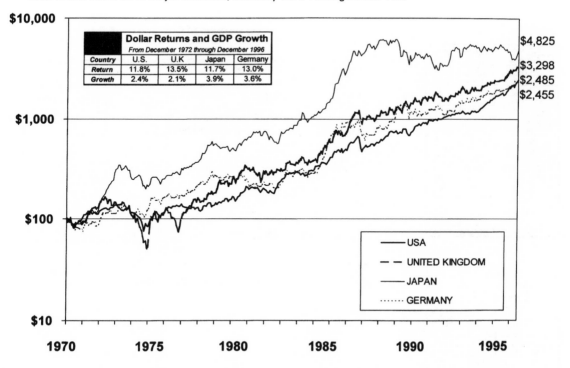

| Dollar Returns and GDP Growth<br>*From December 1972 through December 1996* | | | |
|---|---|---|---|
| Country | U.S. | U.K | Japan | Germany |
| Return | 11.8% | 13.5% | 11.7% | 13.0% |
| Growth | 2.4% | 2.1% | 3.9% | 3.6% |

Over the entire period, Japan has outperformed all other major markets, but all its outperformance occurred between January 1970 and December 1972. Country returns are very sensitive to the time period chosen. Since December 1972 Japan has underperformed all the major markets of the world despite the fact that Japan's economic growth surpassed the U.S., U.K., and Germany.

## ECONOMIC GROWTH AND STOCK RETURNS

Investment advisors often select foreign markets on the basis of the country's prospects for economic growth. But economic growth is no guarantee of superior stock market returns.

Figure 9-2a compares the stock returns and economic growth among the developed countries monitored by the Morgan Stanley

## FIGURE 9-2

Economic Growth and Dollar Stock Market Returns

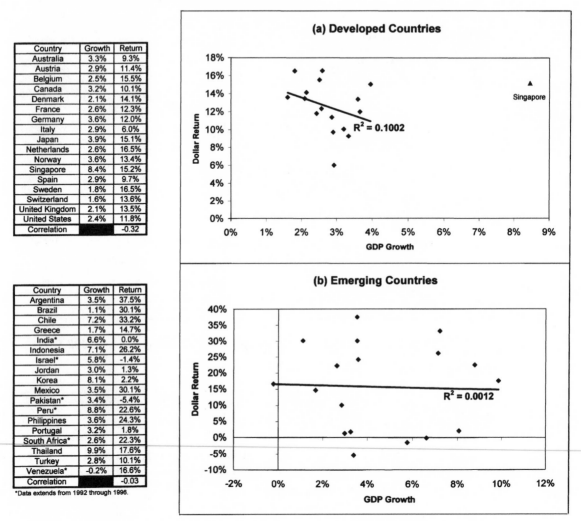

| Country | Growth | Return |
|---|---|---|
| Australia | 3.3% | 9.3% |
| Austria | 2.9% | 11.4% |
| Belgium | 2.5% | 15.5% |
| Canada | 3.2% | 10.1% |
| Denmark | 2.1% | 14.1% |
| France | 2.6% | 12.3% |
| Germany | 3.6% | 12.0% |
| Italy | 2.9% | 6.0% |
| Japan | 3.9% | 15.1% |
| Netherlands | 2.6% | 16.5% |
| Norway | 3.6% | 13.4% |
| Singapore | 8.4% | 15.2% |
| Spain | 2.9% | 9.7% |
| Sweden | 1.8% | 16.5% |
| Switzerland | 1.6% | 13.6% |
| United Kingdom | 2.1% | 13.5% |
| United States | 2.4% | 11.8% |
| Correlation | | -0.32 |

| Country | Growth | Return |
|---|---|---|
| Argentina | 3.5% | 37.5% |
| Brazil | 1.1% | 30.1% |
| Chile | 7.2% | 33.2% |
| Greece | 1.7% | 14.7% |
| India* | 6.6% | 0.0% |
| Indonesia | 7.1% | 26.2% |
| Israel* | 5.8% | -1.4% |
| Jordan | 3.0% | 1.3% |
| Korea | 8.1% | 2.2% |
| Mexico | 3.5% | 30.1% |
| Pakistan* | 3.4% | -5.4% |
| Peru* | 8.8% | 22.6% |
| Philippines | 3.6% | 24.3% |
| Portugal | 3.2% | 1.8% |
| South Africa* | 2.6% | 22.3% |
| Thailand | 9.9% | 17.6% |
| Turkey | 2.8% | 10.1% |
| Venezuela* | -0.2% | 16.6% |
| Correlation | | -0.03 |

*Data extends from 1992 through 1996.

Capital Markets indexes. The results are quite surprising: except for Singapore, over the past 27 years there has been a *negative* correlation between economic growth and dollar stock returns. As Figure 9-2b shows, a negative correlation between growth and stock returns also applies to developing or emerging world economies.

How can this happen? Stronger economic growth often accompanies higher stock returns within a country, but between countries the situation is quite different. Recall that growth stocks do not necessarily have higher returns than value stocks because expected growth is already factored into the price.

The same situation holds between countries. Those with high expected growth rates, such as Japan, have higher P-E ratios than lower-growth countries, such as the U.K. The supercharged Japanese economy of the 1960s and 1970s led to the overly optimistic price-earnings ratios. When economic growth failed to meet expectations, stock prices fell.

A second reason for the lack of correlation between economic growth and stock returns is that even if multinational corporations are headquartered in a particular country, their profits depend on world-wide economic growth. This is particularly true of economies whose firms are oriented to export markets.

These results do not mean that countries that experience economic growth above expectations will not experience higher returns. Do not, however, choose countries solely on the basis of their economic growth, ignoring the fundamentals of the global market in which they compete.

## SOURCES OF DOLLAR RISK IN INTERNATIONAL STOCKS

### Exchange-Rate Risk

Movements of exchange rates are a source of risk for foreign investors, since dollar returns are the sum of local returns and changes in the exchange rate. In the long run, there is wide agreement that the primary source of exchange-rate changes between countries centers on differing rates of inflation. Countries with higher rates of inflation will find that their currencies depreciate relative to countries with lower rates of inflation.

But in the short run, inflation is a very minor factor in exchange-rate movements. Expectations of changing interest rates and central bank policy, trade balances, capital movements, and the relative growth rates of demand and output in each economy also influence the exchange rate. The short-run foreign exchange market is very speculative, and the movements of exchange rates can often exceed that of stock indexes themselves on a daily basis.

Table 9-3 analyzes the stock market risk (measured as the standard deviation) for dollar investors in foreign stocks over the period from January 1970 through December 1996. The *local risk* is the risk calculated

**TABLE 9–3**

Sources of Dollar Risk in Stocks, January 1970 Through December 1996

| Country or Region | Domestic Risk | Exchange Risk | Total Risk | Correlation Coefficient |
|---|---|---|---|---|
| Non-USA World Index | 18.99% | 9.70% | 21.50% | 49% |
| Value Weighted World Index | 16.18% | 5.28% | 16.54% | 80% |
| USA | 16.20% | - - - | 16.20% | 100% |
| Europe | 20.10% | 11.49% | 21.21% | 62% |
| Japan | 29.36% | 13.17% | 36.11% | 23% |

**\*Correlation between US dollar returns and foreign dollar returns.**

from stock returns denominated in the local currencies. The *exchange risk* reflects the fluctuations of the dollar against the country's currency. The total risk of the dollar return of a foreign market reflects both the local risk and the exchange-rate risk.

It is very important to note that the total risk of holding foreign equities is substantially *less than* the sum of the local and exchange risks. This is because these risks are not perfectly correlated, so movements in the exchange rate and the local stock market frequently offset each other. In fact, for some countries, such as the United Kingdom, the exchange risk offsets the local risk so much that a U.S. holder of British equities since 1970 has experienced less volatility in dollar returns than a British investor does in pounds sterling!

## DIVERSIFICATION TO FOREIGN STOCKS

### Optimal Allocation for Foreign Equities

It might surprise investors that the principal reason for investing in foreign stocks is not that their expected return is better than in the U.S. (although that might turn out to be the case), but that investing internationally allows you to diversify your portfolio and therefore reduce risk.

Figure 9-3 shows the risk-return trade-offs for investing in U.S. and foreign equities for dollar-based investors. These are based on the historical returns to these assets over the past 27 years, during which foreign returns did slightly outpace U.S. returns. A minimum risk occurs with 25 percent allocated to foreign stocks, although portfolio theory suggests that investors should increase the foreign allocation to 38.9 percent, called the *efficient portfolio*, if foreign returns higher than those in the past also hold in the future.

Note that the above allocation is determined on the basis of historical data on one-year returns. Chapter 2 warned that one year is rarely the holding period of the average investor. Unfortunately, there is not a long enough data series to develop reliable risk and return measures for

## FIGURE  9–3

Efficient Frontier Between U.S. and International Returns, 1970–1996

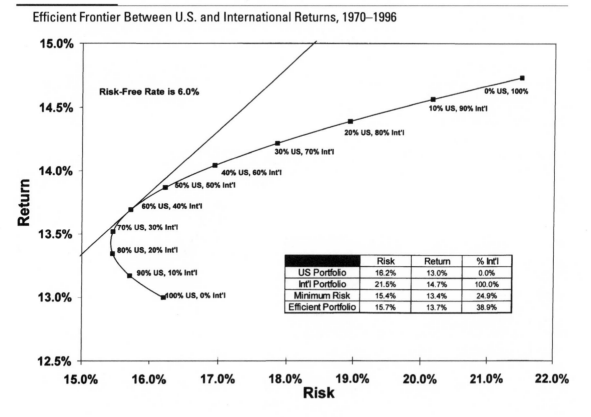

| | Risk | Return | % Int'l |
|---|---|---|---|
| US Portfolio | 16.2% | 13.0% | 0.0% |
| Int'l Portfolio | 21.5% | 14.7% | 100.0% |
| Minimum Risk | 15.4% | 13.4% | 24.9% |
| Efficient Portfolio | 15.7% | 13.7% | 38.9% |

holding periods of ten or more years. In any case, multiple-year analysis involving U.S. and foreign stocks is unlikely to change the allocation appreciably since mean reversion of equity returns prevails in foreign stock markets as well as the U.S.

## Cross-Country Correlations of Stock Returns

Even if foreign returns are not expected to exceed U.S. stock returns, the minimum risk portfolio remains 25 percent allocated to foreign stocks if the risks of U.S. and foreign stocks remain unchanged. This percentage would decline if foreign stocks became more correlated with U.S. stocks. Yet, despite all the talk about the world becoming more integrated, the correlation between foreign and U.S. stocks returns has actually *declined* over time. Figure 9-4 shows the correlation between EAFE dollar stock returns (20 developed economies in Europe, Australasia, and the Far East) and U.S. returns. The trend, if anything, is downward. The corre-

**F I G U R E  9–4**

Correlation Between U.S. and EAFE Stock Returns (Nine-Year Correlation Windows).

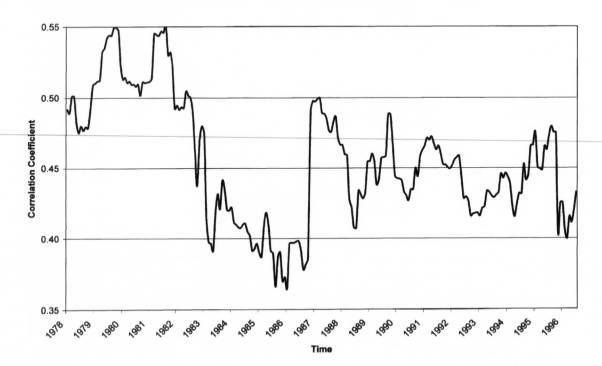

lation takes a jump in 1987 when stock markets around the world crashed in unison, but after that episode the correlation falls again.

The decreased correlation in the 1980s was probably due to the growing size of the Japanese market, which has, as noted in Table 9-3, always moved independently of other world markets. More recently the decreased correlation could be due to the growing importance of domestic monetary and political developments, such as the EMU (European Monetary Union) in Europe. If this is true, cross-country correlation between markets will depend on industry trends instead of national trends. Whatever the reason, there is still enough independence among foreign markets to justify their inclusion into a well-diversified portfolio.

## HEDGING FOREIGN EXCHANGE RISKS

Since foreign exchange risk does add to the dollar risk of holding foreign securities, it appears to pay for an investor in foreign markets to hedge against currency movements. *Currency hedging* means taking a position in a currency market that offsets unexpected changes in the foreign currency relative to the dollar. Stock market fluctuations can cause enough anxiety without worrying about whether a change in foreign exchange rates will reduce the value of your foreign portfolio.

Although hedging seems like an attractive way to offset exchange risk, in the long run it is often unnecessary. For example, in the United Kingdom from 1910 onward, the pound depreciated from $4.80 to about $1.50. It might seem obvious that an investor who hedged the fall of the pound would be better off than one who had not. But this is not the case. Since the interest rate was, on average, substantially higher in the United Kingdom than in the United States, the cost of hedging for a dollar-based investor, which depends on the relative interest rates between the two countries, was high. The unhedged returns for British stocks in U.S. dollars actually exceeded the hedged accumulation, despite the fall of the British pound.

For investors with long-term horizons, hedging currency risk in foreign stock markets is not important. In fact, there is recent evidence that in the long run currency hedges might actually increase the volatility of dollar returns.[5] In the long run, exchange rate movements are determined primarily by changes in local prices. Equities are claims on

---

5 Kenneth A. Froot, "Currency Hedging over Long Horizons," N.B.E.R. working paper no. 4355, May 1993.

real assets that compensate the stockholder for changes in the price level. To hedge such a long-run investment would be self-defeating since by buying a real asset you automatically hedge a depreciating currency.

Hedging currency movements is particularly counterproductive if there is a change in monetary policy. In that case, hedges might actually increase the volatility of your dollar returns. For example, if the Bundesbank, Germany's central bank, tightens credit and raises interest rates, this will cause the deutsche mark to rise. But German stock prices will fall, as rising interest rates lower the value of stocks.

If investors does not hedge, the downward movement in the stock market will be offset by the upward movement of the deutsche mark, thereby reducing fluctuations in the dollar returns on German stocks. On the other hand, if investors hedge, they forgo the appreciation of the deutsche mark that offsets the decline in the value of German stocks.

Although changes in exchange rates and stock prices often move in the opposite direction, this is not always so. An increase in optimism about the growth prospects in a country often increases both stock prices and currency values. When Vice President Al Gore won the debate with Ross Perot by supporting NAFTA in November 1993, both the Mexican peso and Mexican stocks rose. Optimism about economic growth drives up both the exchange rate and stock prices.

Since both monetary and real factors drive exchange rate and stock movements, it is not surprising that the stock and currency markets often move independently of one another. The inability to identify in advance the source of movement in these markets reduces the attractiveness of hedging foreign stock risk.

## STOCKS AND THE BREAKDOWN OF THE EUROPEAN EXCHANGE-RATE MECHANISM

A dramatic example of the offsetting movements of currency and equity markets occurred during the September 1992 breakdown of the European exchange-rate mechanism. The exchange-rate mechanism dictated that member countries must keep their currencies within a narrow band of each other. For some months, many investors had felt that the British pound and the Italian lira were overvalued relative to the deutsche mark. On Sunday night, September 12, the Italian government devalued the lira. Speculators felt it was only a matter of time before the British pound would also be forced to devalue.

Britain's conservative Prime Minister, John Major, and his Chancellor of the Exchequer, Norman Lamont, were determined to hold out and defend the pound against the speculative attack. At 11:00 A.M. on

Wednesday, September 16, Lamont announced a two-point increase in the Bank of England base lending rate, a key short-term rate of great significance to U.K. banks. The Financial Times Stock Exchange Index (FT-SE, often called the *Foot-sie*) immediately fell 1.5 percent after the Bank's announcement. The movements of the British markets are depicted in Figures 9-5a and 9-5b, where the times listed represent U.S. Eastern Standard Time, five hours earlier than the London times quoted earlier in the paragraph.

But the British pound barely budged on the foreign exchange market when the lending rate was increased. Normally an increase in this key rate would cause the pound to rise due to foreign investors flocking to the higher interest rate on sterling balances. But on this day the pound continued to push against the lower limit allowed by European Monetary System, and the Bank of England was forced to accelerate the buying of pounds against the deutsche mark.

To reinforce its conviction to hold sterling, at 2:15 in the afternoon, the Bank of England made its final, desperate move. It raised the rate to 15 percent—the first time in the 300-year history of the Bank that the rate had been raised twice in one day. There was a brief fall in the stock market as investors contemplated the meaning of this dramatic action. But within minutes, stocks began rallying furiously. The market knew that there was no way the British government could hold a 15 percent interest rate in the face of one of its deepest recessions since World War II. Stockholders believed that maintaining such punishing rates in such a bad economy was politically untenable, and they were right.

Britain abandoned support of the pound that evening. The FT-SE 100 stock index rose over 100 points on the following day and continued to rally on Friday while the pound sank lower against both the dollar and the deutsche mark. From the market bottom on Wednesday, September 16 to the top on Friday, the FT-SE index had rallied almost 300 points, or about 13 percent. Over the same time, the pound fell from $1.83 to $1.74, a drop of only 5 percent. Hence British stocks were up about 8 percent in dollar terms during this turbulent period. Despite the continued depreciation of the pound, British stock in dollar terms continued to outpace the U.S. and German markets through the next year.

It is true that a U.S. investor who had hedged his sterling stock investments during the ERM crisis would have done even better than an unhedged investor. But this is not always the case during monetary turmoil. When the French franc came under attack the following week, French interest rates—and hence the cost of covering franc investments—skyrocketed. Yet the Bank of France held firm. The franc was

## F I G U R E   9–5

British Currency and Stocks During the September 1992 ERM Crisis

Figure A

### British Pound Sterling

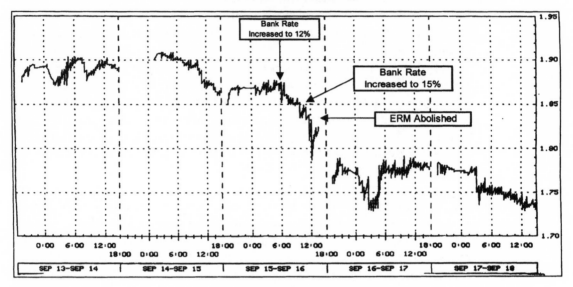

Figure B

### FT-SE 100 Stock Index

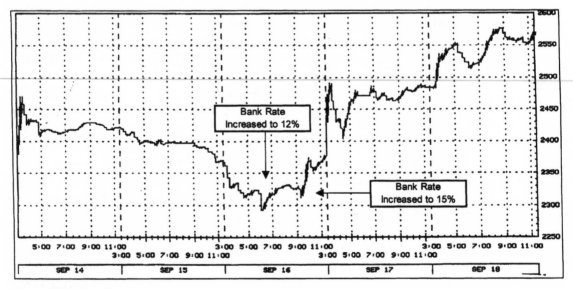

Source: Bloomberg L.P.

not devalued for nearly a year, and speculators who hedged were faced with substantial losses.[6]

The lesson for a dollar investor is that hedging is unnecessary during exchange-rate turbulence. The British stock market rallied as the pound fell. Investors bid stocks up as the prospect of a lower pound and lower interest rates stimulated equity prices. And indeed the Bank of England lowered the base lending rate to 9 percent the following week, a prelude to further cuts. As the next chapter describes, Threadneedle Street greeted the freeing of the pound in much the same way as they did 60 years earlier when Great Britain left the gold standard. Liquidity and low interest rates, as long as they do not lead to inflation, are invariably welcomed by equity markets.

## SUMMARY

Global investment is best viewed as an extension of domestic diversification. Investors can achieve a substantial reduction in risk by investing in foreign equities since foreign markets do not move in tandem with the domestic market. As the United States becomes a smaller and smaller part of the world equity market, sticking only to U.S. equities is akin to restricting your investments to a single industry, a strategy far too risky for the long-term investor.

As the world economy expands, the advantage of international investing increases. No country will be able to dominate every emerging market. And the stock markets of individual countries will likely become more stable as product markets expand worldwide, since the earnings of multinationals will not be held hostage to the state of the economy in one country or in one region. In fact, worldwide integration will most likely lead to a lower total risk in holding equities and an increase in global stock prices.

---

6 Even after the ERM bands were widened in August 1993, the fall in the franc was not nearly sufficient to cover the losses of having continually speculated against the franc.

PART THREE

# ECONOMIC ENVIRONMENT OF INVESTING

# CHAPTER

# MONEY, GOLD, AND CENTRAL BANKS

*In the stock market, as with horse racing, money makes the mare go. Monetary conditions exert an enormous influence on stock prices.*

—Martin Zweig[1]

*If Fed Chairman Alan Greenspan were to whisper to me what his monetary policy was going to be over the next two years, it wouldn't change one thing I do."*

—Warren Buffett[2]

On September 20, 1931, the British government announced that England was going off the gold standard. It would no longer exchange gold for balances at the Bank of England or for British currency, the pound sterling. The government insisted that this action was only "temporary," that it had no intention to abolish forever its commitment to exchange its money for gold. Nevertheless, it was to mark the beginning of the end of both Britain's and the world's gold standard, a standard that had existed for over 200 years.

Fearing chaos in the currency market, the British government ordered the London Stock Exchange closed. New York Stock Exchange officials decided to keep the U.S. exchange open but braced themselves for panic selling. The suspension of gold payments by Britain, the second-greatest industrial power, raised fears that other industrial countries

---

1 *Winning on Wall Street*, New York: Warner Books, 1990, p. 43.
2 Linda Grant, "Striking Out at Wall Street," *U.S. News & World Report*, June 30, 1994, p. 59.

might be forced to abandon gold. For the first time ever, the New York Exchange banned short selling to moderate the expected collapse in share prices. Central bankers called the suspension "a world financial crisis of unprecedented dimensions."[3]

But much to New York's surprise, stocks rallied sharply after an early sinking spell, and many issues ended the day higher. Clearly, British suspension was not seen as negative for American equities.

Nor was this "unprecedented financial crisis" a problem for the British stock market. When England reopened the exchange on September 23, prices soared. The AP wire gave the following colorful description of the reopening of the exchange:

> Swarms of stock brokers, laughing and cheering like schoolboys, invaded the Stock Exchange today for the resumption of trading after the two-day compulsory close-down—and their buoyancy was reflected in the prices of many securities.[4]

Despite the dire predictions of government officials, shareholders viewed casting off the gold standard as good for the economy and even better for stocks. As a result of the gold suspension, the British government could expand credit, and the fall in the value of the British pound would increase the demand for British exports. The stock market gave a ringing endorsement to the actions that shocked conservative world financiers. In fact, September 1931 marked the low point of the British stock market, while the United States and other countries that stayed on the gold standard continued to sink into depression. The lesson from history: money feeds the stock market and shareholders regard inflation as a secondary concern.

## MONEY AND PRICES

In 1950, President Truman startled the nation in his State of the Union address with a prediction that the typical American family income would reach $12,000 by the year 2000. Considering that median family income was about $3,300 at the time, $12,000 seemed like a kingly sum and implied that America was going to make unprecedented economic progress in the next half century. In fact, President Truman's prediction has proved quite modest. The median family income in 1996 was $42,600. Yet that buys less than $7,000 in 1950 prices, a testament to the persistent inflation of the last half century.

---

3 "World Crisis Seen by Vienna Bankers," the *New York Times*, September 21, 1931, p. 2.
4 "British Stocks Rise, Pound Goes Lower," the *New York Times*, September 24, 1931, p. 2.

Rising and falling prices have characterized economic history as far back as economists have gathered data. However, steady inflation is unique to the second half of this century. What has changed over the past 50 years that makes steady inflation the norm rather than the exception? The answer is simple: the control of money has shifted from gold to the government, and with it a whole new system relating money, government deficits, and inflation has come into being.

I examined the overall price level in the U.S. and Great Britain over the last two hundred years in Figure 1-3 of Chapter 1. It is striking how similar the general trends are in these two countries: no overall inflation until World War II and then protracted inflation after. Until the last 50 years, inflation occurred only because of war, crop failures, or other crises. But the behavior of prices in the postwar period has been entirely different. The price level has almost never declined; the only question is the rate at which prices have risen.

Economists have long known that one variable is paramount in determining the price level: the amount of money in circulation. The robust relation between money and inflation is strongly supported by the evidence. Take a look at Figure 10-1, which displays money and prices per unit output in the United States since 1830. The overall trend of the price level has closely tracked that of the money supply.

The strong relation between money and prices is a worldwide phenomenon. No sustained inflation is possible without continuous money creation, and every hyperinflation in history has been associated with an explosion of the money supply. The evidence is overwhelming that countries with high monetary growth experience high inflation and countries with restrained money growth have low inflation.

Why is the quantity of money so closely connected to the price level? Because the price of money, like any good, is determined by supply and demand. The supply of dollars is printed by the central bank. The demand for dollars is derived from households and firms transacting millions of goods and services in a complex economy. If the supply of dollars increases when there is not an equal increase in the quantity of goods transacted, this leads to inflation. The classic description of the inflationary process, "too many dollars chasing too few goods," is as apt today as ever.

## THE GOLD STANDARD

For the nearly 200 years prior to the Great Depression, most of the industrialized world was on a *gold standard*, meaning that the government obligated itself to exchange its own money for a fixed amount of gold.

**F I G U R E   10–1**

Money and Price Indexes for the U.S., 1830–1996

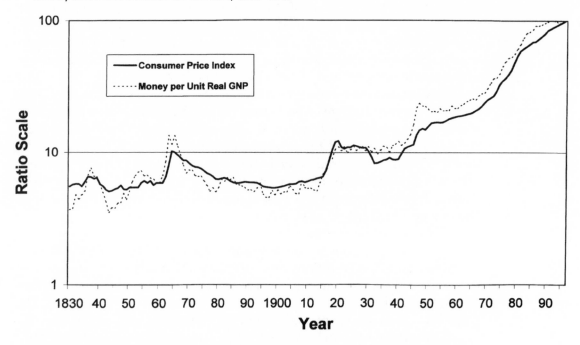

To do this, the government had to keep gold reserves in sufficient quantity to assure money holders that it would always be able to make this exchange. Since the total quantity of gold in the world was fixed (except for new gold finds, which were a small fraction of the total outstanding), prices of goods in terms of either gold or government money held relatively constant or even declined.

Great Britain adopted the gold standard in 1717, setting the price of gold at 3.8938 pounds per ounce. Adherence to the gold standard was considered a sine qua non among policy makers. Sir Robert Peel called "the ancient standard of 3.8938 pounds per ounce a magic price for gold from which England ought never to stray and to which, if she did, she must always return as soon as possible."

The only times when the gold standard was suspended were during crises, such as wars. Great Britain suspended the gold standard during both the Napoleonic and First World Wars, but in both cases returned to original parity with gold after each war.

The United States had also temporarily suspended the gold standard, but, like Great Britain, returned to the standard after the war. When the government issued non-gold-backed money during the Civil

War, this money was called *greenbacks* because the only backing was the green ink printed on the note. Yet just 20 years later, the government redeemed each and every one of those notes in gold, completely reversing the inflation of the Civil War period.

The adherence to the gold standard is the reason why the world experienced no overall inflation during the 19th and early 20th centuries. But overall price stability was not achieved without a cost. By setting the amount of money equal to the quantity of gold, the government essentially relinquished discretionary monetary control. This meant the inability to provide extra money during times of depression or financial crisis, or expand money to stabilize falling prices or accommodate rising output. Adherence to gold turned from being a symbol of government restraint and responsibility to a straitjacket from which the government sought to escape.

## THE ESTABLISHMENT OF THE FEDERAL RESERVE

The problems of liquidity crises caused by strict adherence to the gold standard prompted Congress in 1913 to create the Federal Reserve System. The responsibilities of the Fed were to provide an "elastic" currency, which meant that in times of banking crises the Fed would become the lender of last resort. The central bank would provide currency to enable depositors to withdraw their deposits without forcing banks to liquidate loans and other assets.

In the long run, money creation by the Fed was constrained by the gold standard since Federal Reserve notes promised to pay a fixed amount of gold, but in the short run, the Federal Reserve was free to create money as long as it did not threaten the convertibility. In fact, the Fed was never given any guidance or criteria by which to determine the right quantity of money. This confusion was aptly described by Milton Friedman in his *Monetary History of the United States*:

> The Federal Reserve System, therefore, began operations with no
> effective legislative criterion for determining the total stock of money.
> The discretionary judgment of a group of men was inevitably
> substituted for the quasi-automatic discipline of the gold standard.
> Those men were not even guided by a legislative mandate of intent. . . .
> Little wonder, perhaps, that the subsequent years saw so much backing
> and filling, so much confusion about purpose and power, and so erratic
> an exercise of power.[5]

---

5 *Monetary History of the United States*, Princeton, N.J.: Princeton University Press, 1963, p. 193.

## FALL OF THE GOLD STANDARD

The lack of guidance on how to keep money stable had disastrous consequences just two decades later. In the wake of the stock crash of 1929, the world economies entered a severe recession. Falling asset prices and failing businesses made banks subject to increased suspicion. Depositors withdrew billions of dollars of deposits and placed the banks at peril. In an astounding display of institutional ineptitude, the Fed failed to provide extra reserves needed to stem the currency drainage of the banks. Investors then sought even greater safety, turning their government notes into gold, a process that put extreme pressure on the gold reserves of the gold-standard countries.

The first step towards the abandonment of the gold standard occurred on September 20, 1931, when Britain suspended all payments of gold for sterling. Eighteen months later, on April 19, 1933, the United States also suspended the gold standard as the depression worsened.

The reaction of the U.S. stock market to suspension was even more enthusiastic than that of the British. Stocks soared over 9 percent on that day and almost 6 percent the next. This was the greatest two-day rally in stock market history. Stockholders felt the government could now provide extra liquidity to raise prices and stimulate the economy, which they regarded as a boon for stocks. Bonds, however, fell as investors feared the inflationary consequences of leaving the gold standard. *Business Week*, in a positive editorial on the suspension, asserted:

> With one decisive gesture, [President Roosevelt] throws out of the window all the elaborate hocus-pocus of "defending the dollar." He defies an ancient superstition and takes his stand with the advocates of managed money. . . . The job now is to manage our money effectively, wisely, with self-restraint. It can be done.[6]

### Postdevaluation Policy

Ironically, while the right to redeem dollars for gold was denied U.S. citizens, it was soon reinstated for foreign central banks at the devalued rate of $35 per ounce. As part of the Bretton Woods agreement, which set up the rules of international exchange rates after the close of World War II, the U.S. government promised to redeem for gold all dollars held by foreign central banks at a rate of $35 per ounce as long as they fixed their currency to the dollar.

---

6 "We Start," *Business Week*, April 26, 1933, p. 32.

But postwar inflation made gold seem more and more attractive to foreigners at that price. The United States gold reserves began to dwindle, despite official claims that the U.S. had no plans to change its gold exchange policy. As late as 1965, President Johnson stated unequivocally in the *Economic Report of the President*:

> There can be no question of our capacity and determination to maintain the gold value of the dollar at $35.00 per ounce. The full resources of the Nation are pledged to that end.[7]

Yet four years later, in the 1969 *Economic Report*, President Johnson declared:

> Myths about gold die slowly. But progress can be made—as we have demonstrated. In 1968, the Congress ended the obsolete gold-backing requirement for our currency.[8]

Myths about gold? Obsolete gold-backing requirement? The government finally admitted that monetary policy would not be subject to the discipline of gold, and the guiding principle of international finance and monetary policy for almost two centuries was summarily dismissed as a relic of incorrect thinking.

The United States continued to redeem gold at $35 an ounce, although private investors were paying over $40 in the private markets. Foreign central banks rushed to turn in their dollars for gold. The United States, which held almost $30 billion dollars of gold at the end of World War II, was left with $11 billion by the summer of 1971, and hundreds of millions of dollars were being withdrawn each month.

Something dramatic had to happen. On August 15, 1971, President Nixon, in one of the most extraordinary economic acts since Roosevelt's 1933 Bank Holiday, startled the world financial community by freezing wages and prices and forever closing the "gold window," the method by which foreigners turned in their Federal Reserve Notes for gold. The link of gold to money was permanently—and irrevocably—broken.

But few shed a tear for the gold standard. The stock market responded enthusiastically to Nixon's announcement (which was also coupled with wage and price controls and higher tariffs), jumping almost 4 percent on record volume. But this was not surprising. Suspensions of the gold standard or devaluations of currencies have witnessed some of the most dramatic stock market rallies in history.

---

7 *Economic Report of the President*, Washington: Government Printing Office, 1965, p. 7.
8 *Economic Report of the President*, Washington: Government Printing Office, 1969, p. 16

## Postgold Monetary Policy

With the complete dismantling of the gold standard, there was no longer any constraint on monetary expansion, either in the United States or in foreign countries. The first inflationary oil shock from 1973–74 caught most of the industrialized countries off guard, and all suffered significantly higher inflation as governments vainly attempted to offset falling output by expanding the money supply.

Because of the inflationary bent of monetary policy, Congress tried to control the monetary expansion by the Fed. In 1975, a congressional resolution obliged the Federal Reserve to announce monetary growth targets. Three years later, Congress passed the Humphrey-Hawkins Act, which forced the Fed to testify on monetary policy and state monetary targets before Congress twice annually. It was the first time in over 60 years that Congress gave the Fed some guidance as to the control of the stock of money in the economy. The financial markets closely watch this Humphrey-Hawkins testimony, which is delivered by the Chair of the Federal Reserve System and takes place in February and July.

Unfortunately, the Fed largely ignored the money targets they set in the 1970s. The surge of inflation in 1979 brought increased pressure on the Federal Reserve to change its policy and seriously attempt to break inflation. On October 6, 1979, Paul Volcker, who had been appointed in April to succeed G. William Miller as Chairman of the Board of the Federal Reserve System, announced a radical change in the implementation of monetary policy. No longer would the Federal Reserve set interest rates to guide policy. Instead, the System would exercise control over the supply of money without regard to interest rate movements.

The prospect of sharply restricted liquidity was a shock to the financial markets. Although the Saturday night announcement (later referred to as the "Saturday Night Massacre" by traders in the bond and stock markets) did not immediately capture the popular headlines like Nixon's New Economic Policy, which had frozen prices and closed the gold window, the announcement roiled the financial markets. Stocks went into a tailspin, falling almost 8 percent on record volume in the 2½ days following the announcement. Stockholders shuddered at the prospect that the Fed was suddenly going to take away the money and credit that had sustained inflation during the past decade.

The tight monetary policy of the Volcker years eventually broke the inflationary cycle. The experience of the United States, as well as that of Japan and Germany, who also used monetary policy to stop inflation, proved that restricting money was the only real answer to controlling prices.

## THE FEDERAL RESERVE AND MONEY CREATION

The process by which the Fed changes the money supply and controls credit conditions is straightforward. When the Fed wants to increase the money supply, it buys a government bond in the open market—a market where billions of dollars in bonds are transacted every day. What is unique about the Federal Reserve is that when it buys government bonds it pays for them by crediting the reserve account of the bank of the customer from whom the Fed bought the bond. A *reserve account* is a deposit a bank maintains at the Federal Reserve to satisfy reserve requirements and facilitate check clearing.

If the Federal Reserve wants to reduce the money supply, it sells government bonds from its portfolio. The buyer of these bonds instructs his bank to pay the Fed from his account. The Fed then debits the reserve account of the bank and that money disappears from circulation.

The buying and selling of government bonds are called *open market operations*. An *open market purchase* increases reserves of the banking system, while an *open market sale* reduces reserves.

### How the Fed Affects Interest Rates

When the Federal Reserve buys and sells government securities, it influences the amount of reserves of the banking system. There is an active market for these reserves among banks, where billions of dollars are bought and sold each day. This market is called the *federal funds market* and the interest rate at which these funds are borrowed and lent is called the *federal funds rate*.

Although called the *federal funds market*, this market is not run by the government, nor does it trade government securities. It is a private lending market among banks where rates are dictated by supply and demand. However, it is clear that the Federal Reserve has powerful influence over the federal funds market. If the Fed buys securities, then the supply of reserves is increased and the interest rate on federal funds goes down, as banks have ample reserves to lend. Conversely, if the Fed sells securities, the supply of reserves is reduced and the federal funds rate goes up as banks scramble for the remaining supply.

Although federal funds are borrowed for only one day, the interest rate on federal funds forms the anchor to all other short-term interest rates. These include the prime rate, Treasury bill rates, and Eurodollar lending rates, upon which literally trillions of dollars of loans and securities are based.

## Who Makes the Decisions about Monetary Creation and Interest Rates?

The Board of Governors in Washington, D.C. is the main policy-making arm of the Federal Reserve System. The seven board members, including the chairman, are chosen by the President and confirmed by the Senate. The tenure of board members is 14 years. The policy decisions of the Federal Reserve are final and not subject to review or veto by any congressional or executive body.

The Board of Governors has the power to set the *discount rate*, the interest rate at which our central bank lends funds to banking institutions. This rate receives wide notoriety, but in practice it is quite unimportant. This is because there are very few funds actually borrowed by banks from the Federal Reserve. In recent years, borrowings are far less than 1 percent of the banks' total reserve requirements, and constitute less than 0.01 percent of total banking assets. Over the years, the discount mechanism has evolved into a very-short-term lending facility for failing banks. This does not mean that the market ignores the discount rate, since its level often indicates the future range where the Fed will set the federal funds rate, but it is the federal funds rate, not the discount rate, that influences the market.

The real power of the Fed lies in its ability to control the federal funds rate and supply reserves. The committee that carries on these operations is called the Federal Open Market Committee, or the FOMC. The FOMC consists of the seven board members and the presidents of the 12 regional or district Federal Reserve banks. All 12 bank presidents sit on the meetings of the Open Market Committee, but only five of them vote: four with a rotating one-year term and one, the president of the New York Bank, designated as a permanent voting member. The presidents of the regional banks are not chosen by or even confirmed by the President or Congress. Boards composed of private citizens from the individual district banks choose the regional bank presidents.

The FOMC meets formally eight times a year to determine interest rate policy. The basic decision of the committee is the determination of the federal funds rate. It is the job of the chairman to craft a policy that balances those who want the Fed to pay more attention to fighting inflation and those who want to focus on economic growth. Although a unanimous vote is desirable, this is not always achieved, and dissenting votes, which are duly reported in the minutes of the Fed, are not uncommon in the formulation of Fed policy.

The bond and stock markets watch the members of the open market committee like hawks. Since the direction of Federal Reserve policy is of paramount importance to interest rates, anyone who can predict Fed action has an enormous advantage in the markets. The actions of the Federal Open Market Committee are in many ways the most important taken by any government committee.

## Fed Policy Actions and Interest Rates

In the short and intermediate run, interest rates are the single most important influence on stock prices. This is because the bonds compete with stocks for investment funds. Bonds become more attractive when interest rates rise, so investors sell stocks until their return again becomes attractive relative to bonds. The Fed implements a tightening policy whenever they fear the economy is overheating and inflation threatens.

Over the past 40 years, changes in the Fed funds rates have been a very good predictor of future stock prices. Table 10-1 displays the return on the S & P 500 Index from the beginning of the month *after* the Fed Funds rate has been changed to a date three, six, nine, and twelve months later.

The effects of Fed actions are dramatic: Following increases in the Fed funds rate, the subsequent returns on stocks are significantly less than average; when the Fed funds rate is decreased, stock returns are significantly higher than average. Since 1955, the total returns on stocks has been about 7 percent in the 12 months following the 92 increases in the Fed funds rate, while it has been almost 18 percent following the 85 times the Fed funds rate has been reduced. This compares to an average 12-month return over the period of about 12 percent. If these results persist in the future, investors could significantly beat a buy-and-hold strategy by increasing their stock holdings when the Fed is easing credit conditions and reducing stocks when the Fed is tightening.

Although this strategy has worked quite well in the 1950s, '60s, '70s, and '80s, it has not worked over 9- and 12-month horizons in the 1990s. Perhaps the financial community has become so geared to watching and anticipating Fed policy that the effect of its tightening and easing is already discounted in the market or, if it is not discounted, influences the market over a much shorter period than is considered in this analysis.

But there might be another reason for the reduced impact of Fed policy on stock prices. If the Fed is acting optimally to stabilize the economy, the markets should take a positive view towards *either* tightening

**T A B L E   10–1**

Total S & P Returns and Significant Changes in the Federal Funds Rate

| 1955-1996 | 3-month* | 6-month* | 9-month* | 12-month* |
|---|---|---|---|---|
| Increases (92) | 0.85% | 2.45% | 5.79% | 7.16% |
| Decreases (85) | 5.60% | 10.59% | 13.46% | 17.88% |
| Benchmark | 2.97% | 6.02% | 9.08% | 12.23% |
| | | | | |
| 1955-1959 | 3-month | 6-month* | 9-month* | 12-month* |
| Increases (18) | 5.02% | 7.02% | 10.09% | 11.78% |
| Decreases (8) | 6.41% | 17.43% | 27.76% | 35.97% |
| Benchmark | 3.27% | 6.38% | 8.93% | 11.41% |
| 1960-1969 | 3-month* | 6-month* | 9-month* | 12-month* |
| Increases (22) | -1.22% | 1.24% | 1.36% | 2.61% |
| Decreases (17) | 3.51% | 6.06% | 7.39% | 8.62% |
| Benchmark | 2.16% | 4.09% | 6.18% | 8.43% |
| 1970-1979 | 3-month* | 6-month* | 9-month* | 12-month* |
| Increases (29) | -1.92% | -1.20% | 3.73% | 4.77% |
| Decreases (26) | 6.49% | 11.14% | 13.78% | 17.72% |
| Benchmark | 1.91% | 4.26% | 6.73% | 9.31% |
| 1980-1989 | 3-month | 6-month* | 9-month* | 12-month* |
| Increases (16) | 3.88% | 4.22% | 9.09% | 8.61% |
| Decreases (23) | 6.47% | 12.87% | 14.85% | 21.05% |
| Benchmark | 4.27% | 8.77% | 13.00% | 16.89% |
| 1990-1996 | 3-month* | 6-month | 9-month | 12-month* |
| Increases (7) | 1.23% | 5.56% | 9.60% | 16.21% |
| Decreases (11) | 4.33% | 6.55% | 8.80% | 12.76% |
| Benchmark | 3.66% | 7.28% | 11.38% | 16.32% |

*denotes statistical significance.

or easing, since these actions will keep growth steady and inflation under control. If the market deems Fed tightening insufficient, then the "bond vigilantes," bond traders who assess the inflationary impact of Fed policy, will send interest rates higher and stock prices lower. The same will occur if the Fed lowers interest rates when the market deems such a policy inappropriate.

So the best strategy for stock investors who follow the Fed becomes more complex. The market is responding not just to an increase or decrease in rates, but to whether the policy shift is an appropriate action given economic conditions. The Fed remains crucial to the financial markets, but policy actions, as least so far in the 1990s, have not evoked responses in the equity market that are as predictable as they have been in the past.

## CONCLUSION

The Great Depression dethroned gold as the linchpin of the world's monetary system. The control of money was passed directly to the central bank under authority of the central government.

Release from the shackles of the gold standard has always been marked by celebration in world equity markets. Stocks thrive on the liquidity provided by the central bank, and shareholders will tolerate well any mild inflation that accompanies such monetary accommodations. On the other hand, monetary stringency designed to force commodity prices down to meet exchange rates or inflation guidelines is always painful to the stock market. Volcker's move against inflation in 1979, the Bank of England's vain attempt to stay within the Exchange Rate Mechanism, and, most recently, the failed attempts by Southeast Asian governments to maintain the value of its currency relative to the dollar have always sent stock prices downward. When undue monetary tightness is released, the equity markets often explode to the upside.

Shifts in central bank policy have had a marked effect on the equity market, but there are signs that the market response to Fed actions is not as reliable or as consistent as it has been in the past. Bond traders often punish the Fed for insufficient tightening or excessive easing by selling bonds, thereby raising interest rates and depressing equity prices. In fact, the better the Fed does its job of keeping the economy on an even keel, the less the markets react to policy changes. The lack of market reaction does not spring from the ineffectiveness of the Fed, but from its effectiveness. If the Fed is doing its job, stockholders need not worry.

Despite the inflationary bias of managed money, no country is ever likely to return to the gold standard. The ability to control overall prices is sufficiently beneficial to compensate for the inflationary bias that a managed money standard entails. The success of Paul Volcker and Alan Greenspan at restraining inflation has made the dollar the *de facto* world monetary standard.

# 11
## CHAPTER

# INFLATION AND STOCKS

*In steadiness of real income, or purchasing power, a list of diversified common stocks surpasses bonds.*

—Irving Fisher, 1925[1]

A modern adaptation of a story that has been a perennial favorite among investors for many years tells of a youngish, well-to-do man who wanders off into the forest and falls into a deep sleep, much like Rip Van Winkle. He awakens many years later and his first thoughts turn to his portfolio. He searches out a pay phone and dials his broker's 800 number. The number is still operative and the computer-simulated voice responds to his account number: "Thank you for calling your Merrill Lynch/Dean Witter Morgan Stanley/Paine-Webber/Smith Barney-Shearson/Schwab consolidated account. The value of your stock portfolio is $50 billion . . . short-term bond portfolio $500 million . . . long-term bond portfolio $50,000." Our now aged investor is ecstatic at his newfound wealth until he hears the automated operator come on with the request: "Toll-free calls are limited to 60 seconds; deposit $1 million for the next three minutes, please!"

This story almost always elicits laughter from investors who hear it for the first time. Everyone understands that you cannot know what money will buy unless you know what has happened to the price level. Images of Germans 75 years ago carrying billions of near-worthless Reichsmarks to buy a pint of milk are cruel reminders of the ravages of inflation. And you do not need to go even that far back into history to

---

1 From foreword by Irving Fisher in Kenneth S. Van Strum, *Investing in Purchasing Power*, New York: Barron's, 1925, p. vii.

find rampant inflation. Brazil, Argentina, and many other developing countries have suffered hyperinflation as a result of excessive governmental monetary expansion. Nobody wants to end up with a $50 million portfolio if a phone call costs a million bucks!

But the final values for the stock and bond portfolios in my story were not chosen at random. In the event of hyperinflation, stocks will be, by far, the best-performing financial assets. Over the past several decades, the currencies of Brazil and Argentina have depreciated by more than a billionfold against the dollar, yet their stock markets have appreciated by an even greater extent.

Holders of short-term bonds, such as Treasury bills, will try to keep up with rampant inflation—and will have moderate success in doing so. These investors can reset the interest rate frequently in an attempt to keep pace with rising prices. But long-term bond holders, locked into fixed coupon and principal payments, will see their capital wiped out— their bonds won't be worth enough to pay for a phone call!

## STOCKS AS INFLATIONARY HEDGES

Despite the ever-present threat of inflation, it is surprising how many investors are pleased with an investment that makes only fixed monetary payments. When asked how much $100,000 will buy in 30 years, many realize it will be less than today, but few recognize how much less. At a 3 percent rate of inflation, $100,000 will be worth in 30 years just over $40,000 in today's dollars. And 3 percent inflation is considered by many to be a good average inflation rate for the next 30 years. At 6 percent inflation, $100,000 will command $17,000; at 8 percent it will be less than $10,000; and if inflation averages 10 percent a year (which could mean quite a few good years of moderate price increases combined with a few bad years of double-digit inflation), the purchasing power of $100,000 drops by almost 95 percent to $5,700.

In contrast to the inflation risk of fixed-income assets, the historical evidence is convincing that the returns on stocks over time have kept pace with inflation. Since stocks are claims on the earnings of real assets—assets whose value is intrinsically related to labor and capital—it is reasonable to expect that their return will not be influenced by inflation. The period since World War II has been the most inflationary in our history, yet the real return on stocks has met or exceed that of the previous 150 years, while the real return to bonds has fallen considerably.

Despite the overwhelming evidence that the returns on stocks compensate shareholders for increased inflation, investors' acceptance of stocks as inflation hedges has undergone significant changes. In the 1950s, stocks were praised as hedges against rising commodity prices. For that reason, many investors stayed with stocks, despite witnessing the dividend yield on equities fall below the interest rate on bonds in 1958 for the first time ever. In the 1970s, however, stock prices were ravaged during the inflation triggered by OPEC oil price hikes and perpetuated by bad monetary policy. As a result, it became unfashionable to view equity as an effective hedge against inflation.

When I speak of stocks being a hedge against inflation, I mean that stocks will increase in value sufficiently to compensate investors for any erosion in the purchasing power of money. Although stocks are excellent long-term hedges against inflation, they fail miserably in the short run.

Let us examine the evidence. Figure 11-1 plots the annual compound returns on stocks, bonds, and Treasury bills against the rate of inflation over one- and 30-year holding periods from 1871–1996. The inflation rates are ranked from the lowest to the highest according to quintile groupings. This means that the first point plotted represents the returns associated with the lowest 20 percent of all inflation rates recorded over that holding period, the next point covers the returns over the next lowest inflation rates, and so on.

What do these figures tell us? That neither stocks, bonds, nor bills are good *short-term* hedges against inflation. Real returns on these financial assets are highest when the inflation rates are low, and fall as inflation increases. But the returns on stocks are virtually immune to the inflation rate over longer horizons. Fixed-income assets, on the other hand, simply cannot compete with stocks over any holding period.

This was the principal conclusion of Edgar Smith's book, *Common Stocks As Long-Term Investments*. He showed that stocks outperform bonds in time of falling as well as rising prices, taking the period after the Civil War and before the turn of the century as his test case. Smith's results are quite robust, holding over the past 125 years.

## WHY STOCKS FAIL AS A SHORT-TERM INFLATION HEDGE

### Higher Interest Rates

Although stocks survive inflation well over long periods of time, they are poor *short-term* hedges against inflation. A popular explanation is that since inflation increases interest rates and since the interest rate on bonds competes with stock yields, inflation must depress stock prices. In other words, inflation must send stock prices down sufficiently to in-

**F I G U R E  11–1**

Holding Period Returns and Inflation, 1871–1996

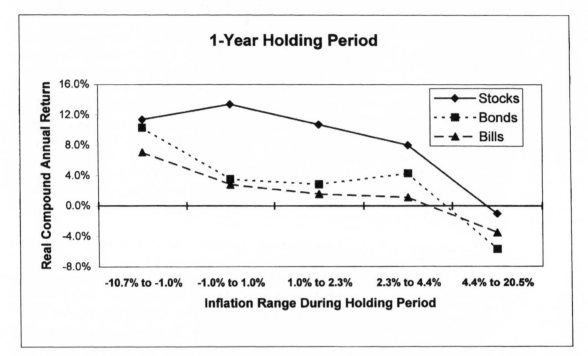

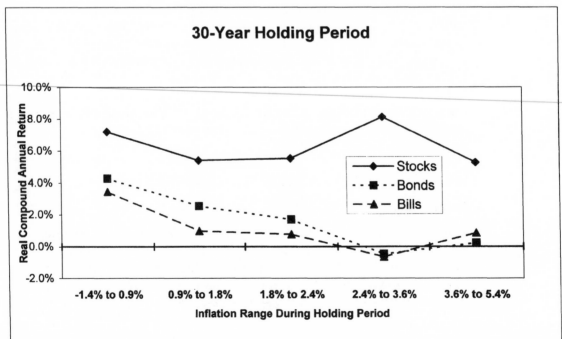

crease their dividend or earning yield to match the higher rate available on bonds.

But this explanation is incomplete. Expectations of rising prices do indeed increase interest rates. It has long been recognized that lenders seek to protect themselves against inflation by adding a premium to the interest rate that they demand. Irving Fisher, the famous early-20th-century American economist indicated that the market interest rate is composed of two parts: the *real rate of interest*—the rate prevailing in an economy with no inflation—plus the *expected rate of inflation*—a premium compensating lenders for the depreciation of the value of money.[2] This relation has been called the *Fisher Equation*, after its discoverer.[3]

Although higher expected inflation raises interest rates, inflation also raises the expected future cash flows available to stockholders. Stocks are claims on the earnings of real assets, whether these assets are the product of machines, labor, land, or ideas. Although inflation raises the cost of inputs, output prices (which are in fact the measure of inflation) must also rise. Therefore future earnings will also rise with the price level.

It can be shown that when inflation impacts input and output prices equally, the present value of the future cash flows from stocks is not adversely affected by inflation. Higher future earnings will offset higher interest rates so that, over time, the price of stocks—as well as the level of dividends—will rise at a rate equaling that of inflation. The returns from stocks will keep up with rising prices and stocks will act as a complete inflation hedge.

## Supply-Induced Inflation

The description in the previous section holds when inflation is purely monetary in nature, influencing costs and profits equally. But there are many circumstances when earnings cannot keep up with inflation. Stocks declined during the 1970s because the restriction in OPEC oil supplies

---

2 Since corporations can deduct interest expense from taxes, interest rates should rise by the expected rate of inflation divided by 1 minus the corporate tax rate (called the *Darby Effect* after Professor Michael Darby) in order to keep the after- tax real cost of capital constant to corporations. Historically, interest rates do not appear to rise this much during inflation, giving firms a net benefit from debt financing during inflation.
3 See Irving Fisher, *The Rate of Interest*, New York: Macmillan, 1907. The exact Fisher Equation for the nominal rate of interest is the sum of the real rate plus the expected rate of inflation plus the cross product of the real rate and the expected rate of inflation. If inflation is not too high, this last term can often be ignored.

dramatically influenced costs. Firms were not able to raise the prices of their output by as much as the soaring cost of their energy inputs.

In the last chapter I noted that inflation is the result of too much money chasing too few goods. A reduction in goods supplied as well as an increase in money issued can cause inflation. A reduction in output can occur because of low productivity or a sharp rise in input prices. In these circumstances, it is not surprising that inflation caused by supply problems should negatively affect the stock market. The inflationary 1970s were just such a period.

U.S. manufacturers, who for years had thrived on low energy prices, were totally unprepared to deal with surging oil costs. The recession that followed the first OPEC oil squeeze pummeled the stock market. Productivity plummeted, and by the end of 1974 real stock prices, measured by the Dow-Jones average, had fallen 65 percent from the January 1966 high—the largest decline since the crash of '29. Pessimism ran so deep that nearly half of all Americans in August 1974 believed the economy was heading towards a depression such as the one the nation had experienced in the 1930s.[4]

### Fed Policy, the Business Cycle, and Government Spending

There are other good reasons why stock prices might react poorly to inflation. One is the fear that the central bank will take restrictive action to curb rising prices, which invariably raises short-term *real* interest rates. Furthermore, inflation often appears late in the business cycle, which is taken as a sign by investors that a recession, with lower profits, is much nearer. Under these circumstances, it is perfectly rational for investors to take stock prices down.

Inflation, especially in less developed countries, is also closely linked with large government budget deficits and excessive government spending. In that case, increased government presence leads to lower growth, lower corporate profits, and higher inflation.

### INFLATION AND THE U.S. TAX CODE

Another very important reason why stocks are poor short-term hedges against inflation is the U.S. tax code. There are two significant areas in which the tax code works to the detriment of shareholders during inflationary times: corporate profits and capital gains.

---

4 Gallup poll taken August 2–5, 1974.

## INFLATIONARY DISTORTIONS TO CORPORATE EARNINGS

When analyzing stocks, analysts often point to the *quality of earnings* that firms report, which is the ability of reported earnings to accurately reflect the earning power of the firm. Reported earnings are often distorted because standard accounting practices, and those accepted by the tax authorities, do not properly take into account the effects of inflation on corporate profits. This distortion shows up primarily in the treatment of depreciation, inventory valuation, and interest costs.

Depreciation of plant, equipment, and other capital investments is based on historical costs. These depreciation schedules are not adjusted for any change in the price of capital that might occur during the life of the asset. During inflation, the cost of replacing capital rises, but reported corporate depreciation does not make any adjustment for this. Therefore, depreciation allowances are understated since firms do not make adequate allowances for the rising cost of replacing capital. As a result, reported depreciation is understated and reported earnings are overstated.

But depreciation is not the only source of bias. In calculating the cost of goods sold, firms must use the historical cost, with either "first in first out" or "last in first out" methods of inventory. In an inflationary environment, the gap between historical costs and selling prices widens, producing inflationary profits for the firm. These "profits" do not represent an increase in the real earning power of the firm, but record just that part of the firm's capital—namely the inventory—that *turns over* and is realized as a monetary profit. This treatment of inventories differs from the firm's other capital, such as plant and equipment, which is not revalued on an ongoing basis for the purpose of calculating earnings.

The Department of Commerce, the government agency responsible for gathering economic statistics, is well aware of these distortions and has computed both a depreciation adjustment and an inventory valuation adjustment. These have been calculated back to 1929 and are currently reported on a quarterly basis along with the comprehensive figures on gross domestic product. But the Internal Revenue Service does not recognize any of these adjustments for tax purposes. Firms are required to pay taxes on *reported* profits, even when these profits are biased upwards by inflation. After-tax earnings, and therefore stock prices, are hurt by inflation because the tax law does not recognize these distortions.

These inflationary biases are often significant. In the inflationary 1970s, reported corporate profits were overstated by up to 50 percent, meaning that the quality of reported earnings during that period was very low. On the other hand, in the low inflation period of the late 1980s and 1990s, reported corporate profits were often below adjusted profits, dramatically increasing the "quality" of reported earnings.

## Inflation Biases in Interest Costs

There is another inflationary distortion to corporate profits that is not reported in government statistics. This is based on the inflationary component of interest costs and, in contrast to depreciation and inventory profits, often leads to a *downward* bias in reported corporate earnings during periods of inflation.

Most firms raise some of their capital by floating fixed-income assets such as bonds and bank loans. This borrowing *leverages* the firm's assets, since any profits above and beyond the debt service go to the stockholders. In an inflationary environment, *nominal* interest costs rise, even if real interest costs remain unchanged. But corporate profits are calculated by deducting nominal interest costs, which overstates the real interest costs to the firm. Hence, reported corporate profits are depressed compared to true economic conditions. Since the firm is paying back debt with depreciated dollars, the higher nominal interest expense is offset by the reduction in the real value of the bonds and loans owed by the firm, and the firm's real profits do not suffer.

Unfortunately, it is not easy to quantify this earnings bias, since it is not easy to identify the share of interest due to inflation and that due to the real interest costs. The extent of the bias depends on the leverage of the firm and might in some cases offset the depreciation and inventory bias, which raise reported corporate profits.

## Inflation and the Capital Gains Tax

In the United States, capital gains taxes are paid on the difference between the cost of an asset and the sale price, with no adjustment made for inflation. If asset values rise with inflation, then the investor accrues a tax liability that must be paid at the time the asset is sold, whether or not the investor has realized a real gain. This means that an asset that appreciates by less than the rate of inflation—meaning the investor is worse off in real terms—will be taxed upon sale.

Higher inflation increases the effective tax on capital assets. Figure 11-2a displays the after-tax real rate of return for various inflation rates and various holding periods under the current tax system.[5]

You can see that the inflation tax has a more severe effect on annual compound returns when the holding period is short. This is because the more an investor turns over an asset, the more the government can capture the nominal capital gains tax. For an investor with a one-year holding period, the real after-tax return with a moderate inflation of 3 percent is reduced by about 70 basis points over the return in a no-inflation environment. For longer holding periods, the annual loss through inflation is reduced since capital gains tax is deferred. As inflation increases, the reduction in real after-tax return increases.

Inflation depresses stock prices because it reduces the real after-tax return on investment. Figure 11-2b shows how much the price of a stock must drop to compensate the holder for the fact that our tax system taxes nominal capital gains. This figure is calculated with 3 percent inflation as the benchmark, so that inflation lower than 3 percent will reduce the effective inflation tax, while inflation higher than 3 percent will increase the effective inflation tax. The exercise assumes that stock prices would have to rise or fall by an appropriate amount to restore the after-tax return to that achieved under a 3 percent benchmark inflation.[6]

As shown in Figure 11-2b, the inflation-depressing effect on stock prices is more severe for stocks held by investors with short holding periods compared to longer holding periods. For a one-year holding period, a rise of inflation from 3 to 6 percent depresses stock prices by about 10 percent. An increase of inflation to 8 percent would depress stock prices by nearly 15 percent, while 10 percent inflation would cause a 20 percent decline. On the other hand, lower inflation improves the after-tax real return and boosts stock prices. Lowering inflation from 3 percent to zero would increase stock prices by over 12 percent if the prices were determined by those with one-year holding periods. It should be noted, however, that all these results ignore the negative impact of inflation on corporate taxes through depreciation, inventory, and nonindexed capital gains taxes.

---

5 Figure 11-2 assumes a total real return of 7 percent (real appreciation of 5 percent and a dividend yield of 2 percent) and tax rates of 20 percent and 28 percent, respectively, on capital gains and dividend income. If inflation is 3 percent, the total return on stocks will be 10 percent in nominal terms.

6 Since expected after-tax returns might fall with inflation, these estimates should be considered upper bounds for the fall in stock prices.

**F I G U R E   11–2**

Taxes and Inflation (2 Percent Dividend Yield, 5 Percent Real Capital Appreciation, 20 Percent Capital Gains Rate, and 28 Percent Dividend Tax Rate)

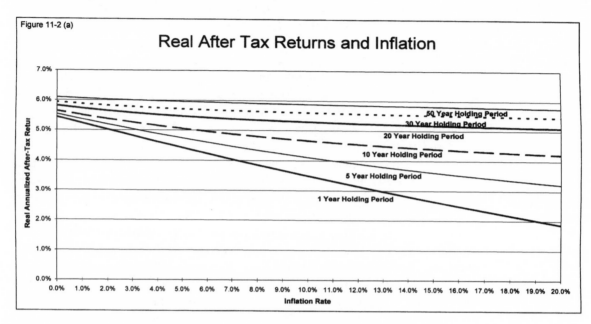

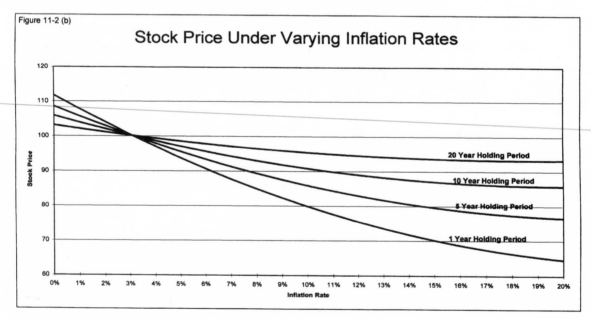

There is considerable support, both inside and outside government, to make some adjustment for inflation in the capital gains tax. In 1986, the U.S. Treasury proposed the indexation of capital gains, but this provision was never enacted into law. In 1997, the House of Representative included capital gains indexation in its tax law, but it was removed by House-Senate conferees under threat of a Clinton veto. Under these plans, investors would pay taxes on only that portion of the gain (if any) that exceeded the increase in the price level over the holding period of the asset. Inflation indexation of the capital gains tax would have a very positive effect on stock prices.

## CONCLUSION

The message of this chapter is that stocks are not good hedges against inflation in the short run—but then no financial asset is. In the long run, stocks are extremely good hedges against inflation, while bonds are not. Stocks are also the best financial asset if you fear rapid inflation, since many countries with high inflation can still have quite viable, if not booming, stock markets. Fixed-income assets, on the other hand, cannot protect investors from excessive monetary issuance.

Inflation, although kinder to stocks than bonds, does have some downsides for equity holders. Fear that the Fed will tighten credit if inflation threatens causes traders to avoid stocks, at least in the short run. Inflation also overstates corporate profits and increases the taxes firms have to pay. Furthermore, because the U.S. capital gains tax is not indexed, inflation causes investors to pay higher taxes than would exist in a noninflationary environment. The distortions of our tax system, which cause both firms and investors to pay higher taxes in an inflationary environment, can be partially remedied by indexing the capital gains and corporate income taxes.

# CHAPTER

# STOCKS AND
# THE BUSINESS CYCLE*

*The stock market has predicted nine out of the last five recessions!*

—**Paul Samuelson**[1]

*I'd love to be able to predict markets and anticipate recessions, but since that's impossible, I'm as satisfied to search out profitable companies as Buffett is.*

—**Peter Lynch**[2]

A well-respected economist is about to address a large group of financial analysts, investment advisers, and stockbrokers. There is obvious concern in the audience. The stock market has been surging to new all-time highs almost daily, driving down dividend yields to record lows and price-earnings ratios skyward. Is this bullishness justified? The audience wants to know if the economy is really going to do well enough to support these high stock prices.

The economist's address is highly optimistic. He predicts that the real gross domestic product of the U.S. will increase over 4 percent during the next four quarters, a very healthy growth rate. There will be no recession for at least three years, and even if one occurs after that it

---

* This chapter is an adaptation of my paper "Does It Pay Stock Investors to Forecast the Business Cycle?" in *Journal of Portfolio Management*, Fall 1991, vol. 18, pp. 27-34. The material benefited significantly from discussions with Professor Paul Samuelson.
1 "Science and Stocks," *Newsweek*, September 19, 1966, p. 92.
2 Peter Lynch, *One Up on Wall Street*, Penguin Books, 1989, p. 14.

will be very brief. Corporate profits, one of the major factors driving stock prices, will increase at double-digit annual rates for at least the next three years. To boot, he predicts that a Republican will easily win the White House in next year's presidential elections, a situation obviously comforting to the overwhelmingly conservative audience. The crowd obviously likes what it hears. Their anxiety is quieted and many are ready to recommend that their clients increase their stake in stocks.

The time of this address is the summer of 1987, with the stock market poised to take one of its sharpest falls in history, including the record-breaking 23% decline on October 19, 1987. In just a few weeks, most stocks can be bought for about half the price paid at the time of the address. But the biggest irony of all is that the economist is dead right in each and every one of his bullish economic predictions.

The lesson is that the markets and the economy are often out of sync. It is not surprising that many investors dismiss economic forecasts when planning their market strategy. The substance of Paul Samuelson's famous words, cited at the beginning of this chapter, still remains true more than 30 years after they were first uttered.

But do not dismiss the business cycle too quickly when choosing your portfolio. The stock market still responds quite powerfully to changes in economic activity. Figure 12-1 shows the reaction of the S & P 500 Index to the business cycle. Although there are many "false alarms" like 1987, when the market collapse was not followed by a recession, stocks almost always fall prior to a recession and rally rigorously at signs of an impending recovery. If you can predict the business cycle, you can beat the buy-and-hold strategy that has been advocated throughout this book.

But this is no easy task, as indicated by Figure 12-1. I will show that to make money by predicting the business cycle, you must be able to identify peaks and troughs of economic activity *before* they actually occur, a skill very few if any economists possess. Yet business-cycle forecasting is a popular Wall Street endeavor not because it is successful —most of the time it is not—but because the potential gains from successfully calling business booms and busts are so large.

## WHO CALLS THE BUSINESS CYCLE?

It is surprising to many that the dating of business cycles is not determined by any of the myriad government agencies that collect data on

**F I G U R E  12–1**

S & P 500 Earnings and Dividends During the Business Cycle, 1938–1996 (NBER Recessions Shaded)

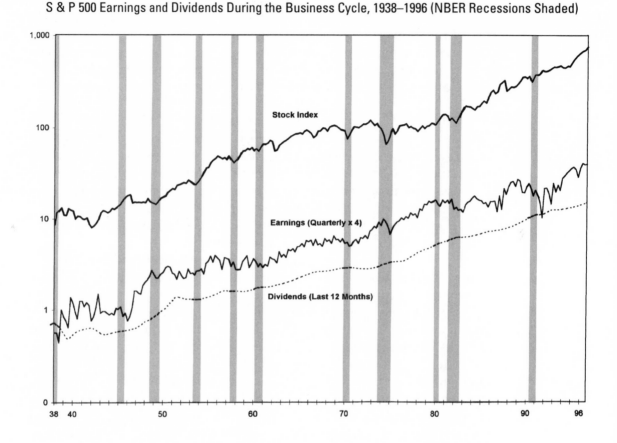

the economy. Instead, the task falls to the National Bureau of Economic Research (the N.B.E.R.), a private research organization founded in 1920 for the purpose of documenting business cycles and developing a series of national income accounts. In the early years of its existence, the Bureau's staff compiled comprehensive chronological records of the changes in economic conditions in many of the industrialized economies. In particular, the Bureau developed monthly series of business activity for the United States and Britain back to 1854.

In a 1946 volume entitled *Measuring Business Cycles*, Wesley C. Mitchell, one of the founders of the Bureau, and Arthur Burns, a renowned business-cycle expert who later headed the Federal Reserve Board, gave the following definition of a business cycle:

> Business cycles are a type of fluctuation found in the aggregate economic activity of nations that organize their work mainly in business enterprises: a cycle consists of expansion occurring at about the same time in many economic activities, followed by similarly general recessions, or contractions, and revivals that merge into the expansion phase of the next cycle; this sequence of changes is recurrent but not periodic; in duration business cycles vary from more than one year to ten or twelve years and they are not divisible into shorter cycles of similar character.[3]

It is commonly assumed that a recession occurs when gross domestic product (or GDP), the most inclusive measure of economic output, declines for two consecutive quarters. But this is not necessarily so. Although this criterion is a reasonable rule of thumb for indicating a recession, it is not the rule used by the N.B.E.R. For example, the 1981 recession occurred when there was only a single quarterly decline in GDP. The Bureau looks at many other indicators, including real personal income and sales, employment, and industrial production in order to date the peaks and troughs of the business cycle.

The Business Cycle Dating Committee of the National Bureau confirms the business-cycle dates. This committee consists of academic economists who are associated with the Bureau and who meet to examine economic data whenever conditions warrant. Over the entire period from 1802 to 1997, the United States has experienced 41 recessions, averaging nearly 18 months in length, while the expansions have averaged almost 38 months. This means that, over these 195 years, almost exactly one-third of the time the economy has been in a recession. However, since World War II, there have been nine recessions, averaging 10 months in length, while the expansions have averaged 50 months. So in the postwar period, the economy has been in a recession only one-sixth of the time.

The dating of the business cycle is of no small importance. The designation that the economy is in a recession or an expansion has political as well as economic implications. For example, when the Bureau called

---

3 Wesley C. Mitchell and Arthur Burns, "Measuring Business Cycles," *N.B.E.R. Reporter*, 1946, p. 3.

the onset of the 1990 recession in July rather than August, it raised quite a few eyebrows in Washington. This is because the Bush administration had told the public that the Iraqi invasion of Kuwait and the surge in oil prices was responsible for the economic recession. This explanation was undermined when the Bureau actually dated the onset of the recession a month earlier.

The Business Cycle Dating Committee is in no rush to call the turning points in the cycle. Never has a call been reversed because of new or revised data that have become available—and the N.B.E.R. wants to keep it that way. As Robert E. Hall, current head of the seven-member Business Cycle Dating Committee indicated, "The N.B.E.R. has not made an announcement on a business cycle peak or trough until there was almost no doubt that the data would not be revised in light of subsequent availability of data."[4]

Recent examples of the N.B.E.R.'s dating make the point. The July 1981 peak was not called until early January 1982, while the November trough was not dated until July 1983. The July 1990 peak of the last recession was not officially called until nine months later. And the March 1991 trough was not designated until December 1992, 21 months later. It is ironic that the N.B.E.R. officially called the peak of the 1990–91 business cycle a month after the trough had already been reached. Clearly, waiting for the Bureau to designate business cycles is far too late to be of any use in timing the market.

## STOCK RETURNS AROUND BUSINESS-CYCLE TURNING POINTS

Almost without exception, the stock market turns down prior to recessions and rises before economic recoveries. In fact, out of the 41 recessions from 1802, 38 of them, or 93 percent, have been preceded (or accompanied) by declines of 8 percent or more in the total stock returns index. The three that were not were the 1829-30 recession, the recession that followed the economic adjustment immediately following World War II, and the 1953 recession, where stock declines fell just shy of the 8 percent criterion.

Table 12-1 summarizes the return behavior for the nine post-World War II recessions. You can see that the stock return index peaked anywhere from 0 to 13 months before the beginning of a recession. The recessions that began in January 1980 and July 1990 are among the very

---

4 Robert Hall, "Economic Fluctuations," *N.B.E.R. Reporter*, Summer 1991, p. 1.

**T A B L E   12–1**

Recessions and Stock Returns

| Recession | Peak of Stock Index (1) | Peak of Business Cycle (2) | Lead Time Between Peaks (3) | Decline in Stock Index From (1) to (2) (4) | Mos. Between 8% Stock Index Decline and (2) (5) | Maximum 12 Month Decline in Stock Index (6) |
|---|---|---|---|---|---|---|
| 1948 - 49 | May 1948 | Nov 1948 | 6 | -8.74% | 0 | -8.19% |
| 1953 - 54 | Dec 1952 | Jul 1953 | 7 | -3.91% | * | -7.18% |
| 1957 - 58 | Jul 1957 | Aug 1957 | 1 | -5.05% | -1 | -13.90% |
| 1960 - 61 | Dec 1959 | Apr 1960 | 4 | -8.28% | 0 | -8.20% |
| 1970 | Nov 1968 | Dec 1969 | 13 | -12.19% | 10 | -25.50% |
| 1973 - 75 | Dec 1972 | Nov 1973 | 11 | -16.20% | 7 | -40.10% |
| 1980 | Jan 1980 | Jan 1980 | 0 | 0.00% | -2 | -8.90% |
| 1981 - 82 | Nov 1980 | Jul 1981 | 8 | -4.08% | -1 | -14.20% |
| 1990 - 91 | Jul 1990 | Jul 1990 | 0 | 0.00% | -3 | -13.92% |
|  |  | **Average** | **5.6** | **-6.49%** | **1.3** | **-15.56%** |
|  |  | Std. Dev. | 4.4 | 5.10% | 4.4 | 10.17 |

*Market never declined 8%

few in U.S. history where the stock market gave no advance warning of the economic downturn.

During the postwar period, if you waits until the stock returns index has declined by 8 percent before signaling a business-cycle peak, then the stock market leads the business cycle by an average of only 1.3 months. This signal ranges from a lead of 10 months in the 1970 recession to a lag of three months in the 1990–91 recession. In all but two of the postwar recessions, an 8 percent decline in the returns index led the business-cycle peak by less than one month, giving little advance warning of an impending recession.

As the Samuelson quote at the beginning of this chapter indicates, the stock market is also prone to false alarms, and these have increased in the postwar period. Excluding the war years, where declining stock markets coincided with expanding war economies, there have been 12 episodes since 1802 when the cumulative returns index for stocks fell by 8 percent or more, but the drop was not then followed by a recession within the next 12 months. This happened five times in the 19th century and seven times in the 20th century. All the occasions in this century have occurred since World War II.

Table 12-2 lists declines greater than 8 percent in the stock returns index during the postwar period that were not followed by recessions. The 1987 decline of 29 percent, from August through November, is the

**T A B L E   12–2**

False Alarms by Stock Market: Postwar Declines of 8 Percent or More When No
Recession Followed Within 12 Months; Ranked by Severity of Decline

| Year of False Alarm | Peak Month Stock Index | Low Month Stock Index | % Decline in Market |
|---|---|---|---|
| 1987 | Aug 1987 | Nov 1987 | -29.10% |
| 1946 | May 1946 | May 1947 | -24.00% |
| 1962 | Dec 1961 | Jun 1962 | -23.10% |
| 1966 | Jan 1966 | Sep 1966 | -15.50% |
| 1978 | Aug 1978 | Oct 1978 | -10.80% |
| 1956 - 57 | Jul 1956 | Feb 1957 | -8.30% |
| 1984 | Nov 1983 | May 1984 | -8.20% |

**T A B L E   12–3**

Expansions and Stock Returns

| Recession | Trough of Stock Index (1) | Trough of Business Cycle (2) | Lead Time Between Troughs (3) | Rise in Stock Index From (1) to (2) (4) | Months Between 8% Stock Index Rise and (2) (5) |
|---|---|---|---|---|---|
| 1948 - 49 | May 1949 | Oct 1948 | 5 | 15.59% | 3 |
| 1953 - 54 | Aug 1953 | May 1954 | 9 | 29.13% | 5 |
| 1957 - 58 | Dec 1957 | April 1958 | 4 | 10.27% | 1 |
| 1960 - 61 | Oct 1960 | Feb 1961 | 4 | 21.25% | 2 |
| 1970 | Jun 1970 | Nov 1970 | 5 | 21.86% | 3 |
| 1973 - 75 | Sep 1974 | Mar 1975 | 6 | 35.60% | 5 |
| 1980 | Mar 1980 | Jul 1980 | 4 | 22.60% | 2 |
| 1981 - 82 | Jul 1982 | Nov 1982 | 4 | 33.13% | 3 |
| 1990 - 91 | Oct 1990 | Mar 1991 | 5 | 25.28% | 3 |
|  | Average | 5.1 | 23.86% | 3.0 |
|  | Std. Dev. | 1.73 | 8.59% | 1.41 |

largest decline in the nearly two- century history of stock returns data
after which the economy did not fall into a recession. Chapter 15 will
discuss the 1987 stock crash and explain why it did not lead to an economic downturn.

Table 12-3 compares the trough in the stock return index and the trough in the N.B.E.R. business cycle. The average lead time between a market upturn and an economic recovery has been 5.1 months, and the range has been quite narrow. This compares to an average 5.6-month lead time between the peak in the market and the peak in the business cycle, with a much greater variability in these figures. As you shall see, stock returns actually rise more in a recession in anticipation of an economic recovery than they fall before an economic downturn.

## GAINS THROUGH TIMING THE BUSINESS CYCLE

Table 12-4 displays the excess returns to investors who can time their investment strategy in relation to the peaks and troughs in economic activity. Since stocks fall prior to a recession, investors want to switch out of stocks and into Treasury bills, returning to stocks when prospects for economic recovery look good. Excess returns are calculated by assuming that investors who lead the business cycle switch out of stocks and into bills before the peak of business expansions, and switch back into stocks before the trough of recessions. In contrast, investors who lag the business cycle switch out of stocks and into bills after the cycle peak, and back into stocks after the cycle

**T A B L E   12–4**

Excess Returns Around Business Cycle Turning Points

|  |  | Lead | | | | Peak | Lag | | | |
|---|---|---|---|---|---|---|---|---|---|---|
|  |  | 4 month | 3 month | 2 month | 1 month | Peak | 1 month | 2 month | 3 month | 4 month |
| Lead | 4 month | 4.8% | 4.0% | 4.2% | 4.1% | 3.3% | 2.7% | 2.1% | 2.2% | 1.9% |
|  | 3 month | 4.0 | **3.3** | 3.5 | 3.3 | 2.6 | 1.9 | 1.4 | 1.5 | 1.3 |
|  | 2 month | 3.3 | 2.6 | **2.8** | 2.6 | 1.9 | 1.2 | 0.7 | 0.8 | 0.7 |
|  | 1 month | 2.5 | 1.8 | 2.0 | **1.8** | 1.1 | 0.5 | 0.0 | 0.1 | 0.0 |
|  | **Trough** | 1.9 | 1.2 | 1.4 | 1.2 | **0.5** | -0.2 | -0.7 | -0.6 | -0.7 |
| Lag | 1 month | 1.5 | 0.8 | 1.0 | 0.8 | 0.1 | **-0.6** | -1.1 | -1.0 | -1.1 |
|  | 2 month | 0.9 | 0.2 | 0.4 | 0.2 | -0.5 | -1.1 | **-1.7** | -1.6 | -1.7 |
|  | 3 month | 0.5 | -0.2 | 0.0 | -0.2 | -0.9 | -1.5 | -2.1 | **-2.0** | -2.1 |
|  | 4 month | 0.3 | -0.4 | -0.2 | -0.3 | -1.1 | -1.7 | -2.2 | -2.1 | **-2.2** |

trough. The excess returns are measured relative to a buy-and-hold stock strategy of the same risk as the timing strategies employed previously.

In the postwar period, the excess return is minimal over a buy-and-hold strategy if investors switch into bills at the peak and into stocks at the trough of the business cycle. In fact, investors switching into bills just one month after the business cycle peak and back into stocks just one month *after* the business cycle trough would have lost 0.6 percent per year compared to the benchmark buy-and-hold strategy.

Interestingly, it is more important to be able to forecast troughs of the business cycle than it is peaks. An investor who buys stocks before the trough of the business cycle gains more than an investor who sells stocks an equal number of months before the business-cycle peak.

The maximum excess return of 4.8 percent per year is obtained by investing in bills four months before the business-cycle peak and in stocks four months before the business-cycle troughs. The strategy of switching between bills and stocks gains almost 30 basis points ($^{30}/_{100}$ of a percentage point) in average annual return for *each week* during the four-month period in which investors can predict the business-cycle turning point.

The extra returns from successfully forecasting the business cycle are impressive. An increase of 1.8 percent per year in returns, achieved by predicting the business-cycle peak and trough only one month before it occurs, will increase your wealth by over 60 percent over any buy-and-hold strategy over 30 years. If you can predict four months in advance, the annual increase of 4.8 percent in your returns will more than triple your wealth over the same time period compared to a buy-and-hold strategy.

## HOW HARD IS IT TO PREDICT THE BUSINESS CYCLE?

Billions of dollars of resources are spent trying to forecast the business cycle. The previous section showed that it is not surprising that Wall Street employs so many economists desperately trying to predict the next recession or upturn since doing so dramatically increases returns. But the record of predicting exact business-cycle turning points is extremely poor.

Stephen McNees, vice president of the Federal Reserve Bank of Boston, has done extensive research into the accuracy of economic forecasters' predictions. He claims that a major factor in forecast accuracy is the time period over which the forecast was made. He concludes, "Errors were enormous in the severe 1973–75 and 1981–82 recessions, much smaller in the 1980 and 1990 recessions, and generally quite minimal apart from business-cycle turning points."[5] But it is precisely these business-cycle turning points that turn a forecaster into a successful market timer.

The 1974–75 recession was particularly tough for economists. Almost every one of the nearly two dozen of the nation's top economists invited to President Ford's anti-inflation conference in Washington in September 1974 was unaware that the U.S. economy was in the midst of its most severe postwar recession to date. McNees, studying the forecasts issued by five prominent forecasters in 1974, found that the median forecast underestimated GNP growth by six percentage points and underestimated inflation by four percentage points. Early recognition of the 1974 recession was so poor that many economists "jumped the gun" on the next recession, which didn't strike until 1980, but most economists thought had begun early in 1979.

For over 15 years, Robert J. Eggert has been documenting and summarizing the economic forecasts of a noted panel of economic and business experts. These forecasts are compiled and published in a monthly publication entitled *Blue Chip Economic Indicators*.

In July 1979, the *Blue Chip Economic Indicators* indicated that a strong majority of forecasters believed that a recession had already started—forecasting negative GNP growth in the second, third, and fourth quarters of 1979. However, the N.B.E.R. declared that the peak of the business cycle did not occur until January 1980 and that the economy expanded throughout 1979.

By the middle of the next year, forecasters were convinced that a recession had begun. But as late as June 1980 the forecasters believed that the recession had started in February or March and would last about a year, or about one month longer than the average recession. This prediction was reaffirmed in August, when the forecasters indicated that the U.S. economy was about halfway through the recession. In fact, the

5 Stephen K. McNees, "How Large Are Economic Forecast Errors?" in the *New England Economic Review*, July/August 1992, p. 33.

recession had ended the month before, in July, and the 1980 recession turned out to be the shortest in the postwar period.

Forecasters' ability to predict the severe 1981–82 recession, when unemployment reached a postwar high of 10.8 percent, was no better. The headline of the July 1981 *Blue Chip Economic Indicators* read "Economic Exuberance Envisioned for 1982." Instead, 1982 was a disaster. By November 1981 the forecasters realized that the economy had faltered, and optimism turned to pessimism. Most thought that the economy had entered a recession (which it had done four months earlier), nearly 70 percent thought that it would end by the first quarter of 1982 (which it would not, instead tying the record for the longest postwar recession, ending in November), and 90 percent thought that it would be mild, like the 1971 recession, rather than severe—wrong again!

In April 1985, with the expansion well underway, forecasters were queried as to how long the economy would be in an expansion. The average response was 49 months, which would put the peak at December 1986, more than 3½ years before the cycle actually ended. Even the most optimistic forecasters picked spring 1988 as the latest date for the next recession to begin. This question was asked repeatedly throughout 1985 and 1986, and no forecaster imagined that the 1980s expansion would last as long as it did.

Following the stock crash of October 1987, forecasters reduced their GNP growth estimates of 1988 over 1987 from 2.8 percent to 1.9 percent, the largest drop in the 11-year history of the survey. Instead, economic growth in 1988 was nearly 4 percent, as the economy failed to respond to the stock market collapse.

As the expansion continued, belief that a recession was imminent turned into the belief that prosperity was here to stay. The continuing expansion fostered a growing conviction that perhaps the business cycle had been conquered—by either government policy or the "recession-proof" nature of our service-oriented economy. Ed Yardeni, senior economist at Prudential-Bache securities, wrote a "New Wave Manifesto" in late 1988, concluding that self-repairing, growing economies were likely through the rest of the decade.[6] On the eve of one of the worst worldwide recessions in the postwar era, Leonard Silk, senior economics edi-

---

6 "New Wave Economist," the *Los Angeles Times*, March 18, 1990, Business Section, p. 22.

tor of the *New York Times* stated in May of 1990 in an article entitled "Is There Really a Business Cycle?":

> Most economists foresee no recession in 1990 or 1991, and 1992 will be another presidential year, when the odds tip strongly against recession. Japan, West Germany, and most of the other capitalist countries of Europe and Asia are also on a long upward roll, with no end in sight.[7]

By November 1990, *Blue Chip Economic Indicators* reported that the majority of the panel believed the U.S. economy had already, or was about to, slip into a recession. But by then, not only had the economy been in recession for four months, but the stock market had already hit its bottom and was headed upward! Had investors given in to the prevailing pessimism at the time when the recession seemed confirmed, they would have sold after the low was reached and stocks were headed for a strong three-year rally.

As we are in the seventh year of this economic expansion, again talk turns to "new era" economics and economies without recession.[8] Yet the business cycle has been a feature of every market-oriented economy since the Industrial Revolution. Although advances in monetary policy can prevent the type of banking collapse that occurred in the 1930s, it is quite premature to assume that fluctuations in business activity will cease to be a problem. Consumer and business spending are subject to the same psychological swings that influence the financial markets. And stock and bond markets do not show any signs of moderating fluctuations.

## CONCLUDING COMMENTS

Stock values are based on corporate earnings, and the business cycle is a prime determinant of these earnings. The gains of being able to predict the turning points of the economic cycle are enormous. Yet doing so with any precision has eluded economists of all persuasions. And de-

---

7 Leonard Silk, "Is There Really a Business Cycle?" in the New York Times, May 22, 1992, p. D2.
8 *USA Today* reported on September 29, 1997 (p. 10B) that nearly two-thirds of 42 economists polled felt there would be no recession, or if it came, it would be after the year 2000, making this the longest expansion in U.S. history. Also see Steven Weber, "The End of the Business Cycle?" in *Foreign Affairs*, July/August 1997.

spite the growing body of economic statistics, predictions are not getting much better over time.

The worst course an investor can take is to follow the prevailing sentiment about economic activity. This will lead to buying at high prices when times are good and everyone is optimistic, and selling at the low when the recession nears its trough and pessimism prevails.

The lessons to investors are clear. Beating the stock market by analyzing real economic activity requires a degree of prescience that forecasters do not yet have. Turning points are rarely identified until several months after the peak or trough has been reached. By then, it is far too late to act in the market.

CHAPTER

# WORLD EVENTS WHICH IMPACT FINANCIAL MARKETS

*I can predict the motion of heavenly bodies, but not the madness of crowds.*

—Issac Newton

On Thursday, July 24, 1997, less than a half hour before the opening of the New York Stock Exchange, the following lead story about the U.S. stock market appeared on a major newswire service:

> 9:07 A.M.
>
>> U.S. stocks are expected to rise, with better-than-expected earnings from companies like Digital Equipment offsetting concern that stocks are overvalued after rallying to records.

The writer interviewed a bullish trader who noted the great earnings and concluded, "We are going to continue to move higher." But stocks opened weak and continued to fall through the morning. Thirty-one minutes after the opening of trading, the same reporter rewrote the opening of his new lead on the stock market:

> 10:01 A.M.
>
>> U.S. stocks fell as concern that stocks are overvalued after rallying to records offset better-than-expected earnings from companies like Digital Equipment.

This time the writer interviewed a bearish analyst who concluded that market valuations were "stretched" and a 5 to 10 percent correction was in the offing. But then in the afternoon, stocks turned around and rallied strongly, ending the day at record levels. The reporter's closing report on the market began:

> 4:13 P.M.
>
>> U.S. stock rose to records, rebounding from early losses as better-than-expected earnings from companies like Digital Equipment offset concern that prices have risen too far.

These flip-flops in the explanation of the market's movements are not at all unusual. During the day, absolutely no news of any major importance was released. The normal, yet unpredictable, ebb and flow of buyers and sellers in the market caused virtually all the day's ups and downs. There was really no "fundamental explanation," in the sense of identifiable economic or political news to justify the market movements at all.

Yet individuals have a deep psychological need to find fundamental explanations for why the market is doing what it is doing. It is very discomforting for many to learn that most movements in the market are random and do not have any identifiable cause or reason. Most investors find comfort when someone explains to them "why," even though on further thought they often know that the explanation given is unlikely to be the true cause of market move.

Financial reporters are more than happy to fill the need for explanations. The level of the market already reflects the interaction of sellers, or *bears*, who have reasons why the market should go down, and buyers, or *bulls*, who believe they have better reasons why the market should go up. All their views have been collected assiduously in newsrooms. If the market falls, reporters pick a reason from the bearish pile; if the market rises, they choose a reason from the bullish set. Or, as the reporter did above, they can just flip the opening sentence around as the market moves up or down, a process made easy by the word processor.

## WHAT MOVES THE MARKET?

Although you might think that economic and political news should be the major source of market movements, it is surprising how much volatility occurs in the absence of any clearly defined news event. Since 1885, when Dow Jones averages were first formulated, there have been 123 days when the Industrial average has changed by 5 percent or more. Of these, only 28 (or less than one in four) can be identified with a specific world political or economic event, such as war, political changes, or governmental policy shifts. Table 13-1a ranks the 40 largest changes,

**T A B L E   13–1A**

Daily Changes over 5 Percent in the Dow Jones Industrial Average, Excluding 15.34 Percent Change from March 3 Through 15, 1933 for U.S. Bank Holiday (Negative Changes are Boldface and Asterisks Denote Changes Associated with News Items)

| Rank | Date | Change | Rank | Date | Change | Rank | Date | Change |
|---|---|---|---|---|---|---|---|---|
| 1 | Oct 19, 1987 | **-22.61%** | 16 | Dec 18, 1899 | **-8.72%** | 31 | Jul 20, 1933 | **-7.07%** |
| 2* | Oct 6, 1931 | 14.87% | 17 | Oct 8, 1931 | 8.70% | 32* | Oct 13, 1989 | **-6.91%** |
| 3 | Oct 28, 1929 | **-12.82%** | 18 | Aug 12, 1932 | **-8.40%** | 33* | Jul 30, 1914 | **-6.90%** |
| 4 | Oct 30, 1929 | 12.34% | 19 | Mar 14, 1907 | **-8.29%** | 34 | Jan 8, 1988 | **-6.85%** |
| 5 | Oct 29, 1929 | **-11.73%** | 20 | Oct 26, 1987 | **-8.04%** | 35 | Oct 14, 1932 | 6.83% |
| 6 | Sep 21, 1932 | 11.36% | 21 | Jun 10, 1932 | 7.99% | 36 | Nov 11, 1929 | **-6.82%** |
| 7 | Oct 21, 1987 | 10.15% | 22 | Jul 21, 1933 | **-7.84%** | 37* | May 14, 1940 | **-6.80%** |
| 8 | Nov 6, 1929 | **-9.92%** | 23 | Oct 18, 1937 | **-7.75%** | 38 | Oct 5, 1931 | **-6.78%** |
| 9 | Aug 3, 1932 | 9.52% | 24* | Sep 5, 1939 | 7.26% | 39* | May 21, 1940 | **-6.78%** |
| 10* | Feb 11, 1932 | 9.47% | 25* | Feb 1, 1917 | **-7.24%** | 40 | Mar 15, 1907 | 6.70% |
| 11* | Nov 14, 1929 | 9.36% | 26 | Oct 27, 1997 | **-7.18%** | 41* | Jun 20, 1931 | 6.64% |
| 12 | Dec 18, 1931 | 9.35% | 27 | Oct 5, 1932 | **-7.15%** | 42 | Jul 24, 1933 | 6.63% |
| 13 | Feb 13, 1932 | 9.19% | 28 | Jun 3, 1931 | 7.12% | 43* | Jul 26, 1934 | **-6.62%** |
| 14* | May 6, 1932 | 9.08% | 29 | Jan 6, 1932 | 7.12% | 44 | Dec 20, 1895 | **-6.61%** |
| 15* | Apr 19, 1933 | 9.03% | 30 | Sep 24, 1931 | **-7.07%** | 45* | Sep 26, 1955 | **-6.54%** |

and Table 13-1b identifies those changes greater than 5 percent associated with specific events.[1] Also note that four out the five largest moves in the stock market over the past century for which there is a clearly identifiable cause have been directly associated with monetary policy.

Of the 10 largest changes, only two can be attributed to news. The record one-day change in the stock market, the October 19, 1987 drop of 22.61 percent in the Dow Industrials, is not associated with a readily identifiable news event. Since 1940, there have been only two days of big moves where the cause is identified: the 6.54 percent drop on September 26, 1955, when President Eisenhower suffered a heart attack, and the 6.91 percent drop on Friday, October 13, 1989. This latter decline has often been attributed to the collapse of the leveraged buyout of United Airlines, although the market was already down substantially before this news was announced late in the day. It is of interest that there has been no 5 percent drop during U.S. involvement in any war during this century.

Nevertheless, there can be sharp disagreement over the cause of market moves. On November 15, 1991, when the Dow fell over 120 points or nearly 4 percent, *Investors Business Daily* titled an article about the market "Dow Plunges 120 in a Scary Stock Sell-off: Biotechs,

---

1 This expands the research originally published in David M. Cutler, James M. Poterba, and Lawrence H. Summers, "What Moves Stock Prices," *Journal of Portfolio Management*, Spring 1989, pp. 4-12.

**T A B L E   13–1B**

Largest News-Related Movements in the Dow Jones Industrial Average (Negative Changes are Boldface)

| Rank | Date | Change | News Headline |
|------|------|--------|---------------|
| 2 | Oct 6, 1931 | 14.87% | Hoover Urges $500M Pool to Help Banks |
| 10 | Feb 11, 1932 | 9.47% | Liberalization of Fed Discount Policy |
| 11 | Nov 14, 1929 | 9.36% | Fed Lowers Discount Rate/Tax Cut Proposed |
| 14 | May 6, 1932 | 9.08% | U.S. Steel Negotiates 15% Wage Cut |
| 15 | Apr 19, 1933 | 9.03% | U.S. Drops Gold Standard |
| 24 | Sep 5, 1939 | 7.26% | World War II Begins in Europe |
| 25 | **Feb 1, 1917** | **-7.24%** | **Germany announces unrestricted submarine warfare** |
| 32 | **Oct 13, 1989** | **-6.91%** | **United Airline Buy-out Collapses** |
| 33 | **Jul 30, 1914** | **-6.90%** | **Outbreak of World War I** |
| 37 | **May 14, 1940** | **-6.80%** | **Germans Invade Holland** |
| 39 | **May 21, 1940** | **-6.78%** | **Allied Reverses in France** |
| 41 | Jun 20, 1931 | 6.64% | Hoover Advocates Foreign Debt Moratorium |
| 43 | **Jul 26, 1934** | **-6.62%** | **Fighting in Austria; Italy mobilizes** |
| 45 | **Sep 26, 1955** | **-6.54%** | **Eisenhower Suffers Heart Attack** |
| 50 | **Jul 26, 1893** | **-6.31%** | **Erie Railroad Bankrupt** |
| 64 | Oct 31, 1929 | 5.82% | Fed Lowers Discount Rate |
| 65 | **Jun 16, 1930** | **-5.81%** | **Hoover to Sign Tariff Bill** |
| 66 | Apr 20, 1933 | 5.80% | Continued Rally on Dropping of Gold Standard |
| 71 | May 2, 1898 | 5.64% | Dewey Defeats Spanish |
| 74 | March 28, 1898 | 5.56% | Dispatches of Armistice with Spain |
| 82 | Dec 22, 1916 | 5.47% | Lansing Denies U.S. Near War |
| 85 | **Dec 12, 1896** | **-5.42%** | **Senate votes for Free Cuba** |
| 86 | **Feb 25, 1933** | **-5.40%** | **Maryland Bank Holiday** |
| 90 | Oct 23, 1933 | 5.37% | Roosevelt Devalues Dollar |
| 92 | **Dec 21, 1916** | **-5.35%** | **Sec. of State Lansing implies U.S. Near War** |
| 101 | Apr 9, 1938 | 5.25% | Congress Passes Bill Taxing U.S. Government Bond Interest |
| 122 | Oct 20, 1931 | 5.03% | ICC Raises Rail Rates |
| 123 | **Mar 31, 1932** | **-5.02%** | **House Proposes Stock Sales Tax** |

Programs, Expiration and Congress Get the Blame."[2] In contrast, a New York writer for the London *Financial Times* titled a front-page article "Wall Street Drops 120 Points on Concern at Russian Moves." What is interesting is that such news, specifically that the Russian government had suspended oil licenses and taken over the gold supplies, was not mentioned even once in the U.S. article! That one major newspaper can highlight "reasons" that another does not even report illustrates the difficulty of finding fundamental explanations for the movements of markets.

## UNCERTAINTY AND THE MARKET

The market fears uncertainty or any event that jars investors from their customary framework for analyzing the world. As noted previously,

---

2 Virginia Munger Kahn, *Investors Business Daily*, November 16, 1991, p. 1.

President Eisenhower's heart attack on September 26, 1955 caused a 6.54 percent decline in the Dow Industrials, the seventh largest in the postwar period. The fall was a clear sign of Eisenhower's popularity with the market. President Kennedy's assassination on November 22, 1963, caused the Dow Industrials to drop 2.9 percent and persuaded the New York Stock Exchange to close two hours early to prevent more panic selling. Yet, when the market reopened the following Tuesday and Lyndon Johnson, as was expected, took over the reins of government, the market soared 4.5 percent, representing one of the best days in the postwar period.

The market almost always declines in reaction to sudden, unexpected changes related to the presidency. When William McKinley was shot on September 14, 1901, the market dropped by more than 4 percent. But stocks regained all of their losses on the following trading day. The death of Warren Harding caused a milder setback, which was soon erased. Sell-offs such as these provide good opportunities for investors to step up and buy stocks because the market usually reverses itself quickly following the change in leadership.[3]

## DEMOCRATS AND REPUBLICANS

It is well known that the stock market prefers Republicans to Democrats. Most corporate executives and stock traders are Republicans, and many Republican policies are perceived to be favorable to stock prices and capital formation. Democrats are perceived to be less amenable to favorable tax treatment of capital gains and more in favor of regulation and income redistribution. Yet the stock market actually does better under Democrats than Republicans.

Figure 13-1 shows the performance of the Dow Jones Industrials during every administration since Grover Cleveland was elected in 1888. The greatest bear market in history occurred during the Hoover administration, while stocks did quite well under Franklin Roosevelt, despite the fact that he was frequently reviled in boardrooms and brokerage houses around the country.

Table 13-2 records the performance of the Dow Industrials during each presidential term since 1888. The immediate reaction of the mar-

---

3 But there are some who the market never forgives. Stocks rallied over 4 percent in the week following the news of the death of Franklin Roosevelt, who was never a favorite on Wall Street.

## FIGURE  13–1

The Dow Jones Industrial Average and Presidential Terms (Lines Represent a Change of Administration, Dark Lines Represent a Change of Party, and Shaded Areas Represent a Democratic President in Office

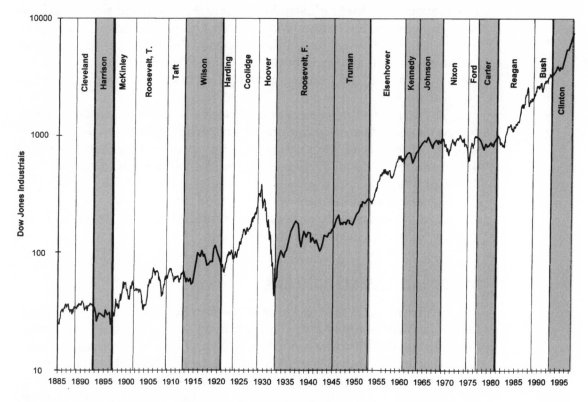

ket—the day before the election to the day after—does indeed conform to the fact that investors like Republicans better than Democrats. Since 1888, the market fell an average of 0.5 percent on the day following Democratic victories, but rose by 0.8 percent on the day following a Republican victory. But the market's reaction to the Republican's success in presidential elections has been muted since World War II. There have been occasions, like Clinton's second-term election victory, when the market soared because the Republicans kept control of Congress, not because Clinton was reelected.

It is also instructive to examine the returns in the first, second, third, and fourth year of a presidential term, also displayed in Table

**TABLE 13-2**

Stock Returns During Presidential Administrations, Measured in Percent by S & P Total Return Index
(Italics Represent Democratic Administrations)

| President's Name | Party | Election Date | From: 1 day before To: 1 day after | First Year of Term | Second Year of Term | Third Year of Term | Fourth Year of Term |
|---|---|---|---|---|---|---|---|
| Harrison | R | 11/6/1888 | 0.4 | 6.9 | -6.2 | 18.7 | 6.2 |
| *Cleveland* | *D* | *11/8/1892* | *-0.5* | *-19.1* | *3.2* | *5.0* | *3.0* |
| McKinley | R | 11/3/1896 | 2.7 | 20.2 | 29.1 | 3.8 | 21.2 |
| McKinley | R | 11/6/1900 | 3.3 | 19.7 | 8.3 | -17.4 | 31.4 |
| Roosevelt T. | R | 11/8/1904 | 1.3 | 21.3 | 0.8 | -24.5 | 38.9 |
| Taft | R | 11/3/1908 | 2.4 | 16.4 | -3.6 | 3.4 | 7.3 |
| *Wilson* | *D* | *11/5/1912* | *1.8* | *-5.1* | *-5.9* | *31.1* | *8.7* |
| *Wilson* | *D* | *11/7/1916* | *-0.4* | *-18.5* | *17.1* | *19.6* | *-14.3* |
| Harding | R | 11/2/1920 | -0.6 | 9.2 | 29.6 | 5.1 | 26.6 |
| Coolidge | R | 11/4/1924 | 1.2 | 25.7 | 11.6 | 37.5 | 43.6 |
| Hoover | R | 11/6/1928 | 1.2 | -8.4 | -24.9 | -43.3 | -8.2 |
| *Roosevelt F.* | *D* | *11/8/1932* | *-4.5* | *54.0* | *-1.4* | *47.7* | *33.9* |
| *Roosevelt F.* | *D* | *11/3/1936* | *2.3* | *-35.0* | *31.1* | *-0.4* | *-9.8* |
| *Roosevelt F.* | *D* | *11/5/1940* | *-2.4* | *-11.6* | *20.3* | *25.9* | *19.8* |
| *Roosevelt F.* | *D* | *11/7/1944* | *-0.3* | *36.4* | *-8.1* | *5.7* | *5.5* |
| *Truman* | *D* | *11/2/1948* | *-3.8* | *18.8* | *31.7* | *24.0* | *18.4* |
| Eisenhower | R | 11/4/1952 | 0.4 | -1.0 | 52.6 | 31.6 | 6.6 |
| Eisenhower | R | 11/6/1956 | -0.9 | -10.8 | 43.4 | 12.0 | 0.5 |
| *Kennedy* | *D* | *11/8/1960* | *0.8* | *26.9* | *-8.7* | *22.8* | *16.5* |
| *Johnson* | *D* | *11/3/1964* | *-0.2* | *12.5* | *-10.1* | *24.0* | *11.1* |
| Nixon | R | 11/5/1968 | 0.3 | -8.5 | 4.0 | 14.3 | 19.0 |
| Nixon | R | 11/7/1972 | -0.1 | -14.7 | -26.5 | 37.2 | 23.8 |
| *Carter* | *D* | *11/2/1976* | *-1.0* | *-7.2* | *6.6* | *18.4* | *32.4* |
| Reagan | R | 11/4/1980 | 1.7 | -4.9 | 21.4 | 22.5 | 6.3 |
| Reagan | R | 11/6/1984 | -0.9 | 32.2 | 18.5 | 5.2 | 16.8 |
| Bush | R | 11/8/1988 | -0.4 | 31.5 | -3.2 | 30.5 | 7.7 |
| *Clinton* | *D* | *11/3/1992* | *-0.9* | *10.0* | *1.3* | *37.6* | *23.0* |
| *Clinton* | *D* | *11/5/1996* | *2.6* | *33.4* | - | - | - |
| Average from 1888 to 1997 | Democratic | | -0.5 | 7.3 | 6.4 | 21.8 | 12.3 |
| | Republican | | 0.8 | 9.0 | 10.3 | 9.1 | 16.5 |
| | Overall | | 0.2 | 8.2 | 8.6 | 14.7 | 14.7 |
| Average from 1948 to 1997 | Democratic | | -0.4 | 15.7 | 4.2 | 25.4 | 20.3 |
| | Republican | | 0.0 | 3.4 | 15.7 | 21.9 | 11.5 |
| | Overall | | -0.2 | 9.1 | 10.9 | 23.3 | 15.2 |

13-2. Since World War II, the returns are clearly the best in the *third* year of a presidential term. The third year would also have been the best over the past century if it had not been for the disastrous 43 percent fall in the market in 1931 during the third term of Hoover's ill-fated administration.

Why the third year stands out is not clear. One would think that the fourth year of a presidential term, when the administration might put pressure on the Fed to stimulate the economy for the upcoming election, should be the best year for stocks. But the fourth year, although good, is clearly not the best. Perhaps the market *anticipates* favorable economic policies in the election year, causing stock prices to rise the year before.

The superior performance under the Democrats in recent years is documented in Table 13-3. This table records the total real and nominal returns in the stock market, as well as the rate of inflation, under Democratic and Republican administrations. Since 1888, the market has fared slightly better in nominal terms under Democrats than Republicans, but since inflation has been lower when the Republicans have held office, real stock returns have been higher under Republicans than Democrats. This has not been true over the past 50 years, when the market performed far better under the Democrats whether or not inflation is factored in. Perhaps this is why the market's reaction to a Democratic presidential victory has not been as negative in recent years as it was in the past.

## STOCKS AND WAR

Since 1885, the U.S. economy has been at war or on the sidelines of a world war about one-fifth of the time. The stock market does equally well in nominal returns whether there is war or peace, but inflation has averaged nearly 6 percent during wartime and less than 2 percent during peacetime, so the real returns on stocks during peacetime greatly outstrip those during wars.

It is of interest that the volatility of the market, measured as the monthly range of the Dow Industrials, has actually been *greater*, on average, during peacetime than during war. The greatest volatility in U.S. markets occurred in the late 1920s and early 1930s, well before the United States was engaged in a worldwide conflict. Only during World War I and the short Gulf War did stocks have higher volatility than average.

In theory, war should have a profound influence on stock prices. Governments commandeer tremendous resources, while high taxes

**TABLE 13–3**

Presidential Administrations and Stock Returns (Stock Returns Taken from Election Date or Date of Taking Office, Whichever is Earlier) 1888–1997

| President's Name | Party | Date | Months in Office | Annualized Nominal Stock Return | Annualized Inflation | Annualized Real Return |
|---|---|---|---|---|---|---|
| Harrison | R | 11/88 - 10/92 | 48 | 5.74 | 0.04 | 5.70 |
| Cleveland | D | 11/92 - 10/96 | 48 | -3.31 | -1.91 | -1.43 |
| McKinley | R | 11/96 - 8/01 | 58 | 20.66 | 0.00 | 20.66 |
| Roosevelt T. | R | 9/01 - 10/08 | 86 | 4.81 | 1.39 | 3.38 |
| Taft | R | 11/08 - 10/12 | 48 | 7.54 | 0.82 | 6.67 |
| Wilson | D | 11/12 - 10/20 | 96 | 4.68 | 9.42 | -4.33 |
| Harding | R | 11/20 - 7/23 | 33 | 5.48 | -4.05 | 9.93 |
| Coolidge | R | 8/23 - 10/28 | 63 | 28.04 | 0.12 | 27.88 |
| Hoover | R | 11/28 - 10/32 | 48 | -20.42 | -6.29 | -15.08 |
| Roosevelt F. | D | 11/32 - 3/45 | 149 | 11.52 | 2.36 | 8.94 |
| Truman | D | 4/45 - 10/52 | 91 | 14.66 | 5.54 | 8.64 |
| Eisenhower | R | 11/52 - 10/60 | 96 | 14.96 | 1.35 | 13.42 |
| Kennedy | D | 11/60 - 10/63 | 36 | 15.15 | 1.11 | 13.88 |
| Johnson | D | 11/63 - 10/68 | 60 | 10.39 | 2.77 | 7.42 |
| Nixon | R | 11/68 - 7/74 | 69 | -1.32 | 6.03 | -6.93 |
| Ford | R | 8/74 - 10/76 | 27 | 17.21 | 7.27 | 9.27 |
| Carter | D | 11/76 - 10/80 | 48 | 11.04 | 10.02 | 0.93 |
| Reagan | R | 11/80 - 10/88 | 96 | 15.18 | 4.46 | 10.26 |
| Bush | R | 11/88 - 10/92 | 48 | 14.44 | 4.22 | 9.81 |
| Clinton | D | 11/92 - 12/97 | 62 | 21.42 | 2.53 | 18.42 |
| Average from 1888 to 1997 | Democrat | | 45.0% | 10.75 | 4.26 | 6.33 |
| | Republican | | 55.0% | 9.97 | 1.54 | 8.28 |
| Overall | | | | 10.32 | 2.76 | 7.40 |
| Average from 1948 to 1997 | Democrat | | 44.0% | 15.27 | 3.76 | 11.22 |
| | Republican | | 56.0% | 11.79 | 4.09 | 7.49 |
| Overall | | | | 13.29 | 3.95 | 9.10 |

and huge government borrowings compete with investors' demand for stock. Whole industries are nationalized to further the war effort. Moreover, if loss of war is deemed a possibility, then stocks could well decline as the victors impose sanctions on the vanquished. However, as demonstrated in Chapter 1, the economies of Germany and Japan were quickly restored to health and stocks boomed following World War II.

## The World Wars

The volatility of the market during World War I greatly exceeded that during World War II. The market rose nearly 100 percent during the early stages of World War I, fell 40 percent when the United States became involved in the hostilities, and finally rallied when the Great War ended. In contrast, during the six years of World War II, the market never deviated more than 32 percent from its prewar level.

The outbreak of World War I precipitated a panic as European investors scrambled to get out of stocks and into gold and cash. After the declaration of war by Austria-Hungary on Serbia on July 28, 1914, all the major European stock exchanges closed. The European panic spread to New York, and the Dow-Jones Industrials closed down nearly 7 percent on Thursday, July 30, the most since the 8.3 percent drop during the Panic of 1907. Minutes before the opening of the New York Stock Exchange on Friday, the exchange voted to close for an indefinite period.

The market did not reopen until December. Never before has the New York Stock Exchange been closed for such an extended period. Emergency trades were permitted, but only by approval of a special committee and only at prices at or above the last trade before the exchange closed. Even then, trading prohibition was observed in the breach as illegal trades were made outside the exchange (on the curb) at prices that continued to decline through October. Unofficially, by autumn prices were said to be 15 to 20 percent below the July closing.

It is ironic that the only extended period during which the New York Stock Exchange was closed occurred when the United States was not at war or in any degree of financial or economic distress. In fact, when the exchange was closed, traders realized that the United States might be the beneficiary of the European conflict. Once investors realized who was going to make the munitions and provide raw materials to the belligerents, public interest in stocks soared.

By the time the exchange reopened on December 12, prices were rising rapidly. The Dow Industrials finished the historical Saturday session about 5 percent higher than the closing prices on the previous July. The rally continued, and 1915 records the best single-year increase in the history of the Dow Industrials, as stocks rose a record 82 percent.

The message of the great boom of 1915 was not lost on traders a generation later. When World War II erupted, investors took their cue from what happened at the beginning of the previous world war. When Great Britain declared war on Germany on September 3, 1939, the rise was so explosive that the Tokyo Exchange was forced to close early.

When the market opened in New York, a buying panic erupted. The Dow Industrials gained over 7 percent and even the European stock exchanges were firm when trading reopened.

The enthusiasm that followed the onset of World War II quickly faded. The day before the Japanese attacked Pearl Harbor, the Dow was down 25 percent from its 1939 high and still less than one-third its 1929 peak. Stocks fell 3.5 percent on the day following Pearl Harbor and continued to fall until they hit a low on April 28, 1942, when Germany invaded and quickly subdued France.

But when the war turned around, the market began to climb. By the time Germany signed its unconditional surrender on May 7, 1945, the Dow Industrials were 20 percent above the prewar level. The detonation of the atomic bomb over Hiroshima, a pivotal event in the history of warfare, caused stocks to surge 1.7 percent as investors recognized the end of the war was near. But World War II did not prove as profitable for investors as the First World War, as the Dow was up only 30 percent during the six years from the German invasion of Poland to V-J Day.

## Post-1945 Conflicts

The Korean War took investors by surprise. When North Korea invaded its southern neighbor on June 25, 1950, the Dow fell 4.65 percent, greater than the day following Pearl Harbor. But the market reaction to the growing conflict was contained, and stocks never fell more than 12 percent below their prewar level.

The War in Vietnam was the longest and least popular of all U.S. wars. The starting point for U.S. involvement in the conflict can be placed at August 2, 1965, when two American destroyers were reportedly attacked in the Gulf of Tonkin.

One and a half years after the Gulf of Tonkin incident, the Dow reached an all-time high of 995, more than 18 percent above its prewar level. But it fell nearly 30 percent in the following months after the Fed tightened credit to curb inflation. By the time American troop strength reached its peak early in 1968, the market had recovered. Two years later, the market fell again when Nixon sent troops into Cambodia, and soaring interest rates coupled with a looming recession sent the market down nearly 25 percent from its prewar point.

The Peace Pact between the North Vietnamese and the Americans was signed in Paris on January 27, 1973. But the gains made by investors over the eight years of war were quite small, as the market was held back by rising inflation, interest rates, and other problems not directly related to the Vietnamese conflict.

If the war in Vietnam was the longest American war, the war against Iraq in the Gulf was the shortest. It began on August 2, 1990, when Iraq invaded Kuwait, sending oil prices skyward and sparking a U.S. military buildup in Saudi Arabia. The rise in oil prices combined with an already slowing U.S. economy to drive the United States deeper into a recession. The stock market fell precipitously and by October 11 the Dow slumped over 18 percent from its prewar levels.

U.S. offensive action began on January 17, 1991. It was the first major war fought in a world where markets for oil, gold, and U.S. government bonds were traded around the clock in Tokyo, Singapore, and London. The markets judged the victors in a matter of hours. Bonds sold off in Tokyo for a few minutes following the news of the U.S. bombing of Baghdad, but the stunning reports of the Allied successes sent bonds and Japanese stocks straight upward in the next few minutes. Oil prices, which were being traded in the Far East, collapsed, as Brent crude fell from $29 a barrel before hostilities to $20 the next day.

On the following day, stock prices soared around the world. The Dow jumped 115 points, and there were large gains throughout Europe and Asia. By the time the United States deployed ground troops to invade Kuwait, the market had known for two months that victory was at hand. The war ended on February 28, and by the first week in March the Dow was more than 18 percent higher than when the war started.

## SUMMARY

When reviewing the causes of major market movements, it is sobering to realize that less than one-quarter can be associated with a news event of major political or economic import. Politics, war, and peace are major backdrops of market action, but few of the big moves occur for these reasons. Surprisingly, volatility during wartime has been less than during peacetime.

All this confirms the unpredictability of the market and difficulty in predicting the major trends. Those who sold in panic at the outbreak of World War I missed out on the greatest year in the market. The victories in World War II did little to revive the market since investors were still fearful of a depression that might follow the end of the war. The postwar boom had to await the 1950s and 1960s, when investors became convinced that inflation, and not depression, was the theme of the future.

# CHAPTER

# STOCKS, BONDS AND THE FLOW OF ECONOMIC DATA

*The thing that most affects the stock market is everything.*
**—James Palysted Wood, 1966**

It's 8:28 A.M. eastern standard time, Friday, July 5, 1996. Normally a trading day wedged between a major U.S. holiday and a weekend is slow, with little volume or price movement. But not today. Traders around the world have anxiously gathered around their terminals, eyes riveted on the scrolling news that displays thousands of headlines every day. It is just two minutes before the most important announcement each month—the U.S. employment statistics.

All week stock, bond, and currency traders have anticipated this day. The Dow has been trading within a few points of its all-time high, reached at the end of May. But interest rates have been rising, giving traders cause for concern. The seconds tick down. At 8:30 sharp, the words come across the screen:

> PAYROLL UP 239,000, UNEMPLOYMENT AT SIX-YEAR LOW OF 5.3
> PERCENT, WAGES UP 9 CENTS AN HOUR, BIGGEST INCREASE IN
> 30 YEARS.

President Clinton hailed the economic news, claiming "We have the most solid American economy in a generation; wages for American workers are finally on the rise again."

But the financial markets were stunned. Figures 14-1a through 14-1d tell the story. Long-term bond prices immediately collapsed on both domestic and foreign exchanges as traders expected higher interest rates.

**FIGURE  14–1**

Market Reaction to Strong Employment Report, July 5, 1996

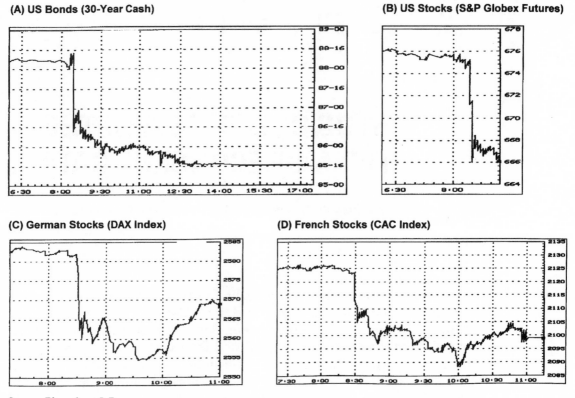

(A) US Bonds (30-Year Cash)

(B) US Stocks (S&P Globex Futures)

(C) German Stocks (DAX Index)

(D) French Stocks (CAC Index)

Source: Bloomberg L.P.

Rates on long and short-term bonds climbed nearly a quarter point. Although the stock market would not open for an hour, S & P 500 Index futures, which represent claims on this benchmark index and are described in detail in the next chapter, fell from 676 to 656, equivalent to about 80 points on the Dow-Jones. European markets, already open, immediately sold off. The benchmark DAX index in Germany, CAC in France, and FT-SE in Britain instantly fell up to 2 percent. Within seconds, world equity markets lost $200 billion and world bond markets fell at least as much.

This episode demonstrates that what most of the population interprets as "good" news often causes security prices to fall, and the news is instantaneously broadcast and processed around the world. The reaction of the markets is strong because the employment statistics contain the most comprehensive and timely data on what is happening in the economy, and provide the best clue as to the future direction of the Federal Reserve's monetary policy.

News moves markets. The timing of much news is unpredictable, like war, political developments, and natural disasters. But most news, especially data about the economy, comes at preannounced times that have been set a year in advance. There are over 300 *scheduled* releases of economic data each year—mostly by government agencies, but increasingly by private firms. Virtually all the announcements deal with economic growth and inflation, and all have the potential to move the market significantly.

Economic data not only frame the way traders view the economy, but also impact traders' expectations of how the Federal Reserve will implement its monetary policy. Stronger economic growth or higher inflation increases the probability that the Fed will either tighten monetary policy or stop easing credit. Economic releases influence the expectations of traders about the future course of interest rates, the economy, and ultimately stock prices.

## PRINCIPLES OF MARKET REACTION

Markets respond to the *difference* between what the participants in the financial markets expect to be announced and what is announced. Whether the news is, by itself, good or bad is of no importance. If the market *expects* that the employment release will report that 200,000 jobs were lost last month, but the report shows that only 100,000 jobs were lost, this will be considered "strong economic news" by the financial markets—having about the same effect on financial markets as a gain of 200,000 jobs when the market expected only 100,000.

The reason why markets react only to data that differ from expectations is that the prices of securities in actively traded markets already include *expected* information. If a firm is expected to report bad earnings, then the market has already priced the stock to reflect this gloomy information. If the earnings report is not as bad as anticipated, the price will rise on the announcement. The same principle applies to the reaction of bonds, stocks, and foreign exchange to economic data.

To understand why the market moves the way is does, you must identify the *market expectation* for the data released. The market expectation, often referred to as the *consensus* estimate, is gathered by news and research organizations. They poll economists, professional forecasters, traders, and other market participants for their estimate of an upcoming government or private release. The results of their survey are sent to the financial press and widely reported in many major newspapers.[1]

## INFORMATION CONTENT OF DATA RELEASES

The economic data are analyzed for their implications for future economic growth, inflation, and Federal Reserve policy. The following principle summarizes the reaction of the bond markets to the release of data relating to economic growth:

*Stronger-than-expected economic growth increases both long- and short-term interest rates. Weaker-than-expected economic growth causes interest rates to fall.*

Faster economic growth raises interest rates for several reasons. First, a stronger economy increases private loan demands. Consumers feel more confident about the economy and are more willing to borrow against future income. Faster economic growth also motivates firms to expand production to meet increased consumer demand. As a result, both firms and consumers increase their demand for credit. The increase in credit demand pushes interest rates higher in the bond market.

A second reason why interest rates rise with a stronger-than-expected economic report is that such growth might be inflationary, especially if it is near the end of an economic cycle. Growth associated with increases in productivity, which often occurs in the early and middle stages of a business expansion, is rarely inflationary.

Inflationary fears were the principal reason why interest rates soared when the Labor Department released its report on July 5. Traders feared that the large increase in wages caused by the tight labor markets and falling unemployment rate would cause inflation, a nemesis to both the bond and the stock market.

These reports have great implications for the actions of the Federal Reserve and therefore central banks around the world. A rise in inflation will make it likely that the Federal Reserve will tighten credit in response. I analyzed in Chapter 10 how the Federal Reserve controls the short-term interest rate through the federal funds rate. If aggregate demand is expanding too rapidly relative to supply, the Fed can use its open market operations to drain reserves from the banking system in order to raise interest rates and prevent the economy from overheating.

---

1 Usually both the median and range of estimates are reported. The consensus estimate does vary a bit from service to service, but the estimates are usually quite close.

Of course, in the case of a weaker-than-expected employment report, the markets will respond favorably, especially if it is associated with lower inflationary fears and comes late in the economic cycle. Such a report increases the probability that the Fed will add reserves to the system, lowering interest rates and increasing the demand for stocks and bonds.

## ECONOMIC GROWTH AND STOCK PRICES

It surprises the general public (and often the financial press) when a strong economic report actually sends the stock market lower. But economic growth has two important implications, and each tugs the stock market in the opposite direction. A strong economy increases future earnings of firms. This is bullish for stocks, but it also raises interest rates, and bonds are the major financial asset that competes with stocks for investors' funds. If interest rates rise, bonds become more attractive, which means that stock prices must fall to attract buyers. On the other hand, a weak economic report lowers future expected earnings, but since interest rates also decline, stock prices might move up.

Sometimes the opposing forces of interest rates and earning prospects will fight each other to a standstill through the day. The impact of interest rate changes often dominates stock trading right on the announcement, while the implications of a strong report for corporate earnings often, but certainly not always, affect the market later.

At the exact time of economic announcements, many stock traders, especially those trading in the stock index futures market, look at the movements in the bond market to guide their trading. This is particularly true of portfolio managers who actively apportion their portfolio between stocks and bonds on the basis of interest rates and expected returns. When bond prices rise after a weak economic report, these investors are ready to buy stocks. Later, as more stock investors recognize that the weak employment report means lower future earnings, many are apt to be more bearish about equity prospects. The stock market often gyrates wildly through such a day as investors digest the implications of the data for stock earnings and interest rates.

## THE EMPLOYMENT REPORT

The employment report compiled by the Bureau of Labor Statistics (BLS) is the key release each month. Of the great importance to traders is the change in the nonfarm payroll (*nonfarm* because the number of farm workers is very volatile and not associated with cyclical economic trends). The payroll survey, sometimes called the "establishment survey," collects payroll data from nearly 400,000 business establishments, covering nearly 50 million workers, about 40 percent of the total. It is this survey that most forecasters use to judge the future course of the economy.

The unemployment rate, however, which is released with the non-farm payroll, usually gets the top billing in the evening news and the financial press. The unemployment rate is determined from an entirely different survey than the payroll data. The unemployment rate is calculated from a "household survey," which contacts about 60,000 households and asks, among other questions, whether anyone in the household has "actively" sought work over the past four weeks. Those who answer in the affirmative are classified as unemployed. The unemployed, divided by the total labor force, yields the unemployment rate. The labor force in the United States, defined as those employed plus unemployed, comprises about two thirds of the adult population, a ratio which has risen steadily as more women have successfully sought work.

Because the payroll and household data are based on totally different surveys, it is not unusual for payroll employment to go up at the same time that the unemployment rate rises, and vice versa. This is because the payroll survey counts jobs, but the household survey counts people, so workers with two jobs are counted once in the household survey but twice in the payroll survey.[2] Furthermore, increases in the number seeking work from the labor market pool will increase the unemployment rate. In fact, it is well known that the unemployment rate often rises in the early stages of an economic recovery due to the influx of job-seekers into an improved labor market.

For these reasons, economists and forecasters have long dismissed the unemployment rate as unimportant in forecasting the business cycle. But this does not diminish the *political* importance of the unemployment rate. It is an easily understood number that represents the fraction of the workforce looking for but not finding work. The public looks more to this rate than any other to judge the health of the economy. As a result, politically motivated pressures can bear on Congress, as well as the Federal Reserve, whenever the unemployment rate rises.

---

2 Early in 1994 the household survey was improved to include this question.

## THE CYCLE OF ANNOUNCEMENTS

The employment report is just one of several dozen economic announcements that come out every month. Table 14-1 displays a typical month and the usual release dates for the data. The number of asterisks represents the importance of the report to the financial market.

The employment statistics are the culmination of important data on economic growth that come out around the turn of the month. On the first business day of each month, a survey by the National Association of Purchasing Managers, or the NAPM, is released. This survey has become increasingly important at providing information to help forecast the all-important employment report.

The NAPM report surveys 250 purchasing agents of manufacturing companies and inquires as to whether orders, production, employment, etc. are rising or falling. A reading of 50 means that half the firms report rising activity and half report falling activity. A reading of 53 or 54 is the sign of a normally expanding economy. A reading of 60 repre-

**T A B L E  14–1**

Monthly Economic Calendar

| Monday | Tuesday | Wednesday | Thursday | Friday |
|---|---|---|---|---|
| **1**<br>10:00 NAPM** | **2**<br>8:30 Leading Economic<br>Indicator* (2 months lag) | **3** | **4**<br>8:30 Jobless Claims**<br><br>4:30 Money Supply* | **5**<br>8:30 Employment Report**** |
| **8** | **9** | **10** | **11**<br>8:30 Jobless Claims**<br><br>4:30 Money Supply* | **12**<br>8:30 Retail Sales**<br>8:30 Producer Prices**** |
| **15** | **16**<br>8:30 Consumer Prices**** | **17**<br>8:30 Housing Starts***<br>9:15 Industrial Production* | **18**<br>8:30 Merchandise Trade*<br>8:30 Jobless Claims**<br>4:30 Money Supply* | **19**<br>10:00 Philadelphia Fed Rep*<br>10:00 Consumer Expect.**<br>(Univ. of Mich., Prelim.) |
| **22** | **23**<br>8:30 Durable Goods Orders** | **24** | **25**<br>8:30 Jobless Claims**<br><br>4:30 Money Supply* | **26**<br>8:30 Gross Dom. Prod.***† |
| **29** | **30**<br>10:00 Consumer Expect.<br>(Conference Board)*** | **31**<br>10:00 Chicago Purchasing<br>Managers** | | |

†First report of quarter (January, April, July, and October) is of moderate importance.  Other months' GDP reports of minor importance.
**Stars Rank Importance to Market (**** = most important)**

sent a strong economy where three-fifths of the firms are experiencing growth. A reading below 50 represents a contracting manufacturing sector, and a reading below 40 is almost always a sign of recession.

Because of the huge importance of the monthly employment report, there is much pressure on traders to obtain earlier data that might give some hint as to the state of the economy and thereby improve the estimate of the monthly payroll change. The NAPM survey fulfills this function. Of particular importance in the NAPM survey is the employment category, for this is the first comprehensive picture of the labor market and provides a clue as to what might be revealed in the important manufacturing category of the employment report.

But traders do have access to even earlier data: the Chicago Purchasing Managers report comes out on the last business day of the previous month, the day before the NAPM report. The Chicago area is well-diversified in manufacturing, so about two-thirds of the time the Chicago index will move in the same direction as the national index.

And if you want an even earlier reading on the economy, there are the consumer sentiment indicators: one from the University of Michigan and another from the Conference Board, a business trade association. These surveys query consumers about their current financial situation and their expectations of the future. The Conference Board survey, released on the last Tuesday of the month, is considered a good early indicator of consumer spending. The University of Michigan index was for many years not released until the month following the survey, but pressure for early data has persuaded the University to release a preliminary report to compete with that of the Conference Board.

## Inflation Reports

Although the employment report forms the capstone of the news about economic growth, the market knows that the Federal Reserve is also preoccupied with inflation. The Fed does not normally ease credit unless it is assured that inflationary pressures are under control. The central bank recognizes that it is the guardian of the currency and cannot ignore inflation. Some of the earliest signals of these pressures arrive with the mid-month inflation statistics.

The first monthly inflation release is the producer price index, or the PPI, formerly the wholesale price index. The PPI measures the prices received by producers at the first commercial sale, usually to retailers. The prices of consumer goods represent about three-quarters of the PPI, while the prices of capital goods comprise the rest. About 15 percent of the PPI is energy-related.

The second monthly announcement, which follows the PPI by a day or so, is the all-important consumer price index, or CPI. In contrast to the producer price index, the CPI does not include the prices of capital goods, but it covers the prices of services as well as goods. Services, which include rent, housing costs, transportation, and medical service, now comprise over half the weight of the CPI.

The consumer price index is considered the benchmark measure of inflation. When price level comparisons are made, both on a historical and an international basis, the consumer price index is almost always the chosen index. The CPI is also the price index to which so many private and public contracts, as well as Social Security, are linked.

The financial market probably gives a bit more weight to the consumer price index than to producer prices because of the CPI's widespread use and political importance. The CPI does have the advantage of including the prices of consumer services, which the PPI does not, but many economists regard the producer price index as more sensitive to early price trends. This is true because increased prices often show up at the wholesale level before they are passed on to the consumer. Furthermore, at the same time the PPI is announced, indexes for the prices of intermediate and crude goods are released, both of which track inflation at earlier stages of production.

## Core Inflation

Of interest to investors are not only the month-to-month changes of the PPI and CPI, but also the changes excluding the volatile food and energy sectors. Since weather has such undue influence on food prices, a rise or fall in the price of food over a month does not have much meaning for the overall inflationary trend. Similarly, oil and natural gas prices fluctuate due to weather conditions and supply disruptions that are not usually repeated in coming months. Hence the Bureau of Labor Statistics, which gathers inflation data, also releases the *core* price index, which excludes food and energy.

Most traders regard changes in the core rate of inflation as more important than changes in the overall index, since core inflation is apt to be persistent and impact long-term inflation trends. Forecasters are usually able to predict the core rate of inflation better than the overall rate, since the latter is influenced by the volatile food and energy sectors. A three-tenths of a percent error in the consensus forecast for the month-to-month rate of inflation might not be that serious, but such an error would be considered quite large for the core rate of inflation and would significantly affect the financial markets.

## Employment Costs

Other important releases bearing on inflation relate to employment costs. The monthly employment report issued by the BLS contains a report on the hourly wage rate. This report indicates wage pressures arising from the labor market. Since labor costs are nearly two-thirds of a firm's production costs, increases in the hourly wage not matched by increases in productivity increase costs and threaten inflation.

Every calendar quarter, the government also releases the Employment Cost Index, or ECI. This index includes benefit costs as well as wages and is considered the most comprehensive report of labor costs. Since the Fed chairman has indicated that this is an important indicator of inflation, the financial markets closely scrutinize these data.

## IMPACT ON FINANCIAL MARKETS

The following summarizes the impact of inflation on the financial markets:

*A lower-than-expected inflation report lowers interest rates and boosts stock prices. Inflation worse than expected raises interest rates and depresses stock prices.*

That inflation is bad for bonds should come as no surprise. Bonds are fixed-income investments whose cash flow is not adjusted for inflation. Bondholders demand higher interest rates in response to worsening news of inflation, not only to protect their purchasing power but also because of the increased concern that the Fed will tighten credit.

But worse-than-expected inflation is also bad for the stock market. As I noted in Chapter 11, stocks have proven to be poor hedges against inflation in the short run. Stock investors fear that worsening inflation will increase the taxes on earning and capital gains and that the Federal Reserve will tighten credit, further reducing corporate profits.

## FED POLICY

Monetary policy is of primary importance to financial markets. There are few fundamental or technical analyses that do not rely heavily on monetary policy indicators, such as the fed funds rate, the discount rate, and sometimes even money supplies, in their forecast of future stock returns.

Martin Zweig, one of the foremost money managers, shares the opinion of others when he states:

> In the stock market, as with horse racing, money makes the mare go.
> Monetary conditions exert an enormous influence on stock prices.
> Indeed, the monetary climate—primarily the trend in interest rates and
> Federal Reserve policy—is the dominant factor in determining the stock
> market's major direction.[3]

Easing monetary policy, by definition, involves lowering short-term interest rates. This is almost always extremely positive for stock prices. As demonstrated in Chapter 10, stocks thrive on liquidity provided by the central bank. Not only does Fed easing lower the rate at which stocks discount future cash flows, but it also provides a monetary stimulus to future earnings. Only if Fed easing is so excessive that the market fears it might spark inflation will stocks react badly. But an investor should prefer being in stocks than bonds under these circumstances, as fixed-income assets are clearly hurt the most by unanticipated inflation.

## SUMMARY

The reaction of financial markets to economic data is not random, but based on sound economic analysis. Strong economic growth invariably raises interest rates, but it has an ambiguous effect on stock prices, depending on whether inflationary fears are increased. Higher inflation is bad for both the stock and bond markets, and Fed easing is very positive for stocks—historically it has sparked some of the strongest rallies the market has experienced.

Although employment data usually comprises the most important monthly report for the market, the focus of traders constantly shifts. In the 1970s, inflation announcements took center stage, but after Fed chairman Paul Volcker shifted the focus to monetary policy, the Thursday afternoon money supply announcements captured the attention of traders. Later, trade statistics and the dollar were given top billing. The 1990-91 recession and subsequent slow economic recovery put employment data back on top with traders. In 1996 and early 1997, traders were looking for every hint of inflation as business activity expanded. Late in 1997 traders turned their attention to the turmoil in the Asian markets.

---

3 Martin Zweig, *Martin Zweig's Winning on Wall Street*, New York: Warner Books, 1986, p. 43

This chapter focused on the very short-run reaction of financial markets to economic data. Many claim that it would be best for investors to ignore such information since the data are often conflicting and revised at a later date. Such advice would be appropriate if you plan to stay invested for the long run, a strategy strongly advocated in this book. But traders trying to beat the market put these bits of information together to form a picture of where the economy and the market are heading. It is fascinating spectacle, but most investors will do much better watching from the sidelines and stick to a long-run investment strategy.

PART FOUR

# STOCK FLUCTUATIONS
# IN THE SHORT RUN

**15** C H A P T E R

# STOCK INDEX FUTURES, OPTIONS AND SPIDERS

*When I was a kid—a runner for Merrill Lynch at 25 dollars a week, I'd heard an old timer say, "The greatest thing to trade would be stock futures—but you can't do that, it's gambling."*

—Leo Melamed[1]

*"Warren Buffett thinks that stock futures and options ought to be outlawed, and I agree with him."*

—Peter Lynch[2]

## STOCK INDEX FUTURES

April 13, 1992 started as a perfectly ordinary day on the exchanges. But at about 11:45 in the morning, the two big Chicago exchanges, the Board of Trade and the Mercantile Exchange, were closed when a massive leak caused runoff from the Chicago River to course through the tunnels under the financial district, triggering extensive power outages. Figure 15-1 shows the intraday movement of the Dow Industrials and the S & P futures. As soon as Chicago futures trading was halted, the movements of stocks were markedly damped.

---

1 Leo Melamed is founder of the International Money Market, the home of the world's most successful stock index futures market. Quoted in Martin Mayer, *Markets*, New York: W. W. Norton, 1988, p. 111.
2 Peter Lynch, *One Up on Wall Street*, Penguin, 1989, p. 280.

**F I G U R E   15–1**

When Stock Index Futures Closed Down, April 13, 1992

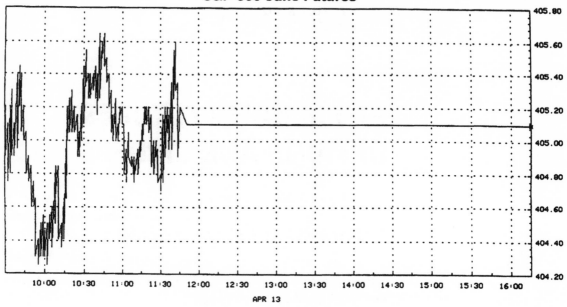

## S&P 500 June Futures

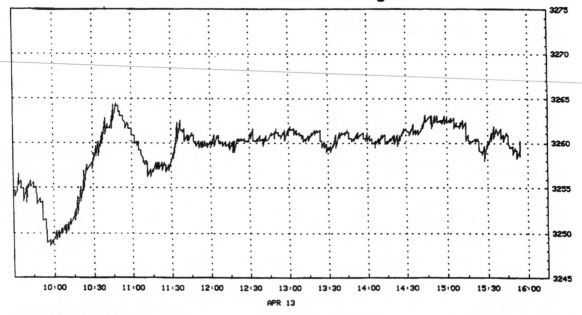

## Dow Jones Industrial Average

Source: Bloomberg L.P.

It almost looks as if the New York Stock Exchange went "brain dead" when there was no lead from Chicago. The volume in New York dropped by more than 25 percent on the day the Chicago futures market was closed, and some dealers claimed that if the futures exchange remained inoperative, it would cause liquidity problems and difficulty in executing some trades in New York.[3] But Michael Metz, a market strategist at Oppenheimer & Co., declared of April 13, "It's been absolutely delightful; it seems so sedate. It reminds me of the halcyon days on Wall Street before the program traders took hold."[4]

Who are these program traders and what do they do? If you step onto the floor of the New York Stock Exchange, you are confronted with a constant din of people scurrying about delivering orders and making deals. But every so often the background noise is punctuated by the rat-tat-tat of dozens of automated machines printing hundreds of buy or sell tickets. These orders are almost always from stock index future arbitrageurs, a type of program trader who relies on differences between the price of stock index futures set in Chicago and the price of stocks set in New York. The tickets signal that the futures market is moving quickly in Chicago and consequently stocks are ready to move in New York. It is an eerie warning, something akin to the buzz of locusts in biblical times, portending decimated crops and famine. And famine it might be, for over the past decade some of the most vicious declines in stock prices have been preceded by computers tapping out orders emanating from the futures markets.

It surprises many that, in the short run, the level of the stock market is not determined on Wall Street, but at the Chicago Mercantile Exchange located on Wacker Drive in Chicago. Specialists on the New York Stock Exchange, those dealers assigned to make and supervise markets in specific stocks, keep their eyes glued on the futures markets to find out where stocks are heading. These dealers have learned from experience not to stand in the way of index futures. If you do, you might get caught in an avalanche of trading such as the one that buried several specialists on October 19, 1987, that fateful day when the Dow crashed nearly 23%.

## THE IMPACT OF INDEX FUTURES

Most investors regard index futures and options as esoteric securities that have little to do with the market in which stocks are bought and

---

3 Robert Steiner, "Industrials Gain 14.53 in Trading Muted by Futures Halt in Chicago," the *Wall Street Journal*, April 14, 1992, p. C2.
4 "Flood in Chicago Waters Down Trading on Wall Street," the *Wall Street Journal*, April 14, 1992, p. C1.

sold. Many do very well trading stocks without any knowledge of these new instruments, but no one can comprehend the short-run market movements without an understanding of stock index futures.

Pick up a newspaper and read of the day's trading in stocks. Chances are good that you will see references to program trading, especially if the market was volatile. Program trading is the way by which large movements that originate in the Chicago futures pit are transmitted to the New York markets.

The following descriptions of volatile markets appeared in the *New York Times* of July 19, 1997:

> Stock prices plunged yesterday in a broad selloff, just two days after the Dow Jones Industrial averaged breached the 8,000-point level. . . . Some of the losses—and part of the volatility that helped the Dow plunge 145 points early in the day—were attributed to heavy program trading and "double witching," the expiration of some options on stocks and stock indexes.[5]

Figure 15-2 shows the behavior of the stock and futures market on that day, which will be described later in this chapter. Virtually all large stock movements are dominated by events that are first felt in the stock index futures markets.

## BASICS OF FUTURES MARKETS

The stock index futures market is the greatest single innovation to come to stock trading since the invention of the ticker tape. Index futures now trade in virtually every major stock market in the world and have become the instrument of choice for global investors who want to change their international stock allocations.

Futures trading goes back hundreds of years. The term *futures* was derived from the promise to buy or deliver a commodity at some future date at some specified price. Futures trading first flourished in agricultural crops, where farmers wanted to have a guaranteed price for the crops they would not harvest until later. Markets developed where buyers and sellers who wanted to avoid uncertainty could come to an agreement on the price for future delivery. The commitments to honor these agreements, called *futures contracts*, were freely transferable and markets developed where they were actively traded.

---

5 David Barboza, "Stocks Tumble, Wiping Out Week's Gain," the New York Times, July 19, 1997, p. 31. See later in the chapter for a description of "double witching."

Trading Bands and Futures Trading, July 18, 1997

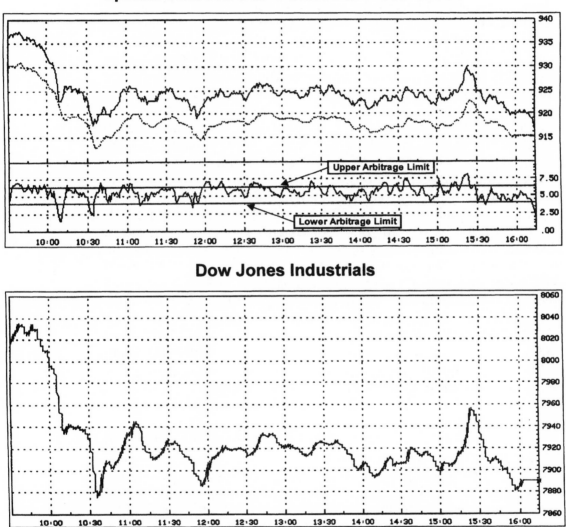

Source: Bloomberg L. P.

Stock index futures were launched in February 1982 by the Kansas City Board of Trade using the Value Line Index of about 1,700 stocks. But two months later in Chicago, at the Chicago Mercantile Exchange, the world's most successful stock index future based on the S & P 500 Index was introduced. Only two years after its introduction, the value of the contracts traded on this index future surpassed the dollar volume on the New York Stock Exchange for all stocks. Today the S & P 500 futures trade about 140,000 contacts a day, worth over $30 billion. Although there are other stock index futures, the S & P 500 Index dominates in the U.S., comprising well over 90 percent of the value of such trading.

All stock index futures are constructed similarly. The S & P Index future is a promise to deliver (in the case of the seller) or receive (in the case of the buyer) a fixed multiple of the value of the S & P 500 Index at some date in the future, called a *settlement date*. The multiple for the S & P Index future is 250 (which was changed from 500 in November, 1997), so if the S & P 500 Index is 1000, the value of one contract is $250,000.

There are four evenly spaced settlement dates each year. They fall on the third Friday of March, June, September, and December. Each settlement date corresponds to a contract. If you buy a futures contract, you are entitled to receive (if positive) or obligated to pay (if negative) 250 times the *difference* between the value of the S & P 500 Index on the settlement date and the price at which you purchased the contract.

For example, if you buy one September S & P futures contract at 1000 and on that third Friday of September the S & P 500 Index is at 1010, then you have made 10 points, which translates into $2,500 profit ($250 times 10 points). Of course, if the index falls to 990 on the settlement date, you would lose $2,500. For every point the S & P 500 Index goes up or down, you make or lose $250 per contract.

On the other hand, the returns to the *seller* of an S & P 500 futures contract are the mirror image of the returns to the buyer. The seller makes money when the index falls. In the previous example, the seller of the S & P 500 futures contract at 1000 will lose $2,500 if the index at settlement date rises to 1010, while he would make the same amount if the index fell to 990.

One source of the popularity of stock index futures is a unique settlement procedure. With standard futures contracts, you are obligated at settlement to receive (if purchased) or deliver (if sold) a specified quantity of the good for which you have contracted. Many apocryphal stories abound about how traders, forgetting to close out their contract, find bushels of wheat, corn, or frozen pork bellies dumped on their lawn on settlement day.

If commodity delivery rules applied to the S & P 500 Index futures contract, delivery would require a specified number of shares for each of the 500 firms in the index. Surely this would be extraordinarily cumbersome and costly. To avoid this problem, the designers of the stock index futures contract specified that settlement be made in "cash," computed simply by taking the difference between the contract price at the time of the trade and the value of the index on the settlement date. No delivery of stock takes place. If a trader fails to close a contract before settlement, his or her account would just be debited or credited on settlement date.

The creation of cash-settled futures contracts was no easy matter. In most states, particularly Illinois where large futures exchanges are located, settling a futures contract in cash was considered a wager—and wagering, except in some special circumstances, was illegal. In 1974, however, the Commodity Futures Trading Commission, a federal agency, was established by Congress to regulate all futures trading. And since there was no federal prohibition against wagering, the state laws were superseded.

## INDEX ARBITRAGE

The prices of commodities (or financial assets) in the futures market do not stand apart from the prices of the underlying commodity. If the value of a futures contract rises sufficiently above the price of the commodity that can be purchased for immediate delivery in the open market (often called the *cash* or *spot* market), traders can buy the commodity, store it, and then deliver it at a profit against the higher-priced futures contract on the settlement date. If the price of a future contract falls too far below its current spot price, owners of the commodity can sell it today, buy the futures contract, and take delivery of the commodity later at a lower price—in essence, earning a return on goods that would be in storage anyway.

Such a process of buying and selling commodities against their futures contracts is one type of *arbitrage*. Arbitrage involves traders who take advantage of temporary discrepancies in the prices of identical or nearly identical goods or assets. Those who reap profits from such trades are called *arbitrageurs*.

Arbitrage is very active in the stock index futures market. If the price of futures contracts sufficiently exceeds that of the underlying S & P 500 Index, then it pays for arbitrageurs to buy the underlying stocks and sell the futures contracts. If the futures price falls sufficiently below that of the index, arbitrageurs will sell the underlying stocks and buy the futures. On the settlement date the futures price must equal the underlying index by the terms of the contract, so the difference between the futures price and the index—called a *premium* if it is positive and a *discount* if it is negative—is an opportunity for profit. Investors who buy and sell futures contracts against the underlying stock index are called *index arbitrageurs.*

In recent years, index arbitrage has become a finely tuned art. The price of stock index futures usually stays within very narrow bands of the index value based on the price of the underlying shares. When the buying or selling of stock index futures drives the futures price outside this band, arbitrageurs step in and hundreds of orders to buy or sell are immediately transmitted to the exchanges that trade the underlying stocks in the index. These simultaneously placed orders are called *buy programs* to buy stock and *sell programs* to sell stock. When market commentators talk about sell programs hitting the market, it means that index arbitrageurs are selling stock in New York and buying futures that have fallen to a discount (or a small enough premium) in Chicago.

As with any arbitrage, speed is of the essence, since both ends of the transaction must be completed quickly in order to lock in a profit. Access to the stocks in the S & P 500 Index, which almost all trade on the New York Stock Exchange, is usually made through an automated order system called the Designated Order Turnaround, or DOT, system. This system used to punch out the buy and sell orders that could be heard on the Exchange floor whenever index arbitrage occurred.

Let's take a look at the market on July 18, 1997. As noted previously, futures trading was a significant factor forcing stock prices down on that day. Figure 15-2 shows the value of the index, the futures prices, and the difference between the two from the 9:30 A.M. opening to the 4:15 P.M. close of the futures market.

Index arbitrageurs do not engage in arbitrage whenever the index and futures prices differ by small amounts. Because of transaction costs, there must be a sufficient spread between the index and the future prices before traders will undertake the arbitrage. Figure 15-2 displays the upper and lower limits under which index arbitrage occurs for reasonable levels of transactions costs, although some engage in index arbitrage before these limits are reached.

Shortly after 10:00 A.M. on July 18, the S & P futures price for September delivery began to break downward in Chicago as traders became pessimistic about the prospect for the market. As a result, the futures price fell well below the price at which arbitrage becomes profitable. Index arbitrageurs then bought the depressed index futures and sold the stocks comprising the index.

Look at the chart of the Dow Jones Industrial Average in Figure 15-2. The character of the intraday movements in the stock average changed markedly when the sell programs kicked in. The sharp downward movements occurred when the arbitrageurs sold stock in response to the falling futures prices. Instead of moving a few points at a time, the industrial average experienced sudden drops of 10 to 15 points in a matter of seconds. This occurred when a number of the Dow stocks, which are weighted heavily in the S & P 500 Index, simultaneously traded lower. The specialists assigned to the big stocks, noting that the futures had fallen to a discount, marked down the price of their stocks in anticipation of imminent sell orders. These adjustments by the specialists speed up the process by which index arbitrage keeps prices in New York aligned with prices of futures in Chicago. It can also been seen that, after the New York Stock Exchange closed, the futures contract again sold at a discount from its fair market range.

## PREDICTING THE NEW YORK OPEN WITH GLOBEX TRADING

Although trading the S & P futures at the Chicago Mercantile Exchange closes at 4:15 P.M. eastern standard time, trading reopens in these futures 30 minutes later in an electronic market called Globex. Globex has no centralized floor; traders post their bids and offers on computer screens where all interested parties have instant access. Trading in Globex proceeds all night until 9:15 A.M. the next morning, 15 minutes before the start of trading at both the New York Stock Exchange and in the S & P futures pit in Chicago.

Unless there is important breaking news, trading is usually slow during the night hours. But it becomes very active around 8:30 A.M. when many of the government economic data, such as the employment report and the consumer and producer price indexes are announced. In the previous section we saw the dramatic fall in the S & P futures traded on Globex in response to the strong July 5, 1996 employment report.

Market watchers can use the Globex S & P futures to predict how the market will open in New York. The *fair market value* of the S & P futures is calculated based on the arbitrage conditions between the futures and the cash market, using the closing of the S & P 500 Index on the previous day. If Globex is trading above the fair market value of the S & P futures based on yesterday's close, the market will likely open strong; if it is trading below the fair market value, the market will likely open weak.

The difference between the close on Globex and the fair market value predicts how much the S & P will open up or down, assuming that no significant news is reported in the 15-minute period before 9:30 A.M. when neither Globex nor the Chicago market is open. Since one S & P 500 index point equals about eight Dow Industrial points, the Globex market can be translated into the opening change in the Dow Jones Industrial Average.

## DOUBLE AND TRIPLE WITCHING

Index futures play some strange games with stock prices on the days when contracts expire. Recall that index arbitrage works through the simultaneous buying or selling of stocks against futures contracts. On the day that a contract expires, arbitrageurs unwind their stock positions at precisely the same time that the futures contract expires.

Index futures contracts expire on the third Friday of the last month of each quarter: in March, June, September, and December. Index options and options on individuals stocks, which are described later in the chapter, settle on the third Friday of every month. Hence four times a year, all three types of contracts expire at once. This expiration has produced violent price movements in the market and is termed *triple witching*. The third Friday of the months when there is no futures contract settlement is called *double witching*, which displays less volatility than triple witching.

There is no mystery why the market is volatile during double or triple witching. On these days, the specialists on the New York Stock Exchange are instructed to buy or sell large blocks of stock on the close, *whatever the price*. If there is a huge imbalance of buy orders, prices will soar; if sell orders predominate, prices will plunge. These swings, however, do not matter to arbitrageurs since the profit on the future position will offset losses on the stock position, and vice versa.

In 1988, the New York Stock Exchange urged the Chicago Mercantile Exchange to change its procedures, ending futures trading at the close of Thursday's trading and settling the contracts at Friday opening prices rather than Friday closing prices. This change gave specialists more time to seek out balancing bids and offers, and has greatly moderated the movements in stock prices on triple witching dates.

## MARGIN AND LEVERAGE

One of the reasons for the popularity of futures contracts is that the cash needed to enter into the trade is a very small part of the value of the contract. Unlike stocks, there is no money that transfers between the buyer and seller when a futures contract is entered. A small amount of good faith collateral, or *margin*, is required by the broker from both the buyer and seller to ensure that both parties will honor the contract at settlement. For the S & P 500 Index, the current initial margin is $12,000, or about 5 percent of the value of the contract. And this margin can be kept in Treasury bills with interest accruing to the investor. So trading a futures contract involves neither a transfer of cash nor a loss of interest income.

The *leverage*, or the amount of stock that you control relative to the amount of margin you have to put down with a futures contract, is enormous. For every dollar of cash (or Treasury bills) that you put in margin against an S & P futures contract, you command about $20 of stock. And for "day trading," when you close your positions by the end of the day, the margin requirements are cut in half, so you can leverage more than 40 to 1. These low margins contrast with the 50 percent margin requirement for the purchase of individual stocks that has prevailed since 1974.

This ability to control $20 or ever $40 of stock with $1 of cash is reminiscent of the rampant speculation that existed in the 1920s before the establishment of minimum stock margin requirements. In the 1920s, individual stocks were frequently purchased with a 10 percent margin. It was popular to speculate with such borrowed money, for as long as the market was rising, few lost money. But if the market drops precipitously, margin buyers can find that not only is their equity wiped out, but that they are indebted to the brokerage firm as well. The tendency of this low margin to fuel market volatility is discussed in Chapter 16.

## ADVANTAGE TO TRADING FUTURES

Although low margins are a great advantage to those who trade in the futures markets, the greatest advantage is the substantial reduction in the cost of trading stocks. Where else can you buy a diversified stock portfolio of 500 firms, such as that represented by the S & P 500 Index, for as little as a few dollars of commission? Each S & P futures contract controls nearly a quarter million dollars of stock at 1997 market levels, and the brokerage costs to an individual are as low as $25 to $30 per round-trip transaction, while professionals pay only a few dollars in commission.

Of even greater importance to investors is the very low bid-ask spreads, or the differences between the buying and selling prices of index futures. The bid-ask spread on an S & P 500 Index futures contract is sometimes as low as one-tenth an S & P point, which correspond to $25 per contract. Compared to paying the bid-ask spread on 500 individual stocks, the cost of trading in the futures market is minuscule.

## SPIDERS

In 1993 the American Stock Exchange introduced a new index security called Standard & Poor's Depositary Receipts, or SPDRs (frequently called "spiders"). SPDRs represent ownership in a trust that matches the performance of the S & P 500 Index by owning all 500 stocks in the appropriate proportion. SPDRs trade like a stock on the American Stock Exchange and have a value of one-tenth the value of the index (In 1997, approximately $90 per share). SPDRs often have a very tight bid-ask spread of ⅟₃₂, or about three cents per share. Normal brokerage commissions apply to their purchase and sale.

One of the advantages of the SPDRs is that you can easily sell (or *short*) its shares even if you do not own any.[6] This is a very convenient way to hedge your overall portfolio. Stock margins, currently 50 percent, apply on either a sale or a purchase. In 1995, the Exchange followed up its extremely successful SPDR with a similar contract on smaller stocks of the S & P Midcap 400, which contains 400 stocks smaller than the S & P 500 Index.

SPDRs and S & P 500 Index futures are very similar in purpose, but each has distinct advantages. A futures contract permits higher leverage and has lower transaction costs. But an SPDR gives you the familiarity of dealing with a stock and more advantageous tax treatment than a futures contract.[7] The Chicago Mercantile Exchange recently introduced the mini S & P 500 futures contract to compete with SPDRs. This contract, which trades electronically, is valued at 50 times the S & P 500 Index and requires only a $2,500 margin.

## USING SPIDERS OR FUTURES

The use of SPDRs or index futures greatly increases your flexibility in managing portfolios. Suppose you have built up some good gains in individual stocks, but are now getting nervous about the market. You do not want to sell your individual stocks because that would trigger a large tax liability. Also, you believe that your stocks will outperform the

---

6 Spiders are exempt from the uptick rule that restricts shorting stock when the price is falling.
7 In contrast to stocks, all profits and losses from futures transactions are marked to market for tax purposes as of December 31, whether realized or not.

market during a decline or when stocks recover. So selling now and buying them back later would entail large transactions costs.

But with spiders (or futures), all this worry becomes unnecessary. You sell the number of shares (or contracts) corresponding to the reduction in the risk that you seek, holding onto your individual stocks. If the market declines, you profit on your spiders' position, offsetting the losses to your individual stocks. If the market instead goes up, contrary to your fears, you will lose on your spiders, but the gains on your individual stock holdings should offset this loss. This sort of activity is called *hedging stock market risk*. Since you never sell your individual stocks, you trigger no tax liability on your stock positions.

Another advantage of SPDRs (or futures) is the ability to profit from a decline in the market even if you do not own any stock. Selling SPDRs substitutes for *shorting* stock, or selling stock you do not own in anticipation that the price will fall and you can buy it back at a lower price. Using SPDRs to bet on a falling market is much more convenient than shorting a portfolio of stocks, since individuals stocks cannot be shorted if the price is declining but SPDRs are exempt from this rule.

## INDEX OPTIONS

Although index futures influence the overall stock market far more than options, the options market has caught the fancy of many investors. And this is not surprising. The beauty of an option is embedded in its very name: you have the option, but not the obligation, to buy and sell at the terms specified.

There are two major types of options: puts and calls. *Calls* give you the right to buy a stock (or stocks) at a fixed price within a given period of time. *Puts* give you the right to sell. Puts and calls have existed on individuals stocks for decades, but organized trading did not exist until the establishment of the Chicago Board Options Exchange (CBOE) in 1974.

What attracts investors to puts and calls is that liability is strictly limited. If the market moves against options buyers, they can forfeit the purchase price, forgoing the option to buy or sell. This contrasts sharply with a futures contract where, if the market goes against buyers, losses can mount quickly. In a volatile market, futures can be extremely risky, and it could be impossible for investors to exit a contract without substantial losses.

In 1978, the CBOE began trading options on the popular stock indexes, such as the S & P 500 Index.[8] Options trade in multiples of $100 per point of index value—cheaper than the $500-per-point multiple on the popular S & P 500 Index futures.

An index allows investors to buy the stock index at a set price within a given period of time. Assume that the S & P 500 Index is now selling for 900, but you believe that the market is going to rise. You can purchase a call option at 920 for three months at about 20 points, or $2,000. The purchase price of the option is called the *premium*, and the price at which the option begins to pay off—in this case 920—is called the *strike price*. At any time within the next three months you can, if you choose, exercise your option and receive $100 for every point that the S & P 500 Index is above 920.

You need not exercise your option to make a profit. There is an extremely active market for options, and you can always sell them before expiration to other investors. In this example, the S & P 500 Index will have to rise above 940 for you to show a profit, since you paid $2,000 for the option. But the beauty of options is that, if you guessed wrong and the market falls, the most you can lose is the $2,000 premium you paid.

An index put works exactly the same way as a call but in this case the buyer makes money if the market goes down. Assume you buy a put on the S & P 500 Index at 880, paying a $2,000 premium. Every point the S & P 500 Index moves below 880 will recoup $100 of your initial premium. If the index falls to 860 by the expiration of the option, you will have broken even. Every point below 860 gives you a profit on your option.

The price that you pay for an index option depends on many factors, including interest rates and dividend yields. But the most important factor is the volatility of the market itself. Clearly the more volatile the market, the more expensive it is to buy either puts or calls. In a dull market, it is unlikely that the market will move sufficiently high (in the case of a call) or low (in the case of a put) to give buyers of the option a profit. If this low volatility is expected to continue, the prices of options fall. In contrast, in volatile markets, the premiums on puts and calls are bid up as traders consider it more likely that the option will have value by the time of its expiration.

---

8 In fact, the largest 100 stocks of the S & P 500 Index, called the S & P 100, comprise the most popularly traded index option. Options based on the S & P 500 Index are more widely used by institutional investors.

The price of options depends on the judgments of traders as to the likelihood that the market will move sufficiently to make the rights to buy or sell stock at a fixed price valuable. But the theory of option pricing was given a big boost in the 1970s when two academic economists, Fischer Black and Myron Scholes, developed the first mathematical formula to price options. The Black-Scholes formula was an instant success. It gave traders a benchmark for valuation where previously only intuition was used. The Black-Scholes formula was programmed on traders' hand-held calculators and PCs around the world. Although there are conditions when the formula must be modified, empirical research has shown that the Black-Scholes formula closely approximates the price of traded options.

Options have opened a new market for investors. Now investors can trade the *volatility* of the market as well as the level. Those who expect that the market will be more volatile than normal will buy puts and calls, while those who feel that the market will be less volatile than usual will tend to sell options. If investors *buy* volatility, they are buying either puts or calls (or both), expecting large market movements over the life of the option. If investors *sell* volatility, they expect a relatively quiet market and expect the options to expire worthless or at prices far below what they paid for them. It is the fascinating truth that, even if the market is unchanged day after day, investors can make large profits by selling options.

## BUYING INDEX OPTIONS

Options are actually more basic instruments than futures. You can replicate any future with options, but the reverse is not true. Options offer the investor far more strategies than futures. Such strategies can range from the very speculative to the extremely conservative.

Suppose an investor wants to be protected against a decline in the market. He or she can buy an index put, which increases in value as the market declines. Of course, you have to pay a premium for this option, very much like an insurance premium. If the market does not decline, you have forfeited your premium. But if it does, the increase in the value of your put has cushioned (if not completely offset) the decline in your stock portfolio.

Another advantage of puts is that you can buy just the amount of protection that you like. If you want to protect yourself against only a total collapse in the market, then you can buy a put that is way "out of the money," in other words, a put whose strike price is far below that of the current level of the index. This option pays off only if the market declines precipitously. In addition, you can also buy puts with a strike price above the current market, so the option retains some value even if the market does not decline. Of course, these "in the money" puts are far more expensive.

There are many recorded examples of fantastic gains in puts and calls. But for every option that gains so spectacularly in value, there are thousands that expire worthless. Some market professionals estimate that 85 percent of individual investors who play the options market lose money. Not only do option buyers have to be right about the direction of the market, but their timing must be nearly perfect and their selection of the strike price must be appropriate.

## SELLING INDEX OPTIONS

Of course, for anyone who buys an option, someone must sell (or write) an option. The sellers, or writers, of call options believe that the market will not rise sufficiently to make a profit for option buyers. Sellers of call options make money most of the time they sell options, since the vast majority of options expire worthless. But should the market move sharply against the option sellers, their losses could be enormous.

For that reason, most sellers of call options are investors who already own stock. This strategy, called "buy and write," is popular with many investors since it is seen as a "win-win" proposition. If stocks go down, they collect a premium from buyers of the call, and so are better off than if they had not written the option. If stocks do nothing, they also collect the premium on the call and are still better off. If stocks go up, call writers still gain more on the stocks they own than they lose on the call they wrote, so they are still ahead. Of course, if stocks go up strongly, they miss a large part of the rally since they have promised to deliver stock at a fixed price. In that case, call writers certainly would have been better off if they had not sold the call. But they still make more money than if they had not owned the stock at all.

The buyers of put options are insuring their stock against price declines. But who are the sellers of these options? They are primarily those who are willing to buy the stock, but only if the price declines. A seller of a put collects a premium, but receives the stock only if it falls sufficiently to go below the strike price. Since put sellers are not as common as call sellers, premiums on puts that are out of the money are frequently quite high.

## LONG-TERM TRENDS AND STOCK INDEX FUTURES

The development of stock index futures and options in the 1980s was a major development for stock investors and money managers. Heavily capitalized firms, such as those represented in the Dow Industrial Average, have always attracted money because of their outstanding liquidity. But with stock index futures, investors can now buy the whole market as represented by the S & P 500 Index. Index futures have higher liquidity than any highly capitalized blue-chip stock. Therefore, when money managers want to take a position in the market, it is most easily done with stock index futures.

International investors and those involved in global asset allocation want index futures and options so they can easily alter the fraction of assets they have invested in each country. For many of these money managers, the first portfolio decision is the percentage of funds invested in each country. Buying or selling stock index futures is clearly the way to alter that percentage. In fact, some money managers shun countries that do not trade index futures, since their absence deprives them of the liquidity they so strongly need.

SPDRs, trading like stocks on the American Stock Exchange, also replicate the S & P 500 Index and have nearly the liquidity and cost savings of futures. These index instruments are much more familiar to individuals who feel uncomfortable dealing with the high volatility and leverage in the futures market. SPDRs make ideal hedges to an investor's overall portfolio by locking in profits on the market without cashing in (and taking the tax consequences) of selling individual stocks.

# MARKET VOLATILITY AND THE STOCK CRASH OF OCTOBER 1987

*The word* crisis *in Chinese is composed of two characters: the first, the symbol of danger . . . the second, of opportunity.*

A comparison of the stock markets of 1922–29 and 1980–87 is shown in Figure 16-1. There is an uncanny similarity between the charts of these two periods. The editors of the *Wall Street Journal* felt the similarity so portentous that they printed a similar comparison in the edition that hit the streets on the morning of October 19, 1987. Little did they know that that day would witness the greatest drop in the history of the stock market, exceeding the great crash of October 29, 1929. In fact, the market of 1987 continued to act like that of 1929 for the remainder of the year. Many forecasters, citing the similarities between the two periods, were certain that disaster loomed and advised their clients to sell everything.

But the similarity between 1929 and 1987 ended at year's end. The stock market recovered from its October crash and by August of 1989 hit new high ground. In contrast, two years after the October 1929 crash, the Dow, in the throes of the greatest bear market in U.S. history, had lost more than two-thirds of its value and was about to lose two-thirds more.

What was different? Why did the eerie similarities between these two events finally diverge so dramatically? The simple answer is that the central bank had the power to control the ultimate source of liquid-

## FIGURE   16–1

### The 1929 and 1987 Stock Crashes

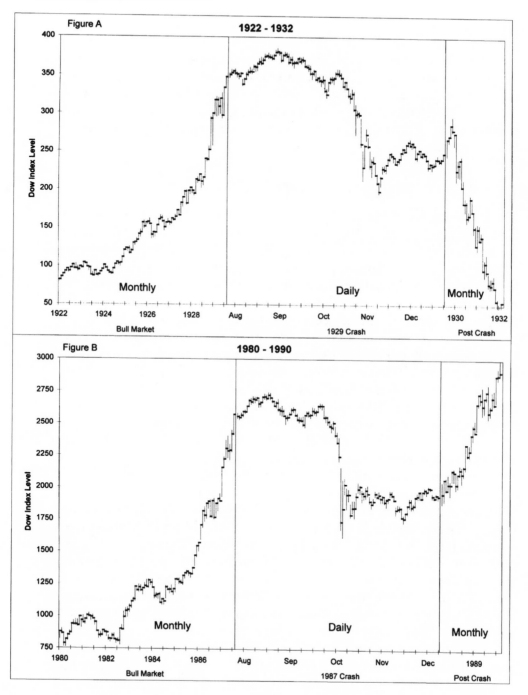

ity in the economy—the supply of money— and, in contrast to 1929, did not hesitate to use it. Heeding the painful lessons of the early 1930s, the Fed temporarily flooded the economy with money and pledged to stand by all bank deposits to ensure that all aspects of the financial system would function properly.

The public was assured. There were no runs on banks, no contraction of the money supply, and no deflation in commodity and asset values. Indeed, the economy itself barely paused as a result of this market debacle. The October 1987 market crash taught many investors an important lesson—that a crisis can be an opportunity for profit, not the time to panic.

## THE STOCK CRASH OF OCTOBER 1987

The stock crash of Monday, October 19, 1987 was one of the most dramatic financial events of the postwar era. The 508-point, or 22.6 percent, decline in the Dow Jones Industrials was by far the largest point drop up to that time and the largest percentage drop in history. Volume on the New York Stock Exchange soared to an all-time record, exceeding 600 million shares on Monday and Tuesday, and for that fateful week the number of shares traded exceeded that for the entire year of 1966.

The crash on Wall Street reverberated around the world. Tokyo, which two years later was going to enter its own massive bear market, fell the least, but still experienced a record one-day drop of 15.6 percent. Stocks in New Zealand fell nearly 40 percent, and the Hong Kong market closed because collapsing prices brought massive defaults in their stock index futures market. In the United States alone, stock values dropped about $500 billion on that infamous day, and the total worldwide decline in stock values exceeded one *trillion* dollars. This is more than the entire gross national product of the continent of Africa.

The fall in the stock market began in earnest the week prior to Black Monday. At 8:30 A.M. on the preceding Wednesday, the Department of Commerce reported that the United States suffered a $15.7 billion merchandise trade deficit, one of the largest in U.S. history and far in excess of market expectations. The reaction to the announcement in the financial markets was immediate. Yields on long government bonds rose to over 10 percent for the first time since November 1985 and the dollar declined sharply in the foreign exchange market. The Dow Industrials fell 95 points on Wednesday, a record point drop at that time.

The situation continued to worsen on Thursday and Friday, as the Dow fell 166 more points. Late Friday afternoon, about 15 minutes prior to close, heavy selling hit the stock index futures markets in Chicago. The indexes had fallen below crucial support levels, which led to the barrage of selling in Chicago by those wanting to get out of stocks at almost any price.

The December S & P 500 Index future fell to an unprecedented 6 points (or almost 3 percent) below the spot index. The development of such a wide discount meant that money managers were willing to sell at a discount in order to execute large orders with speed, rather than risk sell orders that might sit unexecuted in New York. At the close of trading on Friday, the stock market had experienced its worst week in nearly five decades.

Before the opening on Monday, ominous events hung over New York. Overnight in Tokyo, the Nikkei average fell 2½ percent, and there were sharp declines in stock markets in Sydney and Hong Kong. In London, prices had fallen by 10 percent and many money managers were trying to sell U.S. stocks before the anticipated decline hit New York.

Trading on Black Monday was chaotic. No Dow Jones stock opened at the 9:30 bell. Only seven traded before 9:45 and 11 still had not opened by 10:30. Portfolio "insurers," described later in the chapter, were selling heavily, trying to insulate their customers' exposure to the plunging market. By late afternoon, the S & P 500 Index futures were selling at a 25-point or 12 percent discount to the spot market, a spread that was previously considered inconceivable. By the late afternoon, huge sell orders transmitted by program sellers cascaded onto the New York Exchange through the computerized system. The Dow Industrials collapsed almost 300 points in the final hour of trading, bringing the toll to 508 points for the day.

Although October 19 is remembered in history as the day of the great stock crash, it was actually the next day—*terrible Tuesday* as it has become known—that the market almost failed. After opening up over 10 percent from Monday's low, the market began to plunge by midmorning, and shortly after noon fell below its Monday close. The S & P 500 Index futures market collapsed to 181—an incredible 40 S & P points or 22 percent under the reported index value. If index arbitrage had been working, the futures prices would have dictated a Dow at 1,450. Stock prices in the world's largest market, on the basis of this measure, were off nearly 50 percent from their high of 2,722 set just seven weeks earlier.

It was at this point that near meltdown hit the market. The NYSE did not close, but trading was halted in almost 200 stocks. For the first and only time, trading was also halted in the S & P 500 Index futures in Chicago. The only market of any size that remained open was the Major

Market Index futures, representing blue-chip stocks and traded on the Chicago Board of Trade.

After the crash, an investigative report by the *Wall Street Journal* suggested that this futures market was a key to reversing the market collapse.[1] The Major Market Index, a stock index future patterned after the Dow Industrials, was selling at such deep discounts to the prices in New York that the values seemed irresistible. And since it was the only market that remained open, buyers stepped in and the futures market shot up an equivalent of 120 Dow points in a matter of minutes. When traders and the exchange specialists saw the buying come back into the blue chips, prices rallied in New York, and the worst of the market panic passed.

## CAUSES OF THE STOCK CRASH

There was no single precipitating event—such as a declaration of war, terrorist acts, assassination, or bankruptcy—that caused Black Monday. However, ominous trends had threatened the buoyant stock market for some time: sharply higher interest rates caused by a falling dollar in international currency markets, program trading, and portfolio insurance. The latter was born from the explosive growth of stock index futures markets, markets that did not even exist six years earlier.

### Exchange Rate Policies

The roots of the surge in interest rates that preceded the October 1987 stock market crash are found in the futile attempts by the United States and other G7 countries (Japan, the United Kingdom, Germany, France, Italy, and Canada) to prevent the dollar from falling in the international exchange markets.

The dollar had bounded to unprecedented levels in the middle of the 1980s on the heels of huge Japanese and European investment in the United States. Foreign investment was based in the optimism about the U.S. economic recovery and the high real dollar interest rates, in part driven by record U.S. budget deficits. By February 1985, the dollar became massively overvalued and U.S. exports became very uncompetitive in world markets, severely worsening the trade deficit.

Central bankers initially cheered the fall of the overpriced dollar, but they grew concerned when the dollar continued to decline and the

---

1 James Stewart and Daniel Hertzberg, "How the Stock Market Almost Disintegrated a Day After the Crash," the *Wall Street Journal*, November 20, 1987, p. 1.

U.S. trade deficit worsened. Finance ministers met in February 1987 at the Louvre in Paris, with the goal of supporting the price of the dollar. Foreign central bankers were worried that if the dollar became too cheap, their own exports to the United States, which had grown substantially when the dollar was high, would suffer.

The Federal Reserve reluctantly participated in the dollar stabilization program, which was dependent either on an improvement in the deteriorating U.S. trade position or, absent such an improvement, a commitment by the Federal Reserve to raise interest rates to support the dollar. But the trade deficit did not improve; in fact, it worsened after the initiation of the exchange stabilization policies. Traders, nervous about the deteriorating U.S. trade balance sending billions of dollars abroad, demanded higher and higher interest rates to hold U.S. assets. Leo Melamed, chairman of the Chicago Mercantile Exchange, was blunt when asked about the origins of Black Monday: "What caused the crash was all that f——— around with the currencies of the world."[2]

The stock market initially ignored rising interest rates. The U.S. market, like most equity markets around the world, was booming. The Dow Jones Industrials, which started 1987 at 1,933, reached an all-time high of 2,725 on August 22, 250 percent above the August 1982 low reached five years earlier. Over the same five-year period, the British stock market was up 164 percent, the Swiss 209 percent, German 217 percent, Japanese 288 percent, and Italian 421 percent.

But rising bond rates and price-earning ratios spelled trouble for the equity markets. The long-term government bond rate, which began the year at 7 percent, topped 9 percent in September and continued to rise. As the Dow rose, the dividend yield fell, and in August it reached a postwar low of 2.69 percent. The gap between the real yield on bonds and the earning yield on stocks reached a postwar high. By the morning of October 19, the long-term bond yield had reached 10.47 percent. The record gap between earnings and dividend yields on stocks and real returns on bonds set the stage for the stock market crash.

### The Stock Crash and the Futures Market

I cannot overemphasize the importance of the S & P 500 futures market in contributing to the market crash. But to say that heavy futures selling was one reason why stocks crashed begs the question of what caused

2 Martin Mayer, *Markets*, New York: W. W. Norton, 1988, p. 62.

the heavy influx of sales in the futures market. Since the introduction of the stock index futures market, a new trading technique, called *portfolio insurance*, had been introduced into portfolio management.

Portfolio insurance was, in concept, not much different than an oft-used technique called a *stop-loss order*. If investors buy a stock and want to protect themselves from a large loss (or if it has gone up, protect their profit), it is possible to place a sell order below the current market, which is triggered when the price of the stock falls to or below this limit.

But stop-loss orders are not guarantees that you can get out of the market. If the stock falls below your specified price, your stop-loss order becomes a market order to be executed at the *next best price*. If the stock "gaps" downward, your order could be executed far below your speci-fied price. You can see how a panic might develop if many investors place stop-loss orders around the same price. A price decline could trig-ger a flood of sell orders, overwhelming the market.

Portfolio insurers who used the stock index futures market felt they were immune to such problems. It seemed extremely unlikely that the S & P 500 Index futures would ever gap in price and that the whole U.S. capital market, the world's largest, could fail to find buyers.

But the entire market did gap on October 19, 1987. During the week of October 12, the market declined by 10 percent and a large number of sell orders flooded the markets. Portfolio insurers began to sell index fu-tures to protect their clients' profits. The stock index futures market col-lapsed. There was no liquidity.

What was once inconceivable, that many of the stocks of the world's largest corporations would have no market, happened. Portfolio insurers were shell-shocked, and since the prices of index fu-tures were so far below the prices of the stocks selling in New York, in-vestors halted their buying of shares in New York altogether.

Portfolio insurance withered rapidly after the crash. It was shown not to be an insurance scheme at all, since the continuity and liquidity of the market could not be assured. There was, however, an alternative form of portfolio protection: index options. With the introduction of these options markets in the 1980s, you could explicitly purchase insur-ance against market declines by buying puts on a market index. With puts, you never needed to worry about price gaps or being able to get out of your position since the price of the insurance is specified in advance.

Certainly there were factors other than portfolio insurance con-tributing to the stock debacle. But portfolio insurance and its ancestor, the stop-loss order, abetted the fall. All of these schemes are rooted in the basic trading philosophy of letting profits ride and cutting losses short. Whether implemented with stop-loss orders, index futures, or just a mental note to get out of a stock once it declines by a certain amount, this philosophy can set the stage for market gaps.

## Circuit Breakers

As a result of the crash, both the Chicago Mercantile Exchange, where the S & P 500 Index futures are traded, and the New York Stock Exchange have implemented rules that restrict or halt trading when certain price limits have been triggered. To prevent destabilizing speculation when the Dow Jones Industrial Average changes by at least 50 points, the New York Stock Exchange's rule 80a places "trading curbs" on index arbitrage between the futures market and the New York Stock Exchange.

But of greater importance are measures that sharply restrict or stop trading in both the futures and the New York Stock Exchange when market moves are very large. When the S & P 500 Index futures fall by 15 points (approximately 120 Dow points), minimum price limits are imposed for 15 minutes. Similar halts occur when the futures contract falls by 30, 45, and 70 points. The maximum daily price change for the S & P 500 futures contract is 90 points, corresponding to approximately a 10 percent change in market prices.

The New York Stock Exchange imposes trading halts based on changes in the Dow Jones Industrial Average. When the average falls by 350 points, the New York Stock Exchange suspends trading for a half hour. If the Dow falls by 550 points, the Exchange halts trading for one hour. Whenever trading is halted in New York, futures trading in Chicago is also halted. Both of these halts were triggered on October 27, 1997 when the Dow Industrials fell by 554 points.

The rationale behind these measures is that halting trading gives investors time to reassess the situation and formulate their strategy based on significantly different prices. This could bring buyers into the market and help market makers maintain a liquid market.

The argument against halts is that they increase volatility by discouraging short-term traders from buying since they might be preventing from selling during a trading halt in the near future. This sometimes leads to an acceleration of price declines towards the price limits, thereby increasing short-term volatility. This appeared to occur on October 27, 1997.

But restrictions on liquidity might also have a more insidious effect. Many investors will enter only liquid markets that enable them to move quickly in and out. Any restrictions on the liquidity of markets lowers the desirability of these markets and therefore lowers prices. The effect of liquidity on price can be easily seen in the U.S. government bond market, where the latest bond issued (the "on-the-run" bond) sells at a higher price than virtually identical bonds that do not have such liquidity.

## THE NATURE OF MARKET VOLATILITY

Although most investors express a strong distaste for market fluctuations, volatility must be accepted to reap the superior returns offered by stocks. For risk and volatility are the essence of above-average returns: You cannot make any more than the safe rate of return unless there is some possibility that you make less.

While the volatilityof the stock market deters many investors, it fascinates others. the ability to monitor a positionon a minute-by-minute basis fulfills the need of many to know quickly whether their judgment, upon which not only money but also ego lies, has been validated. For many the stock market is truly the world's largest gambling casino.

Yet this ability to know exactly how much you are worth at any given moment can also provoke anxiety. Many investors do not like the instantaneous verdict of the financial market. Some retreat into investments such as real estate, for which daily quotations are not available. They believe that not knowing the current price makes an investment somehow less risky. As Keynes stated over 50 years ago about the investing attitudes of the endowment committee at Cambridge University:

> Some Bursars will buy without a tremor unquoted and unmarketable
> investment in real estate which, if they had a selling quotation for
> immediate cash available at each audit, would turn their hair grey. The
> fact that you do not know how much its ready money quotation fluctuates
> does not, as is commonly supposed, make an investment a safe one.[3]

## HISTORICAL TRENDS OF STOCK VOLATILITY

Is the stock market becoming more volatile over time? Many investors would respond to this question in the affirmative, noting the record one-day drop in 1987 and the sharp intraday movements caused by program selling and index arbitrage. There is evidence that the market has become more volatile *within the trading day*, undoubtedly the result of in-

---

3 "Memo for the Estates Committee, King's College, Cambridge, May 8, 1938," in *Classics*, ed. Charles D. Ellis, Homewood, Ill.: Dow Jones-Irwin, 1989, p. 79.

stantaneous communications and arbitrage from the index futures markets. But there is little evidence that the market has become more volatile measured by monthly or even daily fluctuations.

Figure 16-2 plots the annual variability (measured by the standard deviation) of the monthly returns on stocks, calculated yearly from 1834 to the present. You can see that the period of greatest volatility was during the Great Depression, and the year of highest volatility was 1932. The annualized volatility of 1932 was over 65 percent, 17 times higher than 1964, which is the least volatile year on record. The volatility of 1987 was the highest since the Great Depression. But on the whole, volatility shows no overall trend and dropped to near record lows in 1996.

These trends are confirmed by examining Figure 16-3, which displays the average daily percentage change on the Dow-Jones Industrial

## FIGURE 16–2

Annual Volatility of Stock Returns (Annualized Standard Deviation of Monthly Returns), 1834–1996

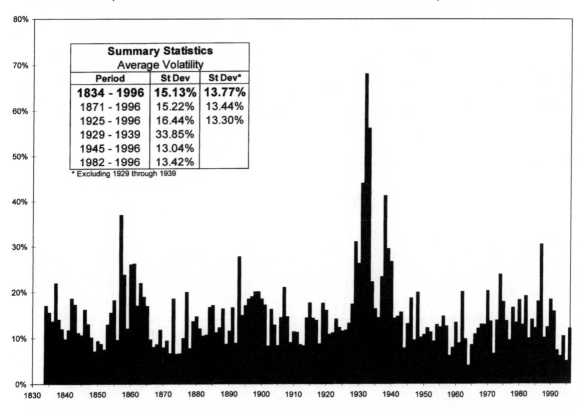

| Summary Statistics | | |
|---|---|---|
| Average Volatility | | |
| Period | St Dev | St Dev* |
| **1834 - 1996** | **15.13%** | **13.77%** |
| 1871 - 1996 | 15.22% | 13.44% |
| 1925 - 1996 | 16.44% | 13.30% |
| 1929 - 1939 | 33.85% | |
| 1945 - 1996 | 13.04% | |
| 1982 - 1996 | 13.42% | |

* Excluding 1929 through 1939

Daily Risk on the DJIA

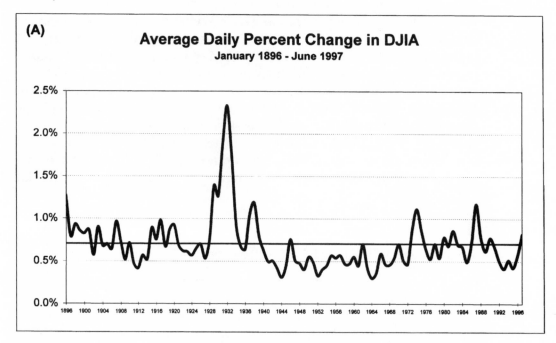

(A) Average Daily Percent Change in DJIA
January 1896 - June 1997

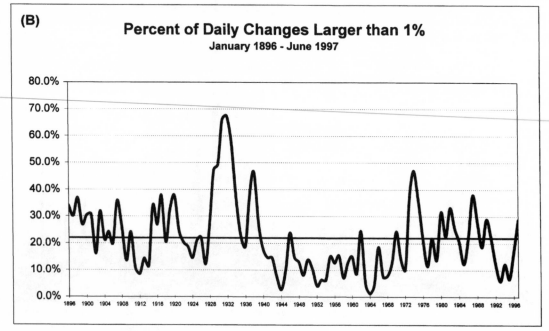

(B) Percent of Daily Changes Larger than 1%
January 1896 - June 1997

Average during each year since 1896. The downward trend in the Dow volatility in the early twentieth century is partially due to the increase in the number of stocks in the Dow Industrials from 12 to 20, and to 30 in 1928. The average daily change in the Dow Industrials over the past 100 years is 0.71 percent, slightly less than three-quarters of one percent. Since the 1930s, there have been only two years, 1974 and 1987, where the average daily change has exceeded 1 percent.

Figure 16-3b shows the percentage of trading days when the Dow Industrials changed by *more than* 1 percent. It has averaged 22 percent over the period, or about once per week. But it has ranged from as low as 1.2 percent in 1964 to a high of 67.6 percent in 1932. In that volatile year, the Dow changed by more than 1 percent in two out of every three trading days.

Most of the periods of high volatility occur when the market has declined. In recessions, the standard deviation of daily returns is about 25% more than during expansions. There are two reasons why volatility increases in a recession. First, as noted in Chapter 12, a decline in the market frequently portends an economic slowdown and therefore generates uncertainty for investors. Secondly, if the market declines because of lower earning forecasts, then investors become much more concerned about the debt and other fixed-income obligations of firms. Since bondholders have first claim on the assets of firms, the probability of severe financial stress and bankruptcy increases when earnings decline. This leads to increased volatility in the equity value of firms.

If the market believes that the value of a firm is at or below that of the indebtedness to bondholders or banks, the stock market can become extremely volatile. Since stockholders lay claim to only the value of a firm above debt obligations, the valuation of the stock of a firm that is in trouble becomes much like that of an "out-of-the-money" option that pays off only if the firm does well, and otherwise is worthless. Such options are extremely volatile.

## DISTRIBUTION OF LARGE DAILY CHANGES

I noted in Chapter 13 that there were 123 days from 1885 through the present when the Dow Jones Industrials changed by 5 percent or more: 59 up and 64 down. Seventy-nine of these days, or nearly two-thirds of the total, were in the period from 1929 through 1933. The most volatile year by far in terms of daily changes was 1932, which contained 35 days when the Dow moved by at least 5 percent. The longest period of time

between two successive changes of at least 5 percent was the 17-year period that preceded the October 19, 1987 stock crash.

Figure 16-4 records some of the properties of large daily changes.
Monday has seen only slightly more large changes than the rest of the
week, and Tuesday has seen significantly fewer. Monday has the largest
number of down days, but Wednesday has by far the highest number of
up days.

Thirty of the large changes occurred in October, which has noto-
riously been a month of great volatility in the stock market. This reputation is fully justified. Not only has October witnessed 30 out of the
123 largest changes, but it has also seen the two greatest stock crashes
in history. It is interesting to note that nearly two-thirds of the total
days with large declines have occurred in the last four months of the

## FIGURE  16–4

Distribution of Dow Industrial Changes over 5 Percent, 1885–1997

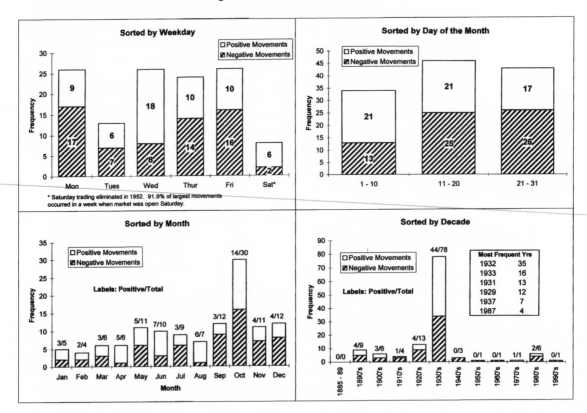

year. I shall present the seasonal aspects of stock price changes in Chapter 18.

One of the most surprising bits of information about large market moves relates to the period of the greatest stock market collapse. From September 3, 1929 through July 8, 1932, the Dow Jones Industrials collapsed nearly 89 percent. During that period, there were 37 episodes when the Dow changed by 5 percent or more. Surprisingly, 21 of those episodes were *increases*!

Many of these sharp rallies were the result of short-covering, as those speculators who thought the market was on a one-way street downward rushed to sell stock they did not own. They were forced to buy back, or cover their positions once the market rallied. It is not uncommon for markets that appear to be trending in one direction to experience occasional sharp moves in the other direction. In a bull market, the expression "up the staircase, down the elevator" is an apt description of price performance. Traders who play the trend are quick to bail out when they see a correction coming, making it hazardous for ordinary investors who believe it simple to spot major trends in financial markets.

## THE ECONOMICS OF MARKET VOLATILITY

Many of the complaints about market volatility are grounded in the belief that the market reacts excessively to changes in news. But how news *should* impact the market is so difficult to determine that few can quantify the proper impact of an event on the price of a stock. As a result, traders often "follow the crowd" and try to predict how *other* traders will react when news strikes.

Over half a century ago, Keynes illustrated the problem of investors who tries to value stock by economic fundamentals as opposed to following the crowd:

> Investment based on genuine long-term expectation is so difficult today as to be scarcely practicable. He who attempts it must surely lead much more laborious days and run greater risk than he who tries to guess better than the crowd how the crowd will behave; and, given equal intelligence, he may make more disastrous mistakes.[4]

In 1981, Robert Shiller of Yale University devised a method of determining whether stock investors tended to overreact to changes in dividends

---

4 John Maynard Keynes, *General Theory*, p. 157.

and interest rates, the fundamental building blocks of stock values.[5] From the examination of historical data, he calculated what the value of the S & P 500 Index *should have been* given the subsequent realization of dividends and interest rates. We know what this value is because, as shown in Chapter 4, stock prices are the present discounted value of future cash flows.

What he found was that stock prices were far too variable to be explained merely by the subsequent behavior of dividends and interest rates. Stock prices appeared to *overreact* to changes in dividends, failing to take into account that most of the deviations from the trend growth in dividends were only temporary. In other words, investors priced stocks in a recession as if they expected dividends to go much lower, completely contrary to historical experience.

The word *cycle* in *business cycle* implies that ups in economic activity will be followed by downs, and vice versa. Since earnings and profits tend to follow the business cycle, they too should behave in a cyclical manner, returning to some average value over time. Under these circumstances, a temporary drop in dividends (or earnings) during a recession should have a very minor effect on the price of a stock, which discounts dividends into the infinite future.

When stocks are collapsing, worst-case scenarios loom large in investors' minds. On May 6, 1932, after stocks had plummeted 85 percent from their 1929 high, Dean Witter issued the following memo to its clients:

> There are only two premises which are tenable as to the future. Either we are going to have chaos or else recovery. The former theory is foolish. If chaos ensues nothing will maintain value; neither bonds nor stocks nor bank deposits nor gold will remain valuable. Real estate will be a worthless asset because titles will be insecure. No policy can be based upon this impossible contingency. Policy must therefore be predicated upon the theory of recovery. The present is not the first depression; it may be the worst, but just as surely as conditions have righted themselves in the past and have gradually readjusted to normal, so this will again occur. The only uncertainty is when it will occur. . . . I wish to say emphatically that in a few years present prices will appear as ridiculously low as 1929 values appear fantastically high.[6]

---

5 Robert Shiller, *Market Volatility*, Cambridge, Mass.: M.I.T. Press, 1989. The seminal article that spawned the excess volatility literature was "Do Stock Prices Move Too Much to Be Justified by Subsequent Changes in Dividends?" in *American Economic Review*, 71 (1981), pp. 421–435.
6 Memorandum from Dean Witter, May 6, 1932.

Two months later the stock market hit its all-time low and rallied strongly. In retrospect, these words reflected great wisdom and sound judgment about the temporary dislocations of stock prices. Yet at the time they were uttered, investors were so disenchanted with stocks and so filled with doom and gloom that the message fell on deaf ears.

## EPILOGUE TO THE CRASH

Despite the drama of the October 1987 market collapse, which has often been compared with 1929, there was amazingly little lasting effect on the world economy or even the financial markets. Because this stock crash did not augur either a further collapse in stock prices or a decline in economic activity, it will probably never attain the notoriety of the crash of 1929. Yet its lesson is perhaps more important. Economic safeguards, such as prompt Federal Reserve action to provide liquidity to the economy and assure the financial markets, *can* prevent an economic debacle of the kind that beset our economy during the Great Depression.

This does not mean that the markets are exempt from violent fluctuations. Since the future will always be uncertain, psychology and sentiment often dominate economic fundamentals. As Keynes perceptively stated 60 years ago in *The General Theory*, "The outstanding fact is the extreme precariousness of the basis of knowledge on which our estimates of prospective yield have to be made."[7] Precarious estimates are subject to sudden change, and prices in free markets will always be volatile.

---

7 Keynes, *The General Theory*, p. 149.

# 17
## CHAPTER

# TECHNICAL ANALYSIS AND INVESTING WITH THE TREND

*Many sceptics, it is true, are inclined to dismiss the whole procedure [chart reading] as akin to astrology or necromancy; but the sheer weight of its importance in Wall Street requires that its pretensions be examined with some degree of care."*

—Benjamin Graham,[1] 1934

## THE NATURE OF TECHNICAL ANALYSIS

Flags, pennants, saucers, and head-and-shoulders formations. Stochastics, moving average convergence divergence indicators, and candlesticks. Such is the arcane language of the technical analyst, an investor who forecasts future returns by the use of past price trends. Few areas of investment analysis have attracted more critics, yet no other area has a core of such dedicated, ardent supporters. Technical analysis, often dismissed by academic economists as being no more useful than astrology, is being given a new look, and some of the recent evidence is surprisingly positive.

Technical analysts, or *chartists* as they are sometimes called, stand in sharp contrast to fundamental analysts, who use such variables as dividends, earnings, and book values to forecast stock returns. Chartists ignore these fundamental variables, maintaining that virtually all useful information is summarized by past price patterns. These patterns might be the result of market psychology or informed traders who accumulate

---

1 Benjamin Graham and David Dodd, *Security Analysis*, 1934, op. cit., p. 618.

and distribute stock. If these patterns are read properly, chartists maintain, investors can use them to share in the gains of those who are more knowledgeable about a stock's prospects.

## CHARLES DOW, TECHNICAL ANALYST

The first well-publicized technical analyst was Charles Dow, the creator of the Dow Jones Averages. But Charles Dow did not analyze only charts. In conjunction with his interest in market movements, Dow founded the *Wall Street Journal* and published his strategy in editorials in the early part of this century. Dow's successor, William Hamilton, extended Dow's technical approach and published *The Stock Market Barometer* in 1922. Ten years later, Charles Rhea formalized Dow's concepts in a book entitled *Dow Theory*.

Charles Dow likened the ebb and flow of stock prices to waves in an ocean. He claimed that there was a primary wave, which like the tide determined the overall trend. Upon this trend were superimposed secondary waves and minor ripples. He also claimed you could identify which trend the market was in by analyzing a chart of the Dow Industrial average, the volume in the market, and the Dow Jones Rail Average (now called the Transportation Average).

It is widely acknowledged that the use of Dow Theory would have gotten an investor out of the stock market before the October 1929 stock crash, but not before the crash of October 1987. Martin J. Pring, a noted technical analyst, argues that, starting in 1897, investors who purchased stock in the Dow Jones Industrial Average and followed each Dow Theory buy and sell signal would have seen an original investment of $100 reach $116,508 by January 1990, as opposed to $5,682 with a buy-and hold strategy (these calculations exclude reinvested dividends).[2] But confirming profits by using Dow Theory is difficult because the buy and sell signals are subjective and not given to precise numerical rules.

## RANDOMNESS OF STOCK PRICES

Although Dow Theory might not be as popular as it once was, the idea that you can identify the major trends in the market, riding bull markets

---

2 Martin Pring, *Technical Analysis Explained*, 3rd ed., New York: McGraw-Hill, 1991, p. 31. Also see David Glickstein and Rolf Wubbels, "Dow Theory Is Alive and Well!" in the *Journal of Portfolio Management*, April 1983, pp. 28-32.

while avoiding bear markets, is still the fundamental thrust of technical analysis. Yet most economists still attack the fundamental tenet of the chartists—that stock prices follow predictable patterns. To these academic researchers, the movements of prices in the market more closely conform to a pattern called a *random walk* than to trends and designs that forecast returns.

The first to make this connection was Frederick MacCauley, an economist in the early part of this century. His comments at a 1925 dinner meeting of the American Statistical Association on the topic of "forecasting security prices" were reported in the Association's official journal:

> MacCauley observed that there was a striking similarity between the fluctuations of the stock market and those of a chance curve which may be obtained by throwing dice. Everyone will admit that the course of such a purely chance curve cannot be predicted. If the stock market can be forecast from a graph of its movements, it must be because of its difference from the chance curve.[3]

More than 30 years later, Harry Roberts, a professor at the University of Chicago, simulated movements in the market by plotting price changes that resulted from completely random events, such as flips of a coin. These simulations looked like the charts of actual stock prices, forming shapes and following trends that are considered by chartists to be significant predictors of future returns. But since the next period's price change was, by construction, a completely random event, such patterns could not logically have any predictive content. This early research supported the belief that the apparent patterns in past stock prices were the result of completely random movements.

But does the randomness of stock prices make economic sense? Factors influencing supply and demand do not occur randomly and are often quite predictable from one period to the next. Should not these predictable factors make stock prices move in nonrandom patterns?

In 1965, Professor Paul Samuelson of MIT showed that the randomness in security prices did not contradict the laws of supply and demand.[4] In fact, such randomness was a result of a free and efficient market in which investors have already incorporated all the *known* factors influencing the price of the stock. This is the crux of the "efficient market hypothesis."

---

3 *Journal of the American Statistical Association*, v. 20, June 1925, p. 248. Comments made at the Aldine Club in New York on April 17, 1925.
4 Paul Samuelson, "Proof that Properly Anticipated Prices Fluctuate Randomly," *Industrial Management Review*, vol. 6 (1965), p. 49.

If the market is efficient, prices will change only when new, unanticipated information is released to the market. Since unanticipated information is as likely to be good or bad, the resulting movement in stock prices is random. Price charts will look like a random walk since the probability that stocks go up or down is completely random and cannot be predicted.[5]

## Simulations of Random Stock Prices

If stock prices are indeed random, then their movements should not be distinguishable from counterfeits generated randomly by a computer. Figure 17-1 extends the experiment conceived by Professor Roberts over 30 years ago. Instead of generating only closing prices, I programmed the computer to generate intraday prices, creating the popular high/low/close bar graphs that are found in most newspapers and chart publications.

Figure 17-1 contains eight charts. A computer, using a random-number generator, has simulated four of these charts. In these graphs, there is absolutely no way to predict the future from the past, since future movements are designed to be totally independent from the past. The other four charts were chosen from actual data of the Dow Jones Industrial Average over recent years. Before reading further, try to determine which are real historical prices and which were created by a computer.

Such a task is quite difficult. In fact, most of the top brokers at a leading Wall Street firm found it impossible to tell the difference between real and counterfeit data. Only Figure 17-1d, which depicts the period around the October 19, 1987 stock crash, was correctly identified by two-thirds of the brokers. With the remaining seven graphs, the brokers showed no ability to distinguish actual from counterfeit data. The true historical prices are represented by graphs B, D, E, and H, while the computer-generated data are graphs A, C, F, and G.[6]

## TRENDING MARKETS AND PRICE REVERSALS

Despite the fact that many "trends" are in fact the result of the totally random movement of stock prices, many traders will not invest against

---

5 More generally, the sum of the product of each possible price change times the probability of its occurrence is zero. This is called a *martingale*, of which a random walk (50 percent probability up, 50 percent probability down) is a special case.
6 Graph 16-1b covers February 15 to July 1, 1991, graph 16-1e covers January 15 to June 1, 1992, and graph 16-1h from June 15 to November 1, 1990.

# F I G U R E   17–1

## Distinguishing Between Real and Random Stock Price Changes

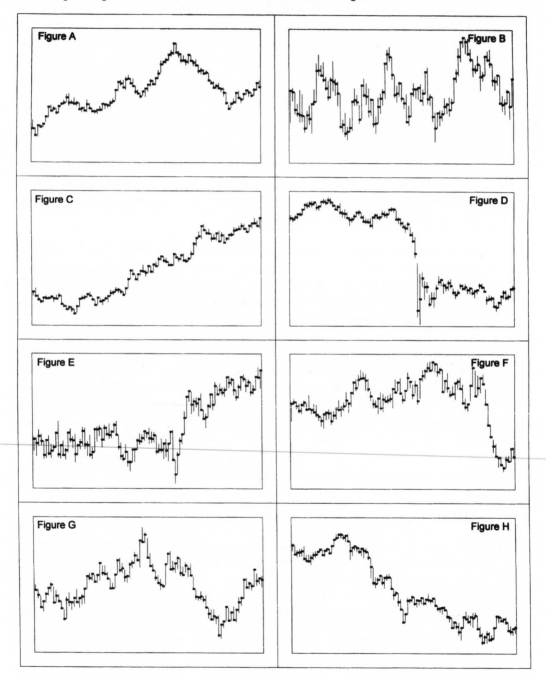

a trend that they believe they have identified. Two of the most well-known sayings of market timers are "Make the trend your friend" and "Trust the thrust."

Martin Zweig, a well-known market timer who uses fundamental and technical variables to forecast market trends, has forcefully stated: "I can't overemphasize the importance of staying with the trend of the market, being in gear with the tape, and not fighting the major movements. Fighting the tape is an open invitation to disaster."[7]

When a trend appears established, technical analysts draw *channels* that enclose the path of stock prices. A channel is drawn to enclose the upper and lower bounds within which the market has traded. The lower bound of a channel is frequently called a *support level* and the upper bound a *resistance level*. When the market breaks the bounds of the channel, a large market move often follows.

The very fact that many traders believe in the importance of trends can induce behavior that makes trend-following so popular. While the trend is intact, traders sell when prices reach the upper end of the channel and buy when they reach the lower end, attempting to take advantage of the apparent back-and-forth motion of stock prices. If the trend line is broken, many of these traders will reverse their positions: buying if the market penetrates the top of the trend line, and selling if it falls through the bottom. This behavior often accelerates the movement of stock prices and reinforces the importance of the trend.

Option trading by trend followers reinforces the behavior of market timers. When the market is trading within a channel, traders will sell put and call options at strike prices that represent the lower and upper bounds of the channel. As long as the market remains within the channel, these speculators collect premiums as the options expire worthless.

If the market penetrates the trading range, option sellers are exposed to great risks. Recall that sellers of options (as long as they do not own the underlying stock) face a huge potential liability, a liability that can be many times the premium that they collected upon sale of the option. When such unlimited losses loom, these option writers "run for cover," or buy back their options, accelerating the movement of prices.

## MOVING AVERAGES

Successful technical trading requires not only identifying the trend but, more importantly, identifying when the trend is about to reverse. A

---

7 Martin Zweig, *Winning on Wall Street*, New York: Warner Books, 1990, p. 121.

popular tool for determining when the trend might change examines the relation between the current price and a moving average of past price movements, a technique that goes back to at least the 1930s.[8]

A *moving average* is simply the arithmetic average of a given number of past closing prices of a stock or index over a fixed interval of time. For example, a 200-day moving average is the average of the past 200 days of closing prices. For each new trading day, the oldest price is dropped and the most recent price is added to compute the average.

Moving averages fluctuate far less than daily prices. When prices are rising, the moving average trails the market and, technical analysts claim, forms a support level for stock prices. When prices are falling, the moving average is above current prices and forms a resistance level. Analysts claim that a moving average allows investors to identify the basic market trend without being distracted by the day-to-day volatility of the market. When prices penetrate the moving average, this indicates that powerful underlying forces are signaling a reversal of the basic trend.

The most popular moving average uses prices for the past 200 trading days, and is therefore called the *200-day moving average*. It is frequently plotted in newspapers and investment letters as a key determinant of investment trends. One of the early supporters of this strategy was William Gordon, who indicated that, over the period from 1897 to 1967, buying stocks when the Dow broke above the moving average produced nearly seven times the return as buying when the Dow broke below the average.[9] Colby and Meyers claim that for the United States the best time period for a moving average of weekly data is 45 weeks, just slightly longer than the 200-day moving average.[10]

## Testing the Moving Average Strategy

In order to test the 200-day moving average strategy, I examined the daily record of the Dow Jones Industrial Average from 1885 to the present. In contrast to the previous studies of this strategy, the holding pe-

---

8 See William Brock, Josef Lakonishok, and Blake LeBaron, "Simple Technical Trading Rules and the Stochastic Properties of Stock Returns," *Journal of Finance*, 47, no. 5 (December 1992), pp. 1731-64. The first definitive analysis of moving averages comes from a book by H. M. Gartley, *Profits in the Stock Market*, New York: H. M. Gartley, 1930.

9 William Gordon, *The Stock Market Indicators*, Palisades, NJ: Investors Press, 1968.

10 Robert W. Colby and Thomas A. Meyers, *The Encyclopedia of Technical Market Indicators*, Homewood, IL: Dow Jones-Irwin, 1988.

riod returns include the reinvestment of dividends when in the market and interest when out of the stock market.[11] Annualized returns are examined over the entire period as well as the subperiods.

Then I adopted the following criteria to determine the buy-sell strategy: Whenever the Dow Jones Industrial Average closed at least 1 percent *above* its 200-day moving average, stocks were purchased at these closing prices. Whenever the Dow Industrials closed by at least 1 percent *below* its 200-day moving average, stocks were sold. Reinvestment out of the market was assumed to be made in Treasury bills.

There are two noteworthy aspects of this strategy. The 1 percent band around the 200-day moving average is used in order to reduce the number of times an investor would have to move in and out of the market. Without this band, investors using the 200-day moving average strategy are often *whipsawed*, a term used to describe the frequent buying and then selling and then buying again of stocks in an attempt to beat the market. Such trades dramatically lower investor returns because of the large transaction costs incurred.

The second aspect of this strategy assumes that an investor buys or sells stocks at the *closing* price rather than at any time reached during the day. Only in recent years has the exact intraday level of the averages been computed. Using historical data, it is impossible to determine times when the market average penetrated the 200-day moving average during the day, but closed at levels that did not trigger a signal. By specifying that the average must close above or below the signal, I present a theory that could have been implemented in practice.[12]

## Backtesting the 200-day Moving Average

Figure 17-2 shows the daily and 200-day moving average of the Dow Jones Industrial during two select periods: from 1924–36 and 1980–97. The time periods when investors are out of the stock market are shaded; otherwise investors are fully invested in stocks.

To the eye, the moving average strategy appears to work extremely well. Investors are in stocks during all the important bull markets, and out of stocks during all the major bear markets.

---

11 The dividend yield was estimated from yearly data of dividend yields, described in Chapter 1.
12 Historically, the daily high and low levels of stock averages were calculated on the basis of the highest or lowest price of each stock reached *at any time* during the day. This is called the *theoretical* high or low. The *actual* high is the highest level reached *at any given time* by the stocks in the average.

**FIGURE   17–2**

Dow Industrials and a 200-Day Moving Average (Shaded Areas are Out of Market)

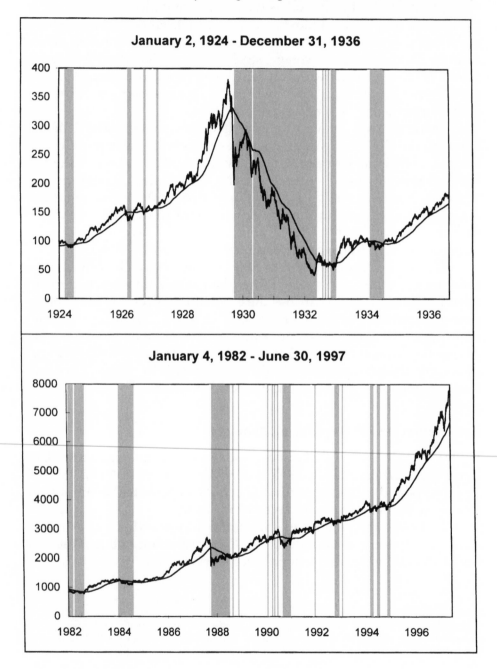

The strategy worked extremely well during the bull and bear market of the 1920s. Using the criteria outlined above, investors would have bought stocks on June 27, 1924 when the Dow was 95.33 and, with only two minor interruptions, ridden the bull market to the top at 381.17 on September 3, 1929. They would have exited the market on October 19, 1927 at 323.87, ten days before the Great Crash. Except for a brief period in 1930, the strategy would have kept investors out of stocks through the worst bear market in history. They would have finally reentered the market on Aug. 6, 1932, when the Dow was 66.56, just 25 points higher than its postcrash low. Over the entire 107-year history of the Dow Jones average, the 200-day moving average strategy had its greatest triumph during the boom and crash of the 1920s and early 1930s.

Investors following the 200-day moving average strategy would also have avoided the October 19, 1987 crash, selling out on the previous Friday, October 16. However, in contrast to the 1929 crash, the market did not continue downward. Although the market fell 23 percent on October 19, investors would not have reentered the market until the following June when the Dow was only about 5 percent below the exit level of October 16. Nonetheless, following the 200-day moving average strategy would have avoided October 19 and 20, traumatic days for many investors who held stocks.

Table 17-1 summarizes the returns from the 200-day moving average strategy and a "buy-and-hold" strategy of not timing the market. From 1885 through June 1997, the 11.51 percent annualized return from the timing strategy beat the return on the holding strategy return of 9.98 percent per year. As noted earlier, however, the timing strategy has its biggest success from avoiding the 1929–32 crash. If that period is excluded, the returns over the whole period are about the same. Since 1982, when the last secular bull market began, the holding strategy beats the timing strategy.

Of course, it would have been no small feat to avoid the Great Crash of 1929. Yet, if you believe that another episode when the Dow drops by nearly 90 percent in less than three years is unlikely (and no other episode before or since has come close), it is important to consider how successful the strategy would be excluding those unique years.

But the major gain of the timing strategy is a reduction in risk. Since you are in the market less than two-thirds of the time, the standard deviation of returns is reduced by about one-quarter. This means that on a risk-adjusted basis the return on the 200-day moving average strategy is quite impressive.

**T A B L E  17–1**

Timing and Holding Strategy Annualized Returns, January 1886 to June 1997

| Period | Holding Strategy | | Timing Strategy | | | | % in Market | # of switches |
| | Annualized | | Annualized Return | | Net Trans Costs | | | |
| | Return | Risk | Return | Risk | Return | Risk | | |
|---|---|---|---|---|---|---|---|---|
| Overall | 9.98% | 22.91% | 11.51% | 17.63% | 10.05% | 18.22% | 63.42% | 292 |
| Subperiods | | | | | | | | |
| 1886 - 1925 | 9.11% | 23.86% | 10.01% | 19.20% | 8.32% | 19.61% | 57.08% | 122 |
| 1926 - 1945 | 6.24% | 32.91% | 11.98% | 22.90% | 10.42% | 23.70% | 62.69% | 56 |
| 1946 - 1997 | 12.16% | 17.24% | 12.50% | 13.96% | 11.26% | 14.62% | 68.66% | 114 |
| Excl. 1929-1932 Crash | | | | | | | | |
| 1926 - 1945 | 18.40% | 27.63% | 16.77% | 22.44% | 15.31% | 23.13% | 72.73% | 53 |
| Overall | 11.91% | 21.65% | 12.19% | 17.46% | 10.75% | 18.01% | 65.05% | 289 |

If the transaction costs of implementing the timing strategy are included in the calculations, the excess returns over the whole period, including the 1929–32 Great Crash, virtually vanish. Transaction costs include brokerage costs and bid-ask spreads, as well as the capital gains tax incurred when stocks are sold, and are assumed to be half a percent when buying or selling the market. This probably underestimates such costs, especially in the earlier years. Each 0.1 percent increase of transaction costs lowers the compound annual returns by 29 basis points.

Nevertheless, there is no question that the 200-day moving average strategy, even with transaction costs, avoids large losses while reducing overall gains only slightly. Figure 17-3 shows the distribution of gains and losses in the timing strategy and the holding strategy. The timing strategy participates in most of the winning markets and avoids most of the big losing markets, but also leads to many more small losses. These occur when the market does not take on a definite trend and, despite the use of the 1 percent band to reduce whipsawing, investors find themselves moving in and out of the market frequently, incurring transactions costs and trading losses. The distribution of gains and losses shown in Figure 17-3 is quite similar to buying index puts on the market. As noted in Chapter 15, index puts are equivalent to buying an in-

## FIGURE 17–3

Distribution of Gains and Losses: Timing Strategy vs. Holding Strategy

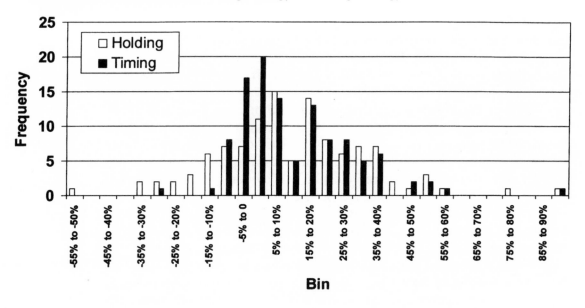

surance policy on the market, but of course you constantly incur the cost of the insurance. Similarly, the timing strategy involves a large number of small losses that comes from moving into and out of the market, while avoiding most severe declines.

## CONCLUSION

Technical analysis, its proponents claim, helps investors identify the major trends of the market and when these trends might reverse. Yet there is considerable debate about whether such trends exist, or whether they are just runs of good and bad returns that are the result of random price movements.

Burton Malkiel has been quite clear in his denunciation of technical analysis. In his best-selling work, *A Random Walk Down Wall Street,* he proclaims:

> Technical rules have been tested exhaustively by using stock price data on both major exchanges, going back as far as the beginning of the 20th century. The results reveal conclusively that past movements in

stock prices cannot be used to foretell future movements. The stock market has no memory. The central proposition of charting is absolutely false, and investors who follow its precepts will accomplish nothing but increasing substantially the brokerage charges they pay.[13]

Yet this contention, once supported nearly unanimously by academic economists, is cracking. Recent econometric research has shown that such simple trading rules as 200-day moving averages can be used to improve returns.[14]

Despite the ongoing academic debate, technical analysis and trend-following draw huge followings on Wall Street and many savvy investors. The analysis in this chapter gives a cautious nod to the strategy based on moving averages, as long as transaction costs are not high. But this strategy must be monitored closely. In October 1987, the Dow fell below its 200-day moving average on the Friday before the crash and gave a sell signal. But if you failed to get through to your broker that Friday afternoon, you would have been swept downward in the 22 percent nightmare of Black Monday.

Furthermore, as I have repeatedly noted throughout this book, actions by investors to take advantage of the past will change returns in the future. As Benjamin Graham stated so well more than 60 years ago:

> A moment's thought will show that there can be no such thing as a scientific prediction of economic events under human control. The very "dependability" of such a prediction will cause human actions which will invalidate it. Hence thoughtful chartists admit that continued success is dependent upon keeping the successful method known to only a few people.[15]

---

13 Burton Malkiel, *A Random Walk Down Wall Street*, 1990, p. 133.
14 William Brock, Josef Lakonishok, and Blake LeBaron "Simple Technical Trading Rules and the Stochastic Properties of Stock Returns," *Journal of Finance*, vol. 47, no. 5 (December 1992), pp. 1731-64.
15 Benjamin Graham and David Dodd, Ibid., p. 619.

CHAPTER

# CALENDAR ANOMALIES

*October. This is one of the peculiarly dangerous months to speculate in stocks. The others are July, September, April, November, May, March, June, December, August, and February.*

—**Mark Twain**

The dictionary defines *anomaly* as something inconsistent with what is naturally expected. And what is more *un*natural than to expect to beat the market by predicting stock prices based solely on the day or week or month of the year? Yet it appears that you can. Recent research has revealed that there are predictable times during which stocks as a whole, and certain classes of stocks in particular, excel in the market.

The most important calendar anomaly is that, historically, small stocks have far outperformed larger stocks in one specific month of the year: January. In fact, January is the only reason that small stocks have greater total returns than large stocks over the past 70 years! This phenomenon has been dubbed the *January Effect*. Its discovery in the early 1980s by Don Keim,[1] based on research he did as a graduate student at the University of Chicago, was the first, and in some ways the most significant, finding in a market where researchers had previously failed to detect any predictable pattern to stock prices.

The January Effect might be the granddaddy of all calendar anomalies, but it is not the only one. For inexplicable reasons, stocks generally do much better in the first few days of the month than the middle or end, and they also fare much better on Fridays than on Mondays.

---

1 Don Keim, "Size-Related Anomalies and Stock Return Seasonality: Further Empirical Evidence," *Journal of Financial Economics*, 1983, v. 12, pp. 13-32.

Furthermore, they do exceptionally well on any day before a big holiday, particularly December 31, which is actually the day that launches
the January Effect.

Why these anomalies occur is not well understood, and whether
they will continue to be significant in the future is an open question. But
their discovery has put economists on the spot. No longer can researchers be so certain that the stock market is thoroughly unpredictable and impossible to beat.

## THE JANUARY EFFECT

Of all of the calendar-related anomalies, the January Effect has been the
most important. From 1925 through 1997, the average return on the S &
P 500 Index in January was 1.6 percent, while the average returns on the
small stocks came to 6.2 percent. The 4.8% percent average excess return
of small stocks in January *exceeds* the entire yearly difference in arithmetic returns between large and small stocks. In other words, from
February through December, the returns on small stocks are lower than
large stocks. On the basis of history, the only profitable time to hold
small stocks is the month of January!

To see how important the January Effect is, look at Figure 18-1. It
shows the total return index on large and small stocks and on small
stocks if the January return on small stocks is replaced with that of the S
& P 500 Index in January. As shown in Chapter 6, a single dollar invested in small stocks in 1926 would grow to $4,881 by the end of 1997,
while the same dollar would grow to only $1,829 in large stocks. Yet if
the small stocks' excess January return is eliminated, the total return to
small stocks accumulates to only $202, merely 11 percent of the return
on large stocks!

Figure 18-1 also shows that if these January small-stock returns
continue in the future, it could lead to some astounding investment results. By buying small stocks at the end of December and transferring
them back to the S & P 500 Index at the end of January, your accumulation would grow to $44,272, or a 16.0 percent annual rate of return! In
fact, history dictates that you should borrow and leverage as much as
you can to take advantage of this January anomaly.

There have been only 14 years since 1925 when large stocks have
outperformed small stocks in January. Furthermore, when small stocks
underperform large stocks, it is usually not by much: the worst underperformance was 5.5 percent in January 1929. In contrast, since 1925,
small-stock returns have exceeded large-stock returns in January for 27

## FIGURE 18-1

Small and Large Stocks, With and Without the January Effect, 1926–1997

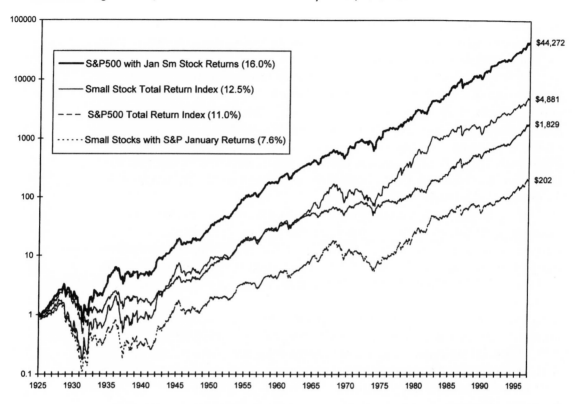

years by at least 5 percent, for 12 years by at least 10 percent, and for two years by over 20 percent.

The January Effect also prevailed during the most powerful bear market in our history. From August 1929 through the summer of 1932, when small stocks lost over 90 percent of their value, small stocks posted consecutive January *monthly* returns of plus 13 percent, 21 percent, and 10 percent in 1930, 1931, and 1932. It is testimony to the power of the January Effect that investors could have increased their wealth by 50 percent during the greatest stock crash in history by buying small stocks at the end of December of those three years and selling them at the end of the month, putting their money in cash for the rest of the year!

A fascinating feature of the January Effect is that you have not had to wait the entire month to see the big returns from small stocks roll in. Most of the buying in small stocks begins on the last trading day of December (often in the late afternoon), as some investors pick up the bargains that are dumped by others on New Year's Eve. Strong gains in small stocks continue on the first trading day of January and with declining force through the first week of trading. On the first trading day of January alone, small stocks earn nearly four percentage points more than large stocks.[2] By the middle of the month, the January Effect is largely exhausted.

When any anomaly such as the January Effect is found, it is important to examine its international reach. When researchers turned to foreign markets, they found that the January Effect was not just a U.S. phenomenon. In Japan, the world's second-largest capital market, the excess returns on small stocks in January come to 7.2 percent per year, more than in the United States. As you shall see later in the chapter, January is the best month for both large *and* small stocks in many other countries of the world.[3]

How could such a phenomenon go unnoticed for so long by investors, portfolio managers, and financial economists? Because in the United States, January is nothing special for large stocks, and these stocks form the base of the popular indexes, such as the Dow Industrials and the S & P 500. That's not to say that January is not a good month for those stocks, too. As explained later, large stocks do quite well in January, particularly in foreign markets. But in the United States, January is by no means the best month for stocks of large firms.

It should be noted that these superior January returns do not always materialize. There are many years when small stocks have underperformed larger stocks in January, and this has happened with greater frequency recently. The widespread publicity of the January Effect may actually lead to its demise.

## Causes of the January Effect

Why do investors tend to favor small stocks in January? No one knows for sure, but there are several hypotheses. Individual investors, in contrast to institutions, hold a disproportionate amount of small stocks, and they are more sensitive to the tax consequences of their trading. Small stocks, especially those that have declined in the preceding 11 months,

---

2 Robert Haugen and Josef Lakonishok, *The Incredible January Effect*, Homewood, IL: Dow Jones-Irwin, 1989, p. 47.

3 For an excellent summary of all this evidence, see Gabriel Hawawini and Don Keim, "The Cross Section of Common Stock Returns: A Review of the Evidence and Some New Findings," May 1997, working paper, Wharton School, University of Pennsylvania.

are subject to tax-motivated selling in December. This selling depresses the price of individual issues.

There is some evidence to support this explanation. Stocks that have fallen throughout the year fall even more in December, and then often rise dramatically in January. Furthermore, there is some evidence that before the introduction of the U.S. income tax in 1913, there was no January Effect. And in Australia, where the tax year runs from July 1 through June 30, there are abnormally large returns in July.

If taxes are a factor, however, they cannot be the only one, for the January Effect holds in countries that do not have a capital gains tax. Japan did not tax capital gains for individual investors until 1989, but the January Effect was still present. Furthermore, capital gains were not taxed in Canada before 1972, and yet there was a January Effect in that country as well. Finally, stocks that have risen throughout the previous year and should not be subject to tax-loss selling still rise in January, although not by as much as stocks that have fallen the previous year.

There are other potential explanations for the January Effect. Individuals often receive an influx of funds, such as bonuses and money that become available from tax-loss selling, at year end. These individuals often wait several days to invest their cash and then buy in the first week of January. Data show that there is a sharp increase in the ratio of public buy orders to public sell orders around the turn of the year. Since the public holds a large fraction of small stocks, this could be an important clue to understanding the January Effect.[4]

Another possible explanation is that portfolio managers often load up with risky stocks, often small stocks, at the beginning of the year, but then sell them by the time their balance sheets are inspected at year end. They do this because if their risky stocks have done well, the managers can lock in their superior performance, in other words "beat the S & P," by indexing on the S & P 500 stocks for the rest of the year. And if risky stocks have not done well, they will also sell them because they do not want their clients to see them on their year-end balance sheet!

Another factor contributing to the January Effect is the fact that returns are calculated on the basis of the last price recorded during the day. If a buyer motivates the last sale, no matter how small, the final price will be registered at the asked or offer price. For small stocks, this could be 5 percent or more above the "bid" price at which the last sale was made. A buying flurry at the end of the day, centered especially in

---

4 Jay Ritter, "The Buying and Selling Behavior of Individual Investors at the End of the Year," *Journal of Finance*, 43 (1988), pp. 701-717.

small stocks, could cause a substantial rise in small stock indexes. This appears to be important at the end of calendar quarters and especially on December 31. But researchers have concluded that it can explain just a small part of the January Effect.[5]

Although all these explanations appear quite reasonable, none jibes with what is called an *efficient capital market*. If money managers know that stocks (especially small ones) will surge in January, they should be bought well before New Year's Day to capture these spectacular returns. That would cause a boom in small stocks in December, which would prompt other managers to buy them in November, and so on. In the process of acting on the January Effect, the price of stocks would be smoothed out over the year and the phenomenon would disappear.

Of course, to eliminate the January Effect, money managers and investors with significant capital must know of the effect and feel comfortable about acting on it. Those in a fiduciary position might feel uneasy justifying what appears to be a very unusual investment strategy to their clients, especially if it does not work out. Others might be reluctant to take advantage of a phenomenon that seems to have no economic rationale.

In fact, the January Effect has been much weaker in recent years. Small stocks (measured as the bottom quintile of capitalization value) underperformed larger stocks in January of 1995, 1996, and 1997, the only consecutive three-year period since 1926 when this has occurred.[6] In the back of many investors' minds is a lingering suspicion that the January Effect won't last when more investors catch on by reading this and other books that have been written about it.

## The January Effect in Value Stocks

In addition to the small stock effect, there is another January Effect in the stock market that has received virtually no publicity. As noted in Chapter 5, value stocks—large as well as small—have a substantially higher return than growth stocks in the month of January. Table 18-1 reports the return on various size-based portfolio for value and growth stocks over the period from June 1963 through June 1996. Over the entire period, value stocks outperform growth stocks for all size firms. But with January removed, large growth stocks, such as those

---

5 Marshall E. Blume, and R. F. Stambaugh, "Biases in Computed Returns: An Application to the Size Effect," *Journal of Financial Economics*, 12 (1983), pp. 387-404.
6 The Ibbotson small-stock index, which since 1982 uses the DFA 9/10 stock fund returns, very slightly outperformed the S & P Index in 1995. But the Russell 2000 Index significantly underperformed large stocks that year.

**T A B L E  18–1**

Annual Compound Returns by Size and Book-to-Market Ratio, July 1963 to June 1996

| All Months | | Size Quintiles | | | | |
|---|---|---|---|---|---|---|
| | | Small | 2 | 3 | 4 | Large |
| Book to Market Quintiles | Value | 19.51 | 16.66 | 16.76 | 16.01 | 12.60 |
| | 2 | 19.07 | 16.63 | 14.51 | 13.32 | 10.67 |
| | 3 | 16.44 | 14.55 | 12.89 | 10.21 | 9.65 |
| | 4 | 12.65 | 11.85 | 11.70 | 9.74 | 9.29 |
| | Growth | 6.67 | 7.62 | 9.60 | 9.71 | 10.18 |

| Excluding January | | Size Quintiles | | | | |
|---|---|---|---|---|---|---|
| | | Small | 2 | 3 | 4 | Large |
| Book to Market Quintiles | Value | 9.69 | 10.17 | 10.82 | 11.24 | 9.17 |
| | 2 | 10.66 | 11.02 | 10.51 | 10.05 | 8.76 |
| | 3 | 8.22 | 10.05 | 9.24 | 7.63 | 7.75 |
| | 4 | 4.92 | 7.98 | 8.96 | 7.42 | 7.99 |
| | Growth | -0.66 | 4.53 | 7.53 | 8.60 | 9.39 |

in the S & P 500 Stock Index, have higher returns than large value stocks. I have noted that the Dow 10 strategy, analyzed in Chapter 3, has large returns in January. The Dow 10 stocks, which have the highest dividend yield among the 30 Dow Industrials, mostly fall in the value category.

Why value stocks do well in the month of January is not known. It might reflect a New Year's reassessment of fundamental value-based criteria. The week between Christmas and New Year has historically been the best week of the year. After such holiday exuberance, portfolio managers start the new year on a sober note, downplaying the earnings projections of high-growth firms and focusing instead on firms that have more conservative valuations. Perhaps this phenomenon is related to the beginning-of- the-year funding of tax-exempt accounts with value stocks to avoid the taxation of dividends. A clearer picture of the reasons for this January Effect in value stocks must await further research.

## MONTHLY RETURNS

There are other seasonal patterns to stock returns besides the January Effect. Figure 18-2 displays the monthly returns on the Dow Industrials and S & P 500 Index. December has been the best month since the Second World War, but only the second best month since 1885. July and August have been very good months, although most of these great summer returns were registered before World War II. In contrast, over the past 50 years, July and August offer investors quite mediocre returns. There is really no evidence of the "summer rally" that is much trumpeted by brokers and investment advisers.

FIGURE  18-2

Monthly Returns on the Dow Jones Industrials and S & P 500

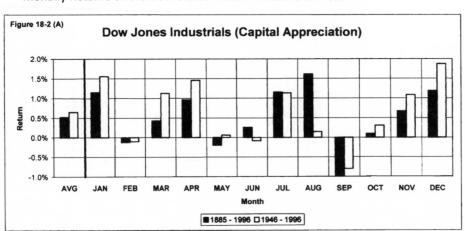

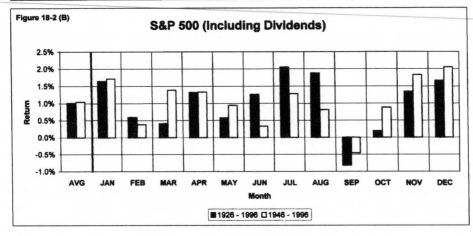

These monthly patterns have a worldwide reach. Although January is a good, but not the best month in the United States, it is a far better month for most countries abroad. Figure 18-3 shows the January returns for the 20 countries covered by the Morgan Stanley Capital Market Index. In every country but Austria, January returns are greater than average. Outside the United States, January returns constitute 30 percent of total stock returns on a value-weighted basis. Investor enthusiasm in January also seems to infect the neighboring months of December and February. Nearly *two-thirds* of all returns outside the United States occur in the three months of December through February.[7]

**F I G U R E   18–3**

International January and September Effects, 1970–1996

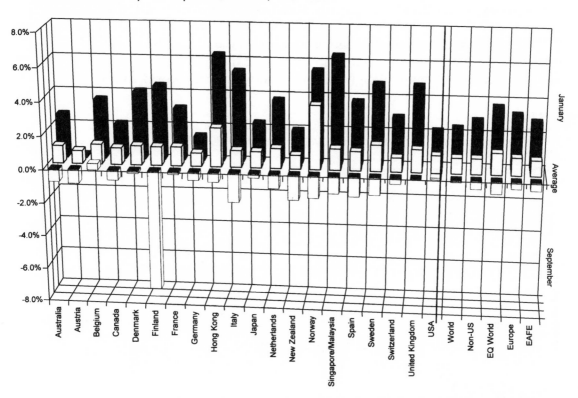

---

7 The data presented in Figure 18-3 are from a value-weighted stock index calculated on large stocks. As noted previously, there is evidence that smaller stocks experience even higher January returns, so the January returns shown in Figure 18-3 are probably much lower than those that can be gained in the average stock.

## The September Effect

Summer months are good, but after the summer holidays, watch out! September is by far the worst month of the year, and in the U.S. is the only month to have a negative return. September is followed closely by October, which, as Chapter 16 indicated, already has a disproportionate percentage of crashes. And, in contrast to the "summer rally," the poor returns in September have persisted over the last century.

Figure 18-4 shows the Dow Jones Industrial average from 1896 through 1997, both including and excluding the month of September. One dollar invested in the Dow Jones Average in 1890 would be worth $179.74 by the end of 1996 (dividends excluded). In contrast, one dollar invested in the Dow only in the month of September would be worth only 26 cents! On the contrary, if you put your money in the stock market the other 11 months of the year, it would have been worth $681.92 at the end of 1996.

The poor returns in September also prevail in the rest of the world. It is amazing that September is the only month of the year that has negative returns in the value-weighted (or equal-weighted) world index

**F I G U R E  18-4**

The September Effect: The Dow Jones Industrial Average, 1890–1996

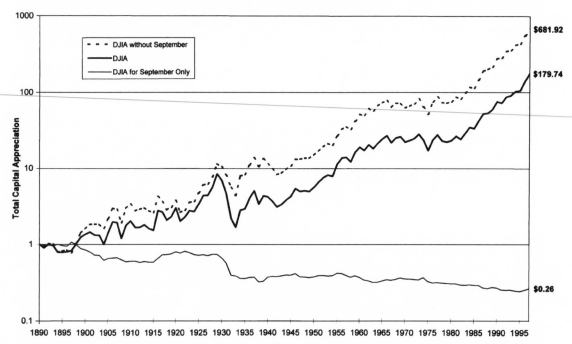

and in most of the 20 countries examined. It should be noted that these data include reinvested dividends, so, historically, stock investors would have been better off in hard cash, which earns nothing, than in the stock market during the month of September. Yet this phenomenon has gone largely unnoticed, and there has been little research to date on this "September Effect."

Why the market experiences these monthly variations is unknown. Maybe the poor returns in late fall have nothing directly to do with economics, but are related to the approach of winter and the depressing effect of rapidly shortening days. In fact, psychologists stress that sunlight is an essential ingredient to well-being. Recent research has confirmed that the New York Stock Exchange does significantly worse on cloudy days than it does on sunny days.[8] But September is also a poor month in Australia and New Zealand, where it marks the beginning of spring and longer days.[9]

Perhaps the poor returns in September are the result of investors liquidating stocks (or holding off buying new stocks) to pay for their summer vacations. As you shall see below, Monday is by far the poorest day of the week. For many, September is the monthly version of Monday: the time you face work after a period of leisure.

## INTRAMONTH RETURNS

Although psychologists say that many silently suffer depression around the joyful season of Christmas and New Year's, stock investors believe `tis the season to be jolly. Daily returns between Christmas and New Year's, as Table 18-2 indicates, average *13* times normal.

Even more striking is the difference between the price change in the first half of the month compared to that in the second half.[10] Figure 18-4 shows the daily changes in the Dow Jones Industrial Average for each day of the month since 1896. Over the entire 107-year period studied, the percentage change in the Dow Jones Industrial Average during the first half of the month—which includes the last trading day of the previous month up to and including the 14th day of the current month— is almost *eight* times the gain which occurs during the second half.[11]

---

8 Edward M. Saunders, Jr., "Stock Prices and Wall Street Weather," American Economic Review, 83 December 1993, pp. 1337-1345.
9 Of course, many investors in the Australian and New Zealand market live north of the equator.
10 R. A. Ariel, "A Monthly Effect in Stock Returns," *Journal of Financial Economics*, 18 (1987), pp. 161-174.
11 The difference in the returns to the Dow stocks between the first and second halves of the month is accentuated by the inclusion of dividends. Currently, about two-thirds of the Dow Industrial stocks pay dividends in the first half of the month, which means that the difference between the first and second half returns are accentuated even more.

**TABLE  18–2**

Average Daily Returns, February 1885 to June 1997

|  | 1885 - 1997 | 1885 - 1925 | 1926 - 1945 | 1946 - 1997 |
|---|---|---|---|---|
| **Overall Averages** | | | | |
| Whole Month | 0.024% | 0.019% | 0.015% | 0.032% |
| First Half of Month | 0.047% | 0.020% | 0.062% | 0.055% |
| Second Half of Month | 0.006% | 0.018% | -0.032% | 0.008% |
| Last Day of Month | 0.120% | 0.087% | 0.163% | 0.127% |
| **Days of the Week** | | | | |
| Monday | -0.110% | -0.087% | -0.211% | -0.089% |
| Tuesday | 0.037% | 0.038% | 0.047% | 0.034% |
| Wednesday | 0.063% | 0.028% | 0.081% | 0.084% |
| Thursday | 0.028% | 0.001% | 0.063% | 0.035% |
| Friday | 0.076% | 0.099% | 0.006% | 0.085% |
| With Sat | 0.070% | 0.099% | 0.006% | 0.099% |
| Without Sat | 0.084% |  |  | 0.084% |
| Saturday | 0.058% | 0.033% | 0.096% | 0.100% |
| **Holiday Returns** | | | | |
| Day before Holiday | | | | |
| July 4th | 0.319% | 0.212% | 0.817% | 0.210% |
| Christmas | 0.306% | 0.452% | 0.363% | 0.303% |
| New Year's | 0.395% | 0.596% | 0.393% | 0.173% |
| Holiday Avg | 0.340% | 0.420% | 0.524% | 0.228% |
| Christmas Week | 0.247% | 0.325% | 0.308% | 0.156% |

Figure 18-5 shows the average percentage change in the Dow Jones Industrial Average over every calendar day of the month. It is striking that the average percentage gain on the last trading day of the month (and the 30th calendar day, when that is not the last trading day) and the first six calendar days is *more than* equal to the entire return for the month. The net change in the Dow Industrials is *negative* for all the other days.

The strong gains at the turn of the month are almost certainly related to the inflow of funds into the equity market that result from monthly flows of income to consumers. It is surprising, however, that these flows have been the dominant source of gains in the market over the past 112 years.

## DAY-OF-THE-WEEK EFFECTS

Many people hate Mondays. After two days of relaxing and doing pretty much what you like, having to face work on Monday is not fun.

**FIGURE  18–5**

Average Daily Returns on the Dow Industrials, 1885–1997

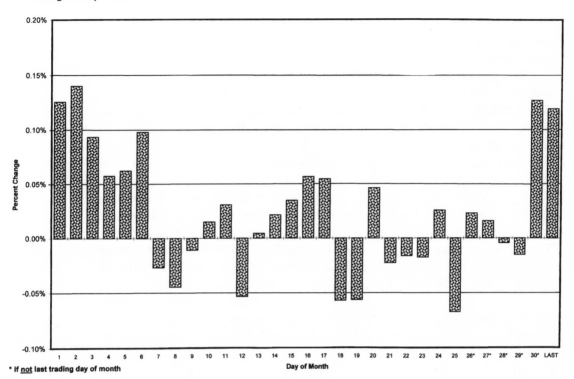

* **if not last trading day of month**

And stock investors apparently feel the same way. Monday is by far the worst day of the week for the market, and has been throughout all the time periods examined. Over the past 112 years, the returns on Monday have been decisively negative—so negative that if Monday returns were instead like Tuesday through Friday, the Dow Industrial Average would be nearly double its current level.

Although investors hate Mondays, they relish Fridays. Friday is the best day of the week, yielding returns about four times the daily average. Even when markets were open on Saturday (every month before 1946 and nonsummer months before 1953), Friday returns were the best.

Once again, the Monday effect is not confined to U.S. equity markets. Throughout most of the world, Monday is a poor day, garnering negative returns not only in the United States but also in Canada, the United Kingdom, Germany, France, Japan, Korea, and Singapore. On the other hand, none of the major countries have negative returns on Wednesday, Thursday, or Friday. Tuesday is also a poor day for the market, especially in Asia and Australia.[12] This might be due to the poor Monday just experienced in Western countries, since daily returns in the United States have been found to influence Asian markets the next day.

The daily patterns in returns, although conforming to the conventional popularity of the work week, do not correspond to economic rationale. Since the return on Monday covers the three-day period from Friday's close, you might think the return should be three times larger than that of other days, given that capital is committed for three times the length of time (and with more risk). But this is not the case.[13]

Fridays are not the only good days in the market. The market does well before virtually any holiday. Returns before the three holidays of the Fourth of July, Christmas, and New Year's are shown in Table 18-2. They are, on average, *18* times the average daily return. Research on behavior before other exchange holidays show the same pattern. And, as was indicated earlier, the last day of the month is a winner, too.

Finally, there appears to be a diurnal pattern of stock returns. Evidence has shown that there is usually a sinking spell in the morning, especially on Monday. During lunch the market firms, then pauses or declines in the mid-afternoon before rising strongly in the last half hour of trading. This often leads the market to close at the highest levels of the day.

## WHAT'S AN INVESTOR TO DO?

These anomalies are an extremely tempting guide to formulating an investing strategy, but those who choose to play by them should be aware of two additional issues: risk and transaction costs. As noted earlier, these calendar-related returns do not always occur and, as investors become more aware of them, they might not occur as frequently or even at all in the future. Also, investing in these anomalies requires the buying and selling of stock, which incurs transaction costs.

---

12 These results are taken from Keim and Hawawini, "On the Predictability of Common Stock Returns: World-Wide Evidence" in R. Jarrow et al., eds., *Handbook in OR & MS*, vol. 9, pp. 497-544.
13 Dividends are fairly evenly spread during the week. They were slightly higher on Monday during the early period, but higher on Friday more recently.

The advent of no-load mutual funds and on-line trading has made the cost of transacting extremely low. However, unless you are investing with tax-sheltered funds, realizing the gains from playing these anomalies can incur significant taxes. Chapter 8 demonstrated that realizing capital gains each year, rather than deferring them to the future, substantially lowers your total returns. Nevertheless, investors who have already decided to buy or sell but have some latitude in choosing the exact time of their transaction would be well advised to take these calendar anomalies into account.

PART FIVE

# BUILDING WEALTH
# THROUGH STOCKS

CHAPTER

# FUNDS, MANAGERS, AND "BEATING THE MARKET"

*"I have little confidence even in the ability of analysts, let alone untrained investors, to select common stocks that will give better than average results. Consequently, I feel that the standard portfolio should be to duplicate, more or less, the DJIA.*

—Benjamin Graham[1]

*How can institutional investors hope to outperform the market . . . when, in effect, they are the market?*

—Charles D. Ellis[2]

There is an old story on Wall Street. Two managers of large equity funds go camping in a national park. After setting up camp, the first manager mentions to the other that he overheard the park ranger warning that black bears had been seen around this campsite. The second manager smiles and says, "I'm not worried; I'm a pretty fast runner." The first manager shakes his head and says, "You can't outrun black bears; they've been known to sprint over 25 miles an hour to capture their prey!" The second manager responds, "Of course I know that I can't outrun the bear. The only thing that's important is that I can outrun *you*!"

In the competitive world of money management, performance is measured not by *absolute* return but the return *relative* to some benchmark. These benchmarks include the S&P 500 Stock Index, the Wilshire

---

1 Benjamin Graham, *The Memoirs of the Dean of Wall Street*, McGraw Hill, 1996, p. 273.
2 Charles D. Ellis, "The Loser's Game," *Financial Analysis Journal*, July/August 1975.

5000, and the latest "style" index popular on Wall Street. But there is a crucially important difference about playing the game of investing compared to virtually any other activity. Most of us have no chance of being as good as the *average* in any pursuit where others practice and hone their skills for many, many hours. But we can be as good as the average investor in the stock market with no practice at all.

The reason for this surprising statement is based on a very simple fact: Since the sum of each investor's holdings must be equal to the market, the performance of the whole market must, by definition, be the average performance of each and every investor. Therefore, for each investor who performs better than the market there must be another investor who performs worse than the market. By matching the market, you are guaranteed to do no worse than average.

But how do you match the market as a whole? Until recently, this goal would be very difficult for the average investor to achieve. No one holds shares in each of the nearly 10,000 firms listed on U.S. exchanges. But over the past several decades, *index* funds whose sole goal is to match the performance of some broad stock index have gained rapid acceptance. This has enabled the average investor to match the market at a very low cost.

## PERFORMANCE OF EQUITY MUTUAL FUNDS

Many claim that striving for *average* market performance is not the best strategy. If there are enough poorly informed traders who consistently underperform the market, then it might be possible, by researching stocks or finding professionals who research stocks and actively manage funds, to outperform the market.

Unfortunately, the past record of the vast majority of such actively managed funds does not support this contention. Table 19-1 shows that, from January 1971 through June 1997, the average equity mutual fund returned 11.68 percent annually, about 1½ percentage points behind the market measured either by the Wilshire 5000 or the S & P 500 Index.[3]

The long-term returns on mutual funds is difficult to measure because of the *survivorship bias* that is inherent in the data. This survivorship bias exists because poorly performing funds are frequently terminated, leaving only the most successful ones with track records over long periods of time. This imparts an upward bias to these fund returns. Table 19-1 shows that the survivor funds did return 1.29 percent

---

3 Fund data provided by the Vanguard Group and Lipper Analytical Services. See John C. Bogle, *Bogle on Mutual Funds*, Burr Ridge, IL: Irwin Professional Publishing, 1994 for a description of these data.

**TABLE 19–1**

Equity Mutual Fund and Benchmark Returns: Annual Compound Return, Excluding Sales and Redemption Fees, January 1971 to June 1997 (Standard Deviation in Parentheses)

| | All Funds | "Survivor" Funds | Wilshire 5000 | S&P 500 | Small Stocks | All Funds - Wilshire 5000 | "Survivor" Funds - Wilshire 5000 |
|---|---|---|---|---|---|---|---|
| **1971-1997** | 11.68% (16.6%) | 12.97% (16.5%) | 13.12% (17.1%) | 13.16% (16.4%) | 15.17% (22.8%) | -1.44% | -0.15% |
| **1975-1983** | 18.83% (12.9%) | 19.97% (13.1%) | 17.94% (15.0%) | 15.74% (15.5%) | 35.32% (14.3%) | 0.89% | 2.03% |
| **1984-1997** | 13.39% (13.5%) | 14.31% (13.6%) | 15.91% (14.2%) | 16.99% (13.3%) | 11.06% (18.1%) | -2.52% | -1.60% |

more annually than the average fund, yet they still underperformed the market averages.

The average mutual fund did outperform the Wilshire 5000 during the 1975–1983 period when small stocks returned over 35 percent per year, more than twice the return of the S & P 500 Index. Equity funds generally do better when small stocks outperform large stocks, as many money managers seek to outperform the averages by buying middle and small-sized firms. Since 1983, when small stocks have done poorly relative to large stocks, however, the performance of the average mutual fund has fallen more than 2½ percent per year behind the market.

Figure 19-1 displays the percentage of general equity funds that have outperformed the Wilshire 5000 and the S & P 500 Index. During this 25-year period, there were only eight years when more mutual funds beat the Wilshire 5000 than fell short. Five of these years occurred during the period when small stocks outperformed large stocks. Since 1982 there have been only two years—1990 and 1993—when the average equity mutual fund outperformed the market.[4]

The underperformance of mutual funds did not begin in the 1970s. In 1970, Becker Securities Corporation startled Wall Street by compiling

---

4 As poor as the data make mutual funds look, they actually overstate the performance of the average equity fund. These mutual fund returns ignore the sales and redemption fees (front- and back-end "loads") that many funds impose. Therefore, most mutual fund returns are even lower than these results indicate.

## FIGURE  19–1

Percentage of General Equity Funds that Outperform the S & P 500 and Wilshire 5000, Excluding Sales and Redemption Fees

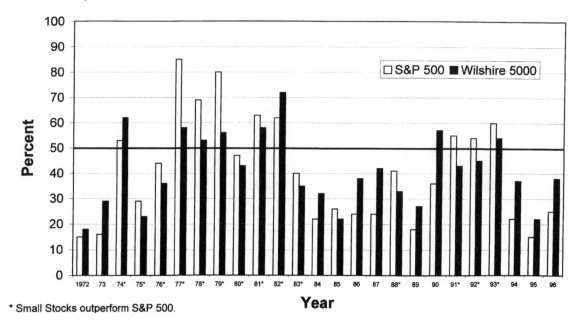

* Small Stocks outperform S&P 500.

the track record of managers of corporate pension funds. Becker showed that the median performance of these managers lagged behind the S & P 500 by one percentage point, and that only one quarter of them was able to outperform the market.[5] This study followed on the heels of academic articles, particularly by William Sharpe and Michael Jensen, which also confirmed the underperformance of equity mutual funds.[6]

Figure 19-2a displays the distribution of the *difference* between the returns of 198 mutual funds that have survived since January 1971 (up until June 1997) and the Wilshire 5000, while Figure 19-2b does the same for the period since January 1984.[7]

You would expect a wide distribution in the performance of these funds. Even if stocks are chosen completely at random, some funds will

5 Malkiel, *A Random Walk Down Wall Street*, p. 362.
6 For an excellent review of the studies on mutual funds, see Richard A. Ippolito, "On Studies of Mutual Fund Performance, 1962-1991," *Financial Analysts Journal*, January-February 1993, pp. 42-50
7 The data on survivor funds were provided by Lipper Analytical Services.

**FIGURE  19–2**

Actual Mutual Fund Performance Relative to Theoretical Expectations

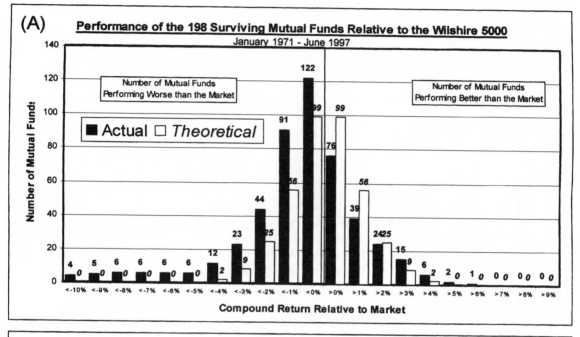

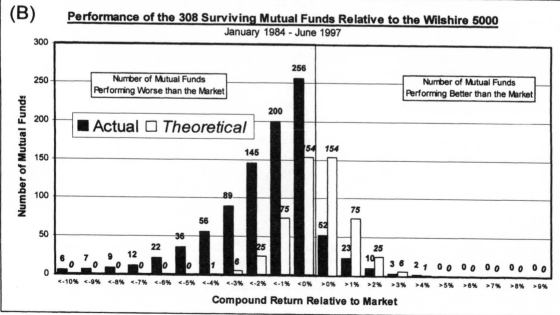

outperform the market, while others will underperform. Based on the risk characteristics of the average mutual funds, a theoretical distribution of what these returns would look like after 20 years if the funds had, on average, the same return as the Wilshire 5000 Index but were randomly invested in a diversified group of stocks.[8]

The entire period from 1971 through June 1997 is favorable for the mutual fund industry because it includes 1975-83, which so favored the small and mid-cap stocks that are held by many mutual funds. Notwithstanding, only 76, or less than 40 percent, of the 198 funds that have survived over the past 20 years have been able to outperform the Wilshire 5000. Less than one in five of these funds has been able to outperform the market by more than 1 percent per year, while less than one in eight has bettered the market by at least 2 percent.[9] In contrast, almost half of the funds lagged the market by 1 percent or more, and more than one in four lagged the market by more than 2 percent.

In the period from 1984 through June 1997, the performance of mutual funds is markedly worse. This is because during this period the S & P 500 Index outperformed mid- and small-cap stocks. As shown in Figure 19-2b, only 52 of the 308 surviving funds outperformed the Wilshire 500 during this period, while almost half of the funds lagged the market by at least 2 percent per year.

Despite the generally poor performance of equity mutual funds, there are some real winners. The most outstanding mutual fund performance over the entire period is that of Fidelity's Magellan fund, whose 19.8 percent annual return from 1971 through June 1997 beat the market by almost 7 percent per year. The probability that this performance was based on luck alone is about one in 200. But this means that, out of the 198 mutual funds that survived the period, there is a very good chance that one would have performed as well as the Magellan Fund by chance alone.

Yet luck could not explain Magellan's performance from 1977 through 1990. During that period, the legendary stock picker, Peter Lynch, ran the Magellan Fund and outperformed the market by an incredible 13 percent per year. Magellan took somewhat greater risks in achieving

---

8 The expected returns are assumed to be identical to that of the Wilshire 5000 Index. The average annual standard deviation of the Wilshire 5000 Index during this period (measured with annual data) is 16.8 percent. The standard deviation of the average mutual fund is slightly higher, assumed to be 18.5 percent, with a correlation coefficient of .88.

9 These performance ratings, as noted earlier, do not include the "load," or front-end (and sometimes back-end) fees and commissions.

this return,[10] but the probability that Magellan would outperform the Wilshire 5000 by this margin over that 14-year period by luck alone is only one in 500,000!

## FINDING SKILLED MONEY MANAGERS

It is easy to determine that Magellan's performance during the Lynch years was due to his skill in picking stocks. But for more mortal portfolio managers, it is extremely difficult to determine with any degree of confidence that the superior returns of money managers are due to skill or luck. Table 19-2 computes the *probability* that managers will outperform the market given that they do pick stocks that in a *probabilistic sense* beat the market, but over short periods of time are subject to normal random movements that mask their higher long-run returns.[11]

**TABLE 19-2**

Probability of Outperforming the Market, Assuming a 14 Percent Expected Return, 16.6 Percent Standard Deviation, and 0.88 correlation coefficient (Based on Data From 1971 to 1996)

| Expected Excess Return | Holding Period | | | | | | |
|---|---|---|---|---|---|---|---|
| | 1 | 2 | 3 | 5 | 10 | 20 | 30 |
| 1% | 54.7% | 56.6% | 58.1% | 60.4% | 64.6% | 70.1% | 74.1% |
| 2% | 59.3% | 63.0% | 65.8% | 70.1% | 77.2% | 85.4% | 90.1% |
| 3% | 63.7% | 69.0% | 72.9% | 78.4% | 86.7% | 94.2% | 97.3% |
| 4% | 68.0% | 74.5% | 79.0% | 85.2% | 93.0% | 98.2% | 99.5% |
| 5% | 71.9% | 79.4% | 84.3% | 90.3% | 96.7% | 99.5% | 99.9% |

10 The standard deviation of the Magellan Fund over Lynch's period is 21.38 percent, compared to 13.88 percent for the Wilshire 5000, while its correlation coefficient with the Wilshire was 0.86.
11 Money managers are assumed to expose their clients to the same risk as the market, and have a correlation coefficient of .88 with market returns, which was typical of equity mutual funds since 1971.

The results are surprising. Even if money managers choose stocks that have an *expected* return of 1 percent per year better than the market, after 10 years there is less than a two-thirds probability that they will exceed the average market return, and after 30 years the probability rises to only 74 percent. If managers pick stocks that will over the very long-run outperform the market by 2 percent per year, after 10 years there is still only a 77 percent chance that they will outperform the market. This means there is almost a one in four chance that they will still fall short of the average market performance. In these situations, the very long run will most certainly outlive managers' trial periods for determining their real worth.

Detecting a bad manager is an equally difficult task. In fact, a money manager would have to underperform the market by 4 percent a year for almost 15 years before you could be *statistically certain* (defined to mean being less than 1 chance in 20 of being wrong) that the manger is actually poor and not just having bad luck. By that time, your assets would have fallen to half of what you would have had by indexing to the market.

Even extreme cases are hard to identify. Surely you would think that a manager who picks stocks that are expected to outperform the market by an average of 5 percent per year, a feat achieved by only one fund other than Magellan since 1970, would easily and quickly stand out. But that is not necessarily so. After one year there is only a 71.9 percent probability that such a manager will outperform the market. And the probability rises to only 79.4 percent that the manager will outperform the market after two years.

Assume you gave a young, undiscovered Peter Lynch with a 5 percent per year edge in picking stocks an ultimatum: that he will be fired if he does not at least match the market after two years. There is a one in five chance of firing such a superior analyst, therefore judging him completely incapable of picking winning stocks!

## REASONS FOR UNDERPERFORMANCE OF MANAGED MONEY

The generally poor performance of funds relative to the market is not due to the fact that managers of these funds pick losing stocks. Their performance lags the benchmarks largely because funds impose fees and trading costs that average 2 percent per year. First, in seeking superior returns, a manager generally actively buys and sells stocks, which involves brokerage commissions and paying the bid-ask spread, or the difference between the buying and the selling price of shares. Second, investors pay management fees (and possibly load fees) to those who are trying to beat the averages. Finally, managers are often competing with other managers with equal or superior skills at choosing stocks. As noted earlier, it is a mathematical impossibility for everyone to do better than the market—for every dollar that outperforms the average, some other investor's dollar must underperform the average.

## A LITTLE LEARNING IS A DANGEROUS THING

Although stocks might appear to be incorrectly priced to an investor who is just beginning to understand market valuation, this is often not the case. For example, take the novice—an investor who is just learning about stock valuation. This is the investor to whom most of the books titled *How to Beat the Market* are sold. A novice might note that the stock has just reported very good earnings, but its price does not rise as much as he believes is justified by this good news. He might think the price should have gone up much more, and so buys the stock.

Yet informed investors know that special circumstances caused the earnings to increase and that these circumstances will not likely be repeated in the future. Informed investors are therefore more than happy to sell the stock to novices, realizing that even the small rise in the price of the stock is not justified. Informed investors make a return on their special knowledge. They make their return from novices who believes they have found a bargain. Uninformed investors, who do not even know what the earnings of the company are, do better than one who is just beginning to learn what equities are worth.

The saying "a little learning is a dangerous thing" proves itself to be quite apt in financial markets. Many seeming anomalies or discrepancies in the price of stocks (or most other financial assets, for that matter) are due to the trading of informed investors with special information. Although this is not always the case, when a stock looks too cheap or too dear, the easy explanation—that emotional or stupid traders have irrationally priced the stock—is often wrong. This is why beginners who try to analyze individual stocks often do quite badly.

## PROFITING FROM INFORMED TRADING

As novices become more informed, they will no doubt find some stocks that are genuinely under- or overvalued. Trading these stocks will begin to offset their transaction costs and poorly informed trades. At one point, a novice might become well enough informed to overcome the transaction costs and match, or perhaps exceed, the market return. The key word here is *might*, however, since the number of investors who have consistently been able to outperform the market is small indeed. And for individuals who do not devote much time to analyzing stocks, the possibility of consistently outperforming the averages is remote.

Yet the apparent simplicity of picking winners and avoiding losers lures many investors into active trading. Many are convinced that they are at least as smart as the next guy who is playing the same investing game. Yet being just as smart as the next guy is not good enough. For being average at the game of finding market winners will result in underperforming the market, since transaction costs diminish returns.

In 1975, Charles D. Ellis, a managing partner at Greenwood Associates, wrote an influential article called "The Loser's Game." In it he showed that, with transaction costs taken into account, average money managers must outperform the market by margins that are not possible given that they themselves are the major market players. Ellis concludes: "Contrary to their oft articulated goal of outperforming the market averages, investment managers are not beating the market; the market is beating them."[12]

## HOW COSTS AFFECT RETURNS

Trading and managerial costs of 2 or 3 percent a year might seem small compared to the year-to-year volatility of the market and for investors who are gunning for 20 or 30 percent annual returns. But such costs are extremely detrimental to long-term wealth accumulation. One thousand dollars invested at a compound return of 11 percent per year, the average nominal return on stocks since World War II, will accumulate $23,000 over 30 years. A 1 percent annual fee will reduce the final accumulation by almost a third. With a 3 percent annual fee, the accumulation amounts to just over $10,000, less than half the market return. Every extra percentage point of return earned each year allows investors aged 25 to retire two years earlier, without sacrificing their standard of living.

## WHAT'S AN INVESTOR TO DO?

The past performance of managed funds might sound discouraging. The fees that most funds charge do not provide investors with superior returns and can be a significant drag on wealth accumulation. Furthermore,

12 Charles D. Ellis, "The Loser's Game," *Financial Analysts Journal*, July/August 1975, p. 19.

a good money manager is extremely difficult to identify, for luck plays some role in all successful investment outcomes.

But there is a solution to this problem. In the next chapter I will discuss ways in which the typical investor can keep costs down and still enjoy the benefits of superior returns on equity. You won't be able to avoid all fees, for no investment can be made for free. But it is not difficult to match the market return and perhaps even beat it by following some simple rules. Performing as well as the top third of equity money managers is a goal well within the reach of all investors.

Does all this mean that financial advisers are useless to the average investor? Not at all. The most important message of this book is to stay invested in stocks. This is extremely difficult for many investors, especially during bear markets. As a result, they jump into and out of even the best of funds as market conditions change, dramatically lowering their returns. For many investors, it is helpful to have an adviser who can lend a steady hand and maintain a proper long-term perspective for a portfolio. It does little good to purchase the right stocks or funds if the next time the market trembles you find yourself scurrying to the safety of money market assets.

CHAPTER

# STRUCTURING A PORTFOLIO FOR LONG-TERM GROWTH

*[The] long run is a misleading guide to current affairs. In the long run we are all dead. Economists set themselves too easy, too useless a task if in tempestuous seasons they can only tell us when the storm is long past, the ocean will be flat.*

**John Maynard Keynes[1]**

*My favorite holding period is forever.*

**Warren Buffett[2]**

No one can argue with Keynes' statement that in the long run we are all dead. But vision for the long run must be used as a guide to current action. Those who keep their focus and perspective during trying times are far more likely to emerge successful. The knowledge that the sea will be flat after the storm is not useless, but of enormous comfort.

It is particularly important that the principles of investment strategy be guided by long-run expectations. Keynes was right when he wrote, "our knowledge of the factors which will govern the yield of an investment some years hence is usually very slight and often negligible."[3] But the fact that such expectations are tenuously held does not justify their abandonment. The well-known statement—that the most successful are those who keep their heads about them when everyone else is losing theirs—is particularly applicable for investment decisions.

1 *A Tract on Monetary Reform*, 1924, p. 80.
2 Linda Grant, "Striking Out at Wall Street," *U.S. News & World Report*, June 20, 1994, p. 58.
3 John M. Keynes, *The General Theory*, New York: MacMillan, 1936, p. 149.

## PRACTICAL ASPECTS OF INVESTING

To be a successful long-term investor is easy in principle, but difficult in practice. It is easy in principle since buying and holding a diversified portfolio of stocks, foregoing any forecasting ability, is available to all investors, no matter what their intelligence, judgment, or financial status. Yet it is difficult in practice since tales of those who have quickly achieved great wealth in the market tempt many people to play a game very different from that of the long-term investor.

Those of us who follow the market closely often exclaim: "I knew that stock (or the market) was going up! If I had only relied on my judgment, I would have made a lot of money." But hindsight plays tricks on our minds. We forget the doubts we had when we made the decision not to buy. Hindsight often distorts the past and encourages us to play hunches and outguess other investors, who in turn are playing the same game.

For most of us, trying to beat the market leads to disastrous results. We take far too many risks, our transaction costs are high, and we often find ourselves giving into the emotions of the moment—pessimism when the market is down and optimism when the market is high. Our actions lead to substantially lower returns than can be obtained by just staying in the market.

Achieving good long-term returns in stocks is simple and available to all who seek to gain through investing. Several principles enable both new and seasoned investors to increase their returns while minimizing their risk. The first one is as follows:

*1.* **Stocks should constitute the overwhelming proportion of all long-term financial portfolios. The new government inflation-indexed bonds should be the asset of choice for long-term investors who want to reduce their exposure to equities.**

Chapter 2 demonstrated that portfolio composition is crucially dependent on the holding period of the investor, and holding periods are often far longer than most investors realize. Uncertain inflation makes standard nominal bonds risky in the long run. Based on historical evidence, even the most conservative investors should place most of their financial wealth in common stocks.

The new government inflation-indexed bonds offer after-inflation returns that are competitive with standard bonds and much safer in terms of purchasing power. Although inflation-indexed bonds currently yield half the long-term return on stocks, these bonds over ten-year periods will outperform equities about one-quarter of the time. Investors worried about equity exposure should consider these bonds as the safe alternative to stocks.

**2. Invest the largest percentage—the *core holdings* of your stock port-folio—in highly diversified mutual funds with very low expense ratios.**

To replicate the returns described in this book, it is necessary to hold a highly diversified portfolio of stocks. Unless you can consistently choose stocks with superior returns, a goal very few investors have reached, maximum diversification is achieved by holding each stock in proportion to its market capitalization.

The mutual fund industry offers investments, called *index funds*, which yield returns extremely close to those of the major market indexes, such as the S & P 500 Index. An index fund does not attempt to beat the market, but by holding a large number of stocks in the proper proportion, such a fund can match the market with an extremely low cost. For the largest of these funds the annual expense ratio is as low as 0.20%. A further advantage of indexed funds is that their turnover is very low and therefore are very "tax-efficient" for investors.

Chapter 19 showed that the Wilshire 5000 has outperformed about two out of three mutual funds since 1976 and a far higher percentage over the past 15 years. By matching the market year after year, as you can with index funds, you are likely to be near the top of the pack when the final returns are tallied. Matching the market is sufficient to obtain the superior returns that have been achieved in stocks over time.

**3. Place up to one-quarter of your stocks in mid- and small-sized stock funds.**

Even though Chapter 6 showed that the outperformance of small stocks is dependent on a particular historical period, the mid- and small-sized stocks still amount to over one-quarter of the total value of U.S. equity. To ignore these stocks completely would likely lead to lower long-term returns for a given level of risk.

To match the total market requires an investment in thousands of stocks, a strategy that would be prohibitively expensive. To approximate total market returns, small-stock index funds choose a representative subset of stocks to approximate the returns of those stocks not in the S & P 500 Index. The small-stock funds, which have somewhat higher expenses than the large-stock index funds, replicate indexes such as the Wilshire 4500 (essentially all stocks not in the S & P 500 Index) and the Russell 2000 (the smallest 2,000 stocks of the top 3,000). For those investors who do not want to combine large and small index funds, there are funds that replicate the Wilshire 5000, the broadest index of all stocks, with extremely low turnover.

Besides diversification, there is another persuasive reason for investing in the mid- and small-cap stocks. Because of the popularity of indexing, stocks jump in price when it is announced that they will be added to or are added to the S & P 500 Index. When index funds acquire these stocks at the higher prices, this might lead to somewhat lower returns for the S & P 500 in the long run. This does not mean that you should necessarily overweight stocks not in S & P 500, since the transactions costs in these smaller stocks are substantially higher. But ignoring smaller issues exposes long-term investors to poorer returns and higher risks than they might otherwise achieve.

It is debatable whether indexing small-cap stocks will be as successful at outperforming active money managers as indexing large stocks has been. There are clearly more inefficiencies in the small-cap markets since far fewer analysts can cover each stock. A good manager is more likely to outperform the averages. But beware, since high fees can easily wipe out the differential return you would achieve by searching out the best of the small-cap managers.

**4.  Allocate about one-quarter of your stock portfolio to international equities, divided approximately equally among Europe, the Far East, and emerging markets.**

This recommendation is based on the analysis in Chapter 9 and the principle of risk diversification. Since almost two-thirds of the world's capital is now located outside of the United States, international equities must be the basis of any well-diversified portfolio. Japanese stocks, despite their long bear market, should not be excluded because they have a low correlation with the rest of the world's markets, making them good diversifiers for a portfolio.

There are three ways to invest in international stocks: open-ended mutual funds, which allow for buying and selling shares from investors at the net asset value of their portfolio; closed-end funds, which trade like shares of a portfolio and are run by an active manager; and the newest innovations, WEBS (World Equity Benchmark Shares) and Country Baskets, which are pools of funds invested in a broad index of foreign stocks.

Closed-end country funds might be good buys if they are selling substantially below the value of their underlying shares. But when foreign investing is in vogue, these funds sell at a premium and investors are often better off investing in regular open-ended mutual funds.

The new WEBS are attractive since they have relatively low expense ratios (less than 1 percent per year) and are indexed to the Morgan Stanley Capital International Indexes. But unless you take a fancy to a particular country, they are too narrow defined to facilitate diversification. Open-ended mutual funds range from index funds issued by large fund groups with expense ratios as low as 0.35%, to the actively managed funds with expense ratios that are in excess of 2 percent per year.

As with smaller capitalization stocks, the evidence in favor of indexing international stocks is not yet as persuasive as among domestic, high-capitalization stocks. This is because there are more inefficiencies in the pricing of international stocks that can be exploited by skillful money managers. Nevertheless, there is not sufficient evidence to determine whether these active managers can overcome their high fees and provide investors with extra value for shareholders.

**5. Do not overweight the emerging markets. High growth is already factored into the prices of many of the stocks of these countries.**

There is a tendency for many investors to overinvest in emerging markets where promises of capital appreciation are high. But the markets of developing countries are extremely risky. The total market capitalization of many small countries is less than some individual firms of developed countries. It is also important to spread your investing globally between Latin America, the Far East, and Central and Eastern Europe. As investors witnessed in 1997, problems can strike whole geographical areas quickly, such as the currency crises that began in Thailand and spread to the other Asian markets. Again, diversification is the key to reducing your risk exposure.

**6.) Large "growth" stocks perform as well as large "value" stocks, and some are worth 30 or more times earnings. On the value side, the *Dow 10 Strategy*, which picks the ten highest-yielding Dow stocks, has worked extremely well, although its popularity may limit future gains.**

Chapter 6 and 7 indicate that large growth stocks, those with low-dividend yields and high price-to-earnings ratios perform just as well over the long run as large value stocks, those with higher-dividend yields and lower P-E ratios. Historically, value stocks surged in the same 1975–83 period that led to the outperformance of small stocks. Large-sized value stocks also do well in January, just as small stocks.

Chapter 4 showed that the Dow 10 strategy of buying the ten highest-yielding Dow Industrial stocks has outperformed the market consistently in the past. Its outperformance is mostly due to the fact that almost all of the Dow Industrials have been superior companies in their respective industries. These stocks are very responsive to a contrarian strategy that accumulates the stocks when they have fallen over a period of several years. A high-dividend yield by itself is not a very important criterion in outperformance.

**7. Small *value* stocks appear to significantly outperform small *growth* stocks. Avoid initial public offerings (IPOs) unless you buy at the offering price.**

In contrast to the big capitalization stocks, value does appear to outperform growth among the mid- and small-cap stocks. The very small growth stocks do the worst of any class of stocks examined. Dreams of buying into another Microsoft or Intel often compel investors to over-pay for these issues.

If you can buy new issues at their offering price, it is usually wise to do so. But don't hold on. IPOs, which often include small growth stocks, are extremely poor performers for long-term investors.

**8. Maximize your contribution to your tax-deferred account (IRA, 401(k), or Keogh). Generally, fund your tax-deferred account with stocks. If your total stock portfolio exceeds your tax-deferred account, hold high-dividend (or value) stocks in the tax-deferred account, and low-dividend (or growth) stocks in your taxable account. But do not overweight tax-deferred account with high-dividend stocks just to shelter dividends.**

Chapter 8 showed how taxes can reduce the returns on your port-folio. You can minimize the tax bite by building a tax-deferred account that accumulates gains at before-tax rates of return. This is best accom-plished through investing in the stock market. The deferral of taxes on capital gains and dividends is usually worth more than the advantage of the lower capital gains tax in the taxable account.

If your stock portfolio exceeds the size of your tax-deferred ac-count, put the high-yielding stocks in that account in order to maximize the deferral of taxes. Stocks with low dividends should be placed in tax-able accounts.

In 1992, Vanguard, in conjunction with BARRA, Inc., divided the S & P 500 Index into growth and value stocks. Combining equal values of each of these funds recreates the total S & P 500 Index. By holding the Value Fund in a TDA and an equal proportion of the Growth Fund in a taxable account, you can replicate the S & P 500 Index with lower taxes.

Do not stretch to fill your tax-deferred account with high-dividend stocks such as REITs or utilities. This will unbalance your portfolio and expose you to too much risk.

## Return-Enhancing Strategies

The following return-enhancing strategies are not necessary to achieve good long-run returns on the market. As this book indicates, you will do quite well with a buy-and-hold strategy pegged to an index or other well-diversified, low-cost fund. But if you like the hunt and get a thrill out of at-tempting to "beat the market," then these strategies, in addition to numbers 6 and 7 in the previous section, have yielded superior returns in the past.

**1. There is some evidence that contrarian strategies of increasing stock exposure when most investors are bearish and decreasing expo-sure when they are bullish can improve long-term returns.**

Chapter 5 concluded that investor sentiment can be an important indicator of the future course of equity values. It has long been noted that investors are often most optimistic when the market is at a peak and pessimistic when it is making a bottom. By pursuing a contrarian strategy, you may realize superior returns.

**2.  Investing when the Fed is easing short-term interest rates has, during most of the last 50 years, produced significantly higher returns than investing when the Fed is restricting credit and interest rates are rising.**

The direction of interest rates is the most significant short-term influence on stock prices. Chapter 10 showed that investing in stocks during periods when the Federal Reserve is tightening credit results in significantly lower returns than investing when the Fed is easing credit.

However, this has not been true during all periods in the past. For reasons ranging from an increased number of Fed watchers to a better strategy by Fed policy makers, this strategy has not worked well over 9 to 12-month periods in the bull market of the 1990s. Any strategy widely followed and acted upon will nullify its own past performance.

**3.  There is significant evidence that many calendar anomalies persist over time. Furthermore, some technical trading rules have been shown to reduce risk and enhance returns.**

For investors who closely follow the market, the evidence presented in Chapters 17 and 18 suggests that there have been regular calendar patterns in stock returns and that pursuing certain trend-following strategies might reduce stock risks. Calendar anomalies include the excess returns to small stocks in the month of January, as well as the superior return to stocks that occur at the very end of the month and the beginning of the next month.

The 200-day moving average has been investigated as a method of timing the market. Although the overall returns are not significantly superior to a buy-and-hold strategy, there is some evidence that risk is reduced.

**4.  All these return-enhancing strategies should be pursued from your tax-deferred account, using no-load mutual funds, SPDRs, or, for those who want to maximize their leverage, S & P 500 index futures.**

These strategies require shifting in and out of equities, which incurs transaction costs in terms of taxes and brokerage or front-load fees in mutual funds. For this reason, pursuing these strategies is best done using no-load mutual funds that do not restrict the number of switches you can make. SPDRs (S & P 500 Depository Receipts) and index futures are low-cost ways of taking a position in this major benchmark, and are discussed in Chapter 15.

Again, it is important to remember that with any system, a significant increase in the number of investors who use that strategy will cause price movements, which will nullify its effect. There is some evidence that the January Effect and other calendar anomalies are becoming weaker over time.

## Implementing the Plan and the Role of an Investment Advisor

I wrote *Stocks for the Long Run* to demonstrate what returns could be reasonably expected on stocks and fixed income assets and to analyze the major factors influencing those returns. Many investors will consider this book a "do-it-yourself guide" to choosing stocks and structuring a portfolio. And for some, this will indeed be the case. But knowing the right *investments* is not the same as implementing the right *investment strategy*. As Peter Bernstein so aptly indicates in his foreword to this edition, there are many pitfalls on the path to successful investing that cause investors to fail to achieve their intended goals.

The first pitfall is the lack of diversification. Many investors are not satisfied earning a ten percent average annual return on stocks when they know there are always individual issues that will double or triple in price over the next twelve months. Finding such gems is extremely gratifying and many dream of buying the next Microsoft or Intel.

But as Chapter 6 indicates, the evidence is overwhelming that most small growth stocks are very risky and have poor long-term returns. Studies of betting at racetracks and in lotteries have confirmed the propensity of bettors to overplay long shots in the hopes of winning big while ignoring safer bets that promise more moderate returns. This propensity leads many individual investors to take far too much risk and suffer far lower returns than can be had from a fully diversified portfolio of stocks.

Investors who have been burned by picking individual stocks often turn to mutual funds in their search for higher returns. But choosing a mutual fund poses similar obstacles. "Hot managers" with superior past performance replace "hot stocks" as the new strategy to beat the market. As a result, many investors end up playing the same game as they had with individual stocks.

Those who finally abandon trying to pick the best funds are tempted to pursue an even more difficult course. They attempt to beat the market by *timing* market cycles. Surprisingly, it is often the *best-informed* investors that fall into this trap. With the abundance of financial news, information, and commentary at our beck and call, it is extraordinarily difficult to stay aloof from market opinion. As a result one's impulse is to capitulate to fear when the market is plunging or to greed when stocks are soaring.

Many try to resist this impulse. The intellect may say, "Stay the course!" but this is not easy to do when one hears so many others—

including well-respected "experts"—advising investors to beat a hasty retreat. And as John Maynard Keynes aptly stated in *The General Theory* sixty years ago, "Worldly wisdom teaches that it is better for reputation to fail conventionally than to succeed unconventionally."[4] Standing against the crowd is hard because failing with others who are also failing is far easier than failing alone.

Poor investment strategy, whether it is for lack of diversification, pursuing hot stocks, or attempting to time the market, often stems from investors' belief that it is necessary to *beat* the market to do *well* in the market. But nothing is further from the truth. The principle lesson of this book is that through time the after-inflation returns on a well-diversified portfolio of common stocks have not only exceeded that of fixed income assets but have actually done so with less risk. *Which* stocks you own is secondary to *whether* you own stocks, especially if you maintain a balanced portfolio. Over time the historical difference between the returns on stocks and the returns on bonds has far exceeded the differences in returns among well-diversified all-stock portfolios.[5]

What does all this mean to the reader of this book? Proper investment strategy is as much of a psychological as an intellectual challenge. As with other challenges in life, it is often best to seek professional help to structure and maintain a well-diversified portfolio. If you should decide to seek help, be sure to select a professional investment advisor who agrees with the basic principles of diversification and long-term investing that I have espoused in these chapters. It is within the grasp of all investors to avoid the pitfalls of investing and reap the generous awards that are only available in equities.

## CONCLUSION

The stock market is exciting. Its daily movements dominate the financial press and record the flows of billions of dollars of investment capital. But the stock market is far more than the quintessential symbol of capitalism or the organization through which investors can stake a claim on the economy's future. It is the driving force behind the allocation of the world's capital and the fundamental engine of economic growth and technological change. As the proliferation of stock markets around the world attests, stocks hold the key to enriching the lives of all peoples everywhere.

---

4 John Maynard Keynes, *The General Theory*, op. cit., p. 158.

5 This is shown first in Gary Brinson in "Determinants of Portfolio Performance," by Gary P. Brinson, L. Randolph Hood, and Gilbert L. Beebower, *Financial Analysts Journal*, July/August 1986 pp. 39–44, and extended by William F. Sharpe in "Asset Allocation: Management Style and Performance Measurement," *Journal of Portfolio Management*, Winter 1992 (18:2), pp. 7–19.

# INDEX

Note: A "q" following page numbers refers to information found in chapter opening quotes; an "f" refers to information found in footnotes. **Boldface** page numbers are graphs or illustrations.

## ABOUT THE AUTHOR

**Jeremy J. Siegel** is a professor of finance at the Wharton School of the University of Pennsylvania. Professor Siegel received his Ph.D. from M.I.T. and taught for four years at the University of Chicago before joining the Wharton faculty in 1976. He has written and lectured extensively about the economy and financial markets, monetary policy and interest rates, and stock and bond returns. Along with heading the macroeconomics module of the Morgan Bank Finance Program in New York, he is the academic director of the U.S. Securities Industry Institute and is on the Advisory Board of the Asian Securities Industry Association. Professor Siegel is courted by nearly every Wall Street firm as a consultant and lecturer and has appeared on CNBC, PBS, *Wall Street Week*, and NPR.